PRAISE FOR

LIMITED WAR

"I hope our government is listening. *Limited War* is a powerful book that I couldn't put down. As you read it, you will realize that history will genuinely repeat itself—especially when it comes to our government getting the nation involved in wars that drag on and on. As a three-time Iraq War veteran, I personally experienced Tom's solid message."

—Nathan Aguinaga, Author, *Division: Life on Ardennes Street* and US Army Master Sergeant (Retired)

"*Limited War* is a blueprint for future successful engagements when war is unavoidable. It is a concise analysis of the negative effects of not understanding the elements necessary for success. It should be required reading for all Federal politicians before taking office."

—Ed Vernon, Amateur Historian

Limited War:
How Cooperation Between the Government, the Military,
and the People Leads to Success

© Copyright 2024 Tom Rogers

ISBN 979-8-88824-096-0

All rights reserved. No part of this publication may be reproduced, stored in a retrieval system, or transmitted in any form or by any means—electronic, mechanical, photocopy, recording, or any other—except for brief quotations in printed reviews, without the prior written permission of the author.

Published by

◤ köehlerbooks™

3705 Shore Drive
Virginia Beach, VA 23455
800-435-4811
www.koehlerbooks.com

Limited War

Limited War

HOW COOPERATION BETWEEN THE GOVERNMENT, THE MILITARY, AND THE PEOPLE LEADS TO SUCCESS

TOM ROGERS

VIRGINIA BEACH
CAPE CHARLES

CONTENTS

PROLOGUE 1

CHAPTER ONE: LIMITED WAR 5
    The Trinity of War 6
    The Steps to Full Understanding 6
    The Consequences of War 8
    Destruction 9
    The Psychological and Physical Damage 9
    Once the War Has Begun 10

CHAPTER TWO: THE AMERICAN REVOLUTION 11
    The Early Settlement of the British Colonies in America 12
    The Move Toward Independence 14
    Great Britain's Decision to Go to War 15
    The American Decision to Rebel 16
    The American War of Independence 18
    No Taxation Without Representation 19
    The Royal Proclamation 22
    The Stamp Act Crisis 23
    The Battles of Lexington, Concord, and Bunker Hill 28
    Additional Factors Leading to War 29
    The American Colonies Mature 30
    The American Revolution, Phase I 31
    George Washington Takes Charge of the
    Continental Army 33
    The American Revolution, Phase II 34
    The Battle of Trenton 36
    The Battle of Princeton 37

The British Forage War 38
The Surrender at Saratoga 40
Origins of the American-French Alliance 40
The American Revolution, Phase III 42
Summary of Battles in the Southern Colonies 43

CHAPTER THREE: THE WAR OF 1812 47
Jefferson's Embargo of 1807 47
An Alternative to War 49
The Embargo's Effect on Canada 51
The Struggle for Sovereignty 52
The Louisiana Purchase: Another Complication 53
Phase I: Westward Movement, Tecumseh,
and the Indian Confederacy 54
The Inevitable Conflict With Native America 55
Phase II: The Canadian Invasion 58
Growing Anger Between Belligerents 59
The First Land Battle of the War 60
Thwarted Plans to Invade Canada 62
Canadian Patriotism and the Battle of Beaver Dams 64
The French Invasion of Russia 65
Phase III: Great Britain 66
March on Washington 68
The Star-Spangled Banner: Francis Scott Key 70
Additional Indian Problems: The Battle at Horseshoe Bend ... 71
The Battle of New Orleans 72
The Aftereffects of the War of 1812 75
Post-War Summary 76

CHAPTER FOUR: THE ANGLO-IRISH WAR 78
The Republican Tradition 80
The Rebellion of 1641 82
The Confederate War, 1642–48 83

The Rebellions of 1868–1870 ... 84
The Fenian Influence ... 85
Gladstone's Impact on Irish Freedom ... 88
Leading up to the Schism ... 90
The Schisms ... 91
The Home Rule Movement ... 92
The Easter Rising of 1916:
Plans for the Rebellion Take Form ... 92
Actions to Arrest Sinn Féin Leaders ... 94
The Aftereffects of the Easter Rising ... 97
The Anglo-Irish War Begins ... 99
IRA Attacks Continue with Increased Force ... 104
The Irish Revolutionary War 1920–1921 ... 104
Archbishop Mannix Pays a Visit ... 105
The Black and Tans Take the Offensive ... 106
The Restoration of Order in Ireland Act ... 107
Restoration of Order Delayed ... 108
Efforts for Compromise ... 112
The Truce at Last ... 113

CHAPTER FIVE: THE KOREAN WAR ... **115**
Prelude to the Korean War ... 116
The United States' Decision to Invade
the Korean Peninsula ... 121
The Korean War: Explained ... 125
The American Response to the Collapse of the ROKA ... 128
The Initial American Offensive in Korea ... 129
China's Decision to Enter the War ... 131
China Enters the War—Phase I of the Chinese Offensive ... 136
First Contact with Chinese Forces ... 136
The Battle of the Chosin Reservoir ... 137
The Second Phase of the Chinese Offensive
(late November 1950) ... 139

The Battle Resumes for the Eighth Army...................................145
The Third Phase of the Chinese Offensive............................145
General MacArthur's Retreat..146
MacArthur's Dismissal and the Limited War Doctrine.........148
The Path to Peace...149
The Long Road to an Armistice: Truce Talks Begin..............153

CHAPTER SIX: THE VIETNAM WAR...................................157
The Complex Nature of the Vietnam War............................159
The United States Decision Process for Intervention..........160
The Possible Consequences of Not Intervening..................161
Direct United States Intervention Begins.............................162
Severe Policy Limitations..163
The Restricted Focus on South Vietnam...............................164
The Civil-Military Disconnect...165
McNamara's "Theory of Victory"...165
The Transfer of Vast Military Resources and
Expertise Proved Insufficient..166
Seeking a Winning American Strategic Policy.....................166
The Battle of Ap Bac..167
The Enemy is Gaining Strength...171
The Viet Cong Find Their Voice...172
The Army of the Republic of Vietnam (ARVN)
Showed Their Weaknesses...173
None Are So Blind as Those Who Will Not See...................173
The ARVN Dereliction of Duty and Viet Cong
Rise to the Occasion...174
The Army of Vietnam is Failing the Test..............................174
Push Back on Reality..175
Tet Offensive: Accelerating Loss of Public Support.............177
The Trinity of War and the Failure of Leadership?.............180
The Beginning of the End..183
Presidential Leadership: The Buck Stops Here.....................185

Conclusions ... 188

CHAPTER SEVEN: THE IRAQ WAR ... 190
Reaching a Decision ... 191
The Neoconservative Influence ... 194
Neoconservative Beliefs and Objectives ... 194
The Neoconservative Intent ... 196
How Much Was George W. Bush Influenced by
Neoconservative Thinking? ... 197
Possession of Weapons of Mass Destruction:
An Intelligence Failure ... 198
The Policy of Containment ... 200
Early Plans for War ... 201
Prelude to War ... 204
Phase I: The Invasion of Iraq ... 207
The Battle of An-Nasiriyah ... 209
The Approach to Baghdad ... 210
The Battles of An-Najaf, As-Samawah, and Karbala ... 210
The Battle of Baghdad ... 211
Post-Invasion Iraq ... 212
Democracy ... 214
Mission Accomplished? ... 215
Too Many Hands on the Steering Wheel ... 216
Fallujah and the Al-Anbar Campaign ... 217
Fallujah: "The Most Dangerous City in Iraq" ... 218
Winning Hearts and Minds ... 219
Operation Vigilant Resolve: The First Battle of Fallujah ... 220
Operation Phantom Fury: The Second Battle of Fallujah ... 220
An Inefficient Way of Operating ... 221
Post-War Iraq: Who Won the War? ... 224
Postscript ... 227

CHAPTER EIGHT:
THE PAST AND FUTURE OF LIMITED WAR 228

ACKNOWLEDGMENTS 241

ENDNOTES 242

PROLOGUE

War, or more properly, the art of using military forces, is a matter of vital importance to the state: the province of life or death; and the road to survival or ruin. It is mandatory that it be thoroughly studied. War is thus a means to a political end. It must adapt itself to its chosen means, a process which can radically change it . . .
—Carl von Clausewitz, On War

W hy should I care more than fifty years later? The point is, I do care. From when I entered college to study political science and history to the time I found out where Vietnam was located, I began to care. I realized the war was not only important to the state but supremely important to "we the people," who are intimately involved.

What follows are issues in limited wars that must be answered by all members of what Carl von Clausewitz called the *trinity of war*: the government, the military, and the people. All involved must comprehend the war's initial objectives, as well as all known consequences of both entering and not entering the conflict. Knowledge of the political objectives of all belligerents is critical if they are to understand and accept the decisions on war or peace. Once the war is entered, these questions must continue to be addressed because war is a dynamic process that changes frequently. If these changes are not known by all elements of the trinity, tremendous discord between its members frequently occurs, often with catastrophic consequences.

Specific objectives of *Limited War* include the intense study of six specific wars: the American Revolution, the War of 1812, the Anglo-Irish War, the Korean War, the Vietnam War, and the Iraq War. Each of these wars was initially researched during my time at the US Naval War College. This book seeks to identify the lessons they have taught that offer a pathway to greater success in future conflicts.

Total war is defined as any war that focuses on the unconditional surrender of the enemy's government and military. In the Second World War, the Axis powers (Germany, Italy, Japan) and the Allied powers (the United States, Great Britain, France, Canada, Australia, and various other nations) joined in a total war against each other. The primary ingredient was that one belligerent group, the Axis powers, was committed to the destruction of their opponents from the beginning. The Allies were then forced to focus their actions on the total surrender of the Axis powers. There was no other alternative available.

Limited war is defined as any war that does not translate into total war for one or all belligerents. Any nation whose strategy limits its own goals for the defeat of its opponents is limited war. Certainly, the six wars discussed in this book meet the narrow war standard. In the Korean War, the United States and other nations wanted to prevent North Korea from taking over South Korea. In addition, the United States had a limited strategy to avoid a larger war with the Soviet Union, led by Joseph Stalin, as well as China, led by Mao Tse-tung.

To avoid such an event, the United States did not seek the destruction of the government and military of North Korea with a massive invasion of the North by the United States Army, Air Force, and Navy. It also did not invade China. Therefore, at least one of the two belligerents had to have limited goals. The strategy of the United States and their United Nations allies was to limit the war's outcome by forcing the North out of the South. They also limited their efforts in the Vietnam War by developing objectives that would force North Vietnam to withdraw its forces from South Vietnam.

The study of limited war is critical because it does not ask for the total surrender of its enemy. It is likely, this side of Armageddon, that most or all future wars will be of a limited nature. Those who engage in future wars must understand the nature and objectives of the participants in these wars; they must know what their limited objectives are and know what the enemy's objectives are as well.

Why is studying past wars so critical as nations continue to deal with the possibility of entering a limited war? Understanding America's many successes and failures in previous wars, and those of other countries, can at least have the potential to develop a winning strategy in the next war. Of course, there is a handicap to that option—the enemy's strategy for victory may succeed if the intentions are not understood.

Once a nation enters a war, it is extremely difficult to withdraw from the fight. That was true with the Vietnam War, the Korean War, and the Iraq War. The British found it difficult to exit the American War of Independence and the Anglo-Irish War. A total net assessment of the enemy's capabilities and intentions must be known and continually updated before and throughout the war. A net assessment of a nation's capabilities and those of any of its allies must also be known. This is true with America's limitations as well.

An early study of the North and South Vietnamese people, government, and military would have helped many in America better understand the Vietnam War. The American people came to believe, over time, that America would not meet its objectives for victory. The North Vietnamese civilians and military were absolutely focused on defeating the United States, as they had defeated France in a colonial war ten years earlier. Eventually, it became evident that North Vietnam was willing to suffer any casualties as long as they were ultimately victorious. In fact, within a five-year period between 1968 and 1973, the North Vietnamese were willing to lose over five hundred thousand of their soldiers. The noncommunist allies, made up largely of the United States, South Korea, the Philippines, and Australia, lost over fifty thousand soldiers throughout the whole war. This was a horrible loss for them and for North Vietnam as well.

Ultimately, America realized it would surely leave the Vietnam War without victory. Its allies in the South were incapable of defeating the North. They were corrupt, poorly trained, and virtually unwilling to fight the well-trained North or its local guerrilla forces, the Vietcong. The United States was incapable of developing a winning strategy, largely because they did not understand the enemy's strategy for victory.

My fervent hope for my country and for the world is that we can go beyond war to simply choosing peace and fellowship with one another; there is so much to be gained for us all if that wish comes true. I also believe that for this to happen, we must all reach into our spiritual beliefs; there we will find hope and the belief that universal peace can become a reality. Until that time comes, the governments, militaries, and people of the world's nations must carefully select wars that are necessary for their survival, not wars that are either unnecessary or impossible to win. Examples of both are described in *Limited War*.

CHAPTER ONE

LIMITED WAR

Within the context of limited war, the failure of the military leader to comprehend the political objective and the inability of the civilian leader to comprehend what can and cannot be achieved by force either already has or will have the potential for catastrophic results. Numerous examples of civilian and military leaders failing to understand each other's critical function are discussed in the case studies that follow.

Carl von Clausewitz, the foremost political theorist on the dynamics of war, determined over a century and a half ago that politics must define the ultimate objectives of every war. Political objectives must also stay within the parameters of military capabilities. Clausewitz believed that "war was merely politics by a different means, and that the use of these military means may be inappropriate for meeting certain political objectives."[1]

In studying each of six wars—the American Revolution, the War of 1812, the Anglo-Irish War, the Korean War, the Vietnam War, and the Iraq War—it becomes apparent that both civilian and military leaders, together, must understand the capabilities of themselves and their enemies. The more civilian and military leaders collaborate, the more likely they will work together successfully. To Clausewitz, this collaboration is essential to victory in any war.

The final element necessary for victory is the full participation of the people. Their inclusion makes up the trinity of war. With it, victory is almost always attained.[2]

The Trinity of War

For Carl von Clausewitz, attaining this trinity is not an abstract idea. The civilian and military leadership must include the people of the nation. They are the foundation for the development and execution of a strategy for ultimate victory. Without the trinity of war, victory is unlikely to be realized.

His notion of the trinity of war is the intimate cooperation of the government (in the American case, the executive branch and Congress), the military, and most importantly, the people of the nation. Each member of this trinity will then be able to develop and better understand the issues prior to engaging in a full-blown war.

Citizens must also know the risks involved in pursuing any war. This pursuit then becomes the individual citizen's responsibility, and one way to be prepared is to understand past wars and the many mistakes and successes experienced by all participants. This will make it possible to hold the civilian and military leaders responsible for their actions. The nation's population must be kept fully aware of the strategy for victory as well. If left out of the process, the people will be ignorant of the actions taken by leadership and will seriously delay the people's inclusion in the trinity. This historical accountability, or lack thereof, will be clearly apparent in each of the six wars discussed.[3]

The main conclusion and the primary idea of the trinity of war are what this book is about. The members of the trinity must answer the questions raised below if a decision is to be made to enter or forego the war. Within the process, the members of the trinity must also effectively communicate with each other, or the process of decision-making will surely fail.[4]

The Steps to Full Understanding

What follows are questions that must be answered by all members of the trinity. They must know the political objectives of all belligerents if they can make the decision of whether to go to war. Once the war is entered, these questions must continue to be addressed because war is a dynamic process that changes frequently. B. A. Lee, from the US Naval War College,[5] has thoughtfully formulated a set of fourteen questions that serve as a guiding compass for such assessment, worthy of a thorough exploration when deliberating the path to war. I've expanded upon this list with a question of my own, which may also be of use regarding the inherent bias in making this determination.

First, there are the basic questions that should be considered:

- Can political objectives be achieved by means other than military action, with a successful result?
- What limitations, if any, were placed on the use of force, if that direction was chosen?
- Was success made less probable by including these limitations?
- Can all parties understand and articulate the political goals of military action?
- Is regime change necessary, or can political objectives be satisfied otherwise?
- Are the benefits and rewards worth the costs and risks that we expect to see?

Next, there are questions based on intelligence, assessment, and plans:

- What is the quality of the intelligence, including its interpretation, that has led us to this point?
- Are we accurately assessing our military capabilities, as well as those of our allies, in creating our strategy?

Based on the instruments of war, they should ask:

- Do all leaders understand the capabilities of their military forces?
- Strategically, are leaders able to plan to integrate these capabilities?
- What prevents the leadership from fully integrating these capabilities?

Concerning the military's ability to make battlefield adjustments:

- How malleable are the prewar plans in the face of military decisions made by the enemy?

On the international, strategic dimension:
- What pressures are exerted upon the various phases of war by international political entities?
- What effects will the outcome of the conflict have on the international political environment?

Finally, there is one question I have added that solidifies the arguments previously presented:

- How does human bias affect the decisions made by the government, the military, and the people of whether or not to go to war?

The Consequences of War

Even with thorough assessments, belligerents in any war never really know how the war will progress. Because of the limitations placed on American efforts to defeat North Vietnam by invasion, they were prevented from truly defeating them. Instead, they launched seriously controlled and limited air strikes without intending to actually vanquish the enemy, hoping to force them to surrender. They never came to that point, and real American progress ended in a quagmire. America saw that it could not win and could not exit this never-ending war.

Was military force the best means to achieve the political objectives, or were other means at least as promising? Great Britain chose war over negotiation during the Anglo-Irish War. If started early enough, they probably could have developed an agreement with the Irish satisfactory to both the Irish and the British. Was strategy based upon an objective net assessment of friendly and enemy strengths and weaknesses? In the American War of Independence, Great Britain did not understand the true nature of their enemy; therefore, they did not make the appropriate changes to their strategy.

Destruction

In both the Vietnam War and the Korean War, the wars were primarily destructive. Participants suffered terrible losses of both soldiers and civilians. Through continued napalm air attacks, all but one major North Korean city was leveled in the effort to turn back invading North Korean and Chinese soldiers. The Vietnam War was equally destructive as hundreds of thousands of both military and civilians died from bombings, chemical attacks, and starvation. The United States met its Korean War goals but did not achieve similar success in the Vietnam War.[6]

The Psychological and Physical Damage

The aftereffects of war on soldiers and civilians alike often lead to social and psychological incidents of posttraumatic stress disorder (PTSD). Common symptoms of PTSD are nightmares and vivid memories, or flashbacks, of the event that make sufferers feel like it is happening all over again. They often feel emotionally cut off from others, numb, constantly on guard, and irritated. They may lose interest in things they used to care about, have angry outbursts, difficulty sleeping, and trouble concentrating, and may become easily startled. These incidents, if not treated, often result in family separations. The symptoms also can lead to suicide attempts.

Because of the enormous stress caused by the Vietnam, Korean, and Iraq wars, returning soldiers often commit suicide. Many others remain afflicted with the symptoms of PTSD for life. Some victims go without psychological assistance, or there are long delays in contact with medical services. The victims, their families, and the nation are often left with enormous financial debt from medical and psychological care.[7]

The Iraqi people were no exception to these problems and still live with this burden of debt and casualties. America has suffered soldier and civilian deaths, serious wounds, and at least $1.2 trillion-plus debt from the Iraq War alone.[8]

Once the War Has Begun

If the civilian and military leaders of a nation, in collaboration with the people, do not evaluate their decisions to either fight in or abstain from the war, it will commence without a good strategy for ending it. Therefore, the issues will not be satisfactorily addressed. All must take heed of the enemy's desire to fight the war to the end. It is also necessary to evaluate allies in the war. The United States did not do that with their South Vietnamese civilian and military partners. In fact, these allies were largely corrupt and incapable of fighting the North Vietnamese Army and their VC guerrillas in the South. The South Vietnamese Army was rarely victorious during the battle with these opponents.[9]

Leadership needed to successfully evaluate these forces and their intent to fight on to the end. In most cases, the American military understood that the South Vietnamese were hopelessly corrupt and unwilling to fight. They fought the war largely alone without the South's effective participation. The North Vietnamese civilian and military leaders ended up knowing America's capabilities much better than the Americans understood theirs. That resulted in a long war, many civilian and military deaths, and an inability to end the war.

If the citizens of the United States had known the enemy and what it would take to defeat them, they would have had time to oppose entry into the war in the first place rather than just be satisfied by what civilian and military leaders decided.

The ultimate point is that war must not begin until all reasons for involvement are fully analyzed by government leaders, military leaders, and the people. All three are critical within the context of war and peace. This analysis must also continue throughout the war because war is a dynamic event that changes throughout its existence. During the Second World War, the trinity of war successfully worked to provide that cohesion throughout the war. Of course, Japan and Germany threatened allied sovereignty, so there was little choice but for all three pillars to work together. That was not true, however, in the Korean, Vietnam, and Iraq wars.[10]

CHAPTER TWO

THE AMERICAN REVOLUTION

Great Britain characterized the uprising in the American colonies initially as a police action against certain "criminals in Boston." As the rebellion grew in intensity, the British crown eventually reacted to a small conventional force of regulars and various regional militias under General George Washington, with an army of approximately ten thousand British Redcoats and a supporting Royal Navy. As this British response to the colonial rebellion continued to expand, a long war of attrition ensued.[11]

It was a limited war for the British because their goal was to maintain control over the colonies by maintaining the status quo. The British failed to understand their army was inappropriate for a combination of the conventional and small-unit guerrilla war strategy devised by the Americans. Britain's miscalculation of the growing American resolve proved fatal. Britain's ever-changing tactics, limited objectives, and weak resolve to see the war through to its definite conclusion resulted in its colonial war defeat.[12]

The decisions made by the king and leading representatives of the British Parliament failed to realize what could and could not be achieved by force. An infinitely more peaceful resolution to the conflict, one more aligned with the will of the colonies that allowed for some degree of independence or representation in Parliament, was contemplated but never seriously considered by the king or Parliament. England believed the approach was correct until its great army faced ultimate defeat on the battlefield of Yorktown.[13]

The Early Settlement of the British Colonies in America

Except for New York, which was inhabited primarily by the Dutch and some Frenchmen, all other colonies were inhabited mainly by people of British descent. This was especially true in New England, which was almost exclusively English. Pennsylvania had a substantial Welsh element, and Catholic Irish people made up a large portion of the population in Maryland. Both Irish and Scottish emigrants lived throughout the Southern colonies. After 1709, large numbers of Germans emigrated to the colonies. More than thirteen thousand came from the Rhine area of Germany via England.

The people of England and people of English heritage in the colonies formed parts of "one nation"—Great Britain. But by 1760, many of the American colonists had come to think of themselves as something different. "In all that constitutes nationality, two nations now owed allegiance to the British crown,"[14] at least temporarily. This distinction was to have dramatic consequences throughout the 1770s and early 1780s, and have lasting effects for Great Britain, the American colonies, and the world.

The evolution of the colonies was not limited to becoming "a distinct race." They also became aware of their knowledge of democratic systems. James A. Williamson wrote, "Colonial administration on either side of the Atlantic had grown up piecemeal and uncoordinated. No single element, the assembly, governor, Board of Trade, or secretary of state, could claim to be in the last resort a supreme authority with the ultimate power to resolve a disputed question."[15]

The lack of a competent central authority solely responsible for the management of politics in the colonies proved to be an Achilles' heel for the British in the American colonies. One major weakness on their part was the management of the "proprietary governors" themselves.

Williamson continues, "Every proprietary Governor . . . has two masters, one who gives him his Commission, and one who gives him his Pay. Salaries of the governor and royal officials, the right of colonies to issue paper money, and the right of the Crown to veto colonial legislation were three issues of dispute that continually reoccurred."[16]

Politically, the American colonies eventually learned the inner workings of self-government. This knowledge included mimicking and self-designing political systems that worked for them. In each province, a governor representing the Crown advised the government by assisting in legislation and acting as the supreme court of law. A lower chamber or assembly was composed of colonial-elected natives. Eventually, this and other democratic systems were taken over by the colonies, as they directly affected internal colonial issues.

By the time Thomas Jefferson completed the Declaration of Independence, experiences with self-government were encouraging to the leaders of each of the thirteen colonies. This confidence in their ability to self-govern moved the colonials toward a war of independence from Great Britain.

British efforts to promote the vetoing of colonial legislation were a source of perpetual ill-feeling for the colonials. Despite these efforts, colonial control of internal political issues continued to grow as Britain's efforts to sustain its influence over the colonial government became less and less effective. This failure continued until the colonies attained complete independence with total separation from the British government at the end of the American Revolution in 1783.

The Commons of England's Parliament had fought the battle to legislate and won in the seventeenth century. With this legislative victory against Charles I, members of Parliament chose not to share the success with the American colonists. In March of 1642, Parliament declared that its ordinances were valid on their own merits and did not require the king's approval.

Eventually, the colonists won because of their steady persistence. Colonial governors, receiving no money from home, accepted temporary grants in default of a permanent salary. Because of their deficiencies, the central English government took the colonial view.

Jonathan Belcher, governor of Massachusetts Bay, New Hampshire, and later, New Jersey, as well as other governors throughout the colonies, were themselves colonists, but the attitude of their subjects remained the same:

"The colonists did not deny the crown [through Parliament] a right to veto. They found means of circumventing it by passing temporary Acts and renewing them as often as they fell to the ground relying upon the fact that an interval of two or three years commonly elapsed before the decision of the home government."[17]

The Move Toward Independence

The move toward independence was not without its challenges. For many colonists, at least the appearance of loyalty to the British crown existed primarily due to the fears and distrust of French intentions in North America. The colonists believed they needed the security the British provided despite their underlying opinion that Britain's control of them must end. They felt they must maintain the essence of independence while outwardly appearing allegiant to England.

Ultimately, the colonies would choose war with England. But, the act of war must be studied thoroughly before a final commitment, as there is no turning back once decided. Carl von Clausewitz cited, "War, or more properly the art of using military forces, is vital to the state: the province of life or death; the road to survival or ruin. War is thus a means to a political end."[18]

Key leaders of the fast-approaching rebellion took stock of the inherent dangers to them and their efforts toward independence. As open rebellion by the colonists grew closer, American leadership in the newly formed Continental Congress knew if they were to fail, the resistance against Great Britain would be a matter of life and death. The rebellion was also political—not just a threat to life but hopefully a way to political and economic freedom.[19]

The colonists soon realized the war was a viable way to end significant political control against taxation without representation and a way to withdraw from the many economic restrictions Great Britain had placed on them. Success in overturning these controls would also free them to trade with the rest of Europe and nations worldwide, such as the French West Indies, which was prohibited by Britain.

With success, it would also finally provide a means by which they could overcome the severe population growth in the colonies and the growing pressures to open up the western lands for development. These pressures were applied to quickly push development, despite the resistance from the native populations or Britain's disapproval.[20]

Great Britain's Decision to Go to War

As important as understanding the nature of the colonies' decision to declare independence from Britain is, it is also essential that we understand that those in power must make the decision to go or not to go to war. These political issues began with Britain's unwillingness to consider solutions short of military intervention. This position centered on its constitution and how the colonies fit within it.

"The king and a majority in the British Parliament saw the rebellion as a local police action that could be quickly put down through force. The British were responding to a revolt that would disappear once they jailed its leaders. As this response to the colonial revolution continued to be ineffective, a long and bloody war ensued. At that point, the British came to believe that the rebellion was the beginning of a civil war, not a contest between nation-states. Their military strategy would be different than fighting an international war: Parliament and its ministers' problem was not to conquer a foreign enemy but to reestablish the authority of the crown at home."[21]

From the British point of view, the rebellion directly subjected their constitution to a profound crisis. The law was a direct result of the Settlement of 1689, which gave Parliament the power to tax its citizens, including those in the American colonies. Their view was that this settlement was at the core of all British liberties. The preservation of its constitution was absolute. They were using age-old constitutional processes and used power to levy taxes.

It is also essential to understand that this was a parliamentary power, not a royal power. Parliament possessed total legislative sovereignty over all who lived within the protection of the empire. Again, in this rebellion, few in Britain found a "foreign enemy" in the Americans. However, they did see the beginnings of a civil war manifesting heavily based on the colonists' opposition to taxation. It was a political act that was unconstitutional to the British.

The most fundamental constitutional issue was the British political assumption that liberty must survive against those that threatened it. Britain identified the threat coming from the criminal elements in America, such as John Adams, Samuel Adams, and all of those who are now known as the American Founding Fathers. The virtual independence of the thirteen colonies was the one factor that Prime Minister Frederick North could not understand as they proceeded forward to war. Liberty was the root of Britain's inability and unwillingness to consider solutions short of military intervention.[22]

Boston Tea Party, 1773[23]

The American Decision to Rebel

The British had a different perspective than those supporting the Declaration of Independence in the colonies. Americans did not feel their actions equated to a constitutional crisis. They opposed the British Settlement of 1689 and its constitution, feeling it was irrelevant to them and was at the foundation of their loss of real liberties. John Adams clearly described the American opposition to the British Constitution as early as December 1765 by stating that this year was "a remarkable year of my life. The enormous engine, fabricated by the British Parliament for battering down all the rights and liberties of America . . . has raised and spread thro [sic] the whole continent, a spirit that will be recorded to our honour, with all future generations."[24]

David McCullough maintains that Alexander Hamilton sought to justify their intentions to rebel against the British Constitution. Hamilton's complete explanation of the rebellion was written seventeen months before the Declaration of Independence, in December 1774, under the nom de plume "A Friend of America." Hamilton intended to defend congressional resolutions calling for a boycott of British goods in America and an embargo on exports to the British Empire. The recommendations were to respond to the continuing parliamentary efforts to tax the American colonies without their consent.[25]

Hamilton responded directly to the pamphlet "Free Thoughts on the Seabury." Hamilton wrote under the pseudonym A. W. Farmer, and his response was entitled "The Farmer Refuted." Seabury argued that the American Continental Congress had "ignorantly misunderstood, carelessly neglected, or basely betrayed" the colonies' interests. Seabury also defended the supreme legislative authority of Great Britain to make laws for its territories.[26] Hamilton felt obligated to support congressional legislative actions from the charge of injustice. Hamilton contended that self-preservation was more important than American duties to Englishmen. Hamilton insisted that the Colonial Congress' responsibility was to take any action necessary to secure American rights. To defend Congress and its activities, Hamilton generated three assumptions: "First, that Parliament had no right to tax the American colonies; second, that Congress had a right to enact sanctions against the British and their dominions; and third, that such sanctions were justified even if it caused much suffering for ordinary British subjects. Congress is responsible for taking all necessary measures to secure American rights in the quarrel with England."[27]

The die was cast for what would begin as a rebellion and progressively continue to a full-blown war against Great Britain. Alexander Hamilton decried British aggression as an attempt to "reduce the King's deluded subjects [the Americans] to their natural obedience."[28]

As the American uprising grew, Britain's commitment to stop what they saw as a police action and a civil war by an American population that was part of the empire increased. This growing commitment became increasingly complicated as they set out to begin military action three thousand miles across the Atlantic Ocean. Although this was an unequaled accomplishment, by 1760, the colonies were distinct from England's specified Great Britain. In reality, this fact should have been included in Britain's decision whether to go to war or to seek a peaceful settlement.[29]

The American War of Independence

The American War of Independence was mainly one theater of war in a three-pronged global conflict. It was England's war to retain the status quo in North America, defend its colonies worldwide, and prevent France's invasion of the British Isles.

As the American conflict increased, Great Britain responded with ten thousand regulars and the British Navy. The British should have understood that strategy was inappropriate for fighting a war on the North American continent. It contained vast lands with forests, rivers, and a large hostile colonial population. Britain's trained soldiers and sailors were adept at fighting a conventional war, not a traditional war and a guerrilla war simultaneously.

They also terribly miscalculated the American resolve and its military's ability to fight. That British perception stemmed from years of believing American soldiers were vastly inferior to their British regulars. The British war assessment was seriously flawed by analyzing the current capabilities of the American military rather than estimating how their abilities might change as the war progressed. *What if* scenarios might have aided them as they decided on war or peace. This failure directly led to Britain's ultimate defeat against this increasingly powerful enemy. Their overall war assessment should have included questions like: What if the rebels were not inferior? What if other nations came to support the rebellion? What if the logistics trail proved overwhelming to their transportation system? What if a long, drawn-out, and complicated war became a reality?[30]

Further complicating Britain's difficulties, the British people, the British Parliament, and the king were committed to keeping the Americans within the fold. However, Britain's obligations to a three-pronged responsibility, namely 1) opposing the American Revolution, 2) maintaining their worldwide war for commerce and territory, and 3) preventing through strength a possible French (and Spanish) invasion of the British Isles, proved to be impossible for them. This possibility was additionally tricky because of France's massive expansion of its navy, both in the number of warships and of competent admirals.[31]

The British Navy needed to prepare to meet this French naval threat. Over the preceding ten years following the worldwide Seven Years War, the British Navy had deteriorated due to inactivity, inadequate funding, and financial corruption. The British Navy would need to meet their North American obligations and defend their responsibilities at home and their colonies throughout the world. To eliminate the growing French naval threat, the conflict with America could no longer be their priority. The second and third obligations were critical to their national survival—the American War was not.

No Taxation Without Representation

Strong feelings existed within the general British public, members of Parliament, and King George III that the colonies must pay their fair share for the cost of their protection.

The British Parliament initiated a series of legislative acts designed to bring in revenue from the American colonies. This anticipated revenue was to decrease Britain's financial burdens associated with the French and Indian War and fund the ongoing protection of the colonies. Obligations, such as the presence of the British Army and Navy, were necessary to respond to threats such as regional Indian attacks and potential and realized invasions into the colonies from Canada.

The American colonists had their grievances associated with paying for new financial burdens. They also had ongoing concerns about the local economic conditions caused by the financial downturn due to years of war from 1754 to 1763. As tempers grew within the American community, the presence of British soldiers living in American colonists' homes was angrily perceived not as an attempt to protect them but as an effort to stop the anticipated rebellion soon to come. This rebellion occurred first in Boston and then spread throughout the colonies.

Although the Molasses Act was ignored until after 1763, the British Parliament began to enforce revenue collection through the replacement Sugar Act. The strictly controlled revenue collection in the provinces was due to Britain's understanding that anticipated profits would be achieved only with stern management.[32]

Despite their efforts to control revenue collection, the British representatives in North America and Parliament soon realized that the parliamentary reforms were barely sufficient to pay for the collection costs. It certainly would not support the ten thousand British regulars in the colonies. It would have little effect on their national budget deficits.

Three-fourths of the ten thousand soldiers were already in America. The rest were assigned to the West Indies so that Britain could more closely monitor American trade there. Keeping a watchful eye on trade revenues lost with American businesses outside the British West Indies was necessary because this illegal trade resulted in substantial financial losses.

Although most colonists initially wished to remain subjects of the British crown, many developed deep resentment toward Parliament for forcing unpopular and burdensome taxes on them. Implementing the highly contentious Stamp Act of 1765 and the Townsend Acts of 1767 created widespread opposition.

Bad feelings worsened when the colonial sloop *Liberty* was seized by the British and confiscated for smuggling in 1768. That event and the legislation of 1765 and 1767 ultimately resulted in growing support for the rebellion throughout the thirteen colonies. The ship's wealthy owner, John Hancock, became a hero to those who supported their complete separation from Great Britain. Ultimately, John Hancock would join Samuel Adams and others to lead much of the resistance to British rule. The driving force behind the growing protest was that Americans were already overwhelmed by taxes. They now needed financial assistance, not additional burdens.[33]

Britain's implementation of the Stamp Act also presented a different situation than such legislation as the Sugar Act for the colonies. It was different from all previous acts of Parliament affecting the thirteen colonies. "It was an internal tax for the sole purpose of raising a revenue, lacking any commercial compensations which had flowed from the manipulation of tariffs, and was granted to the Crown by a House of [Commons] revenue collections which included not a single member [representing] the areas affected."[34]

As trivial as the stamp duties may have appeared, they generated an enormous backlash from the colonial population. To demonstrate how the thirteen colonies were uniting, each had an "identical grievance" to promote collective resistance. Associated with this resistance was a simple mantra: *No taxation without representation.*[35]

The establishment of the Sons of Liberty became a vital tool to promote this resistance and a key enforcement group under the leadership of John Hancock, Samuel Adams, Paul Revere, and others. These leaders of rebellion molded their followers into an active organization for change.

The focus of this resistance and the growing number of members joining the newly formed Sons of Liberty quickly evolved into intimidating mob attacks on those collecting the taxes on stamps, molasses, and its follow-up, sugar.

George Grenville, the British chancellor of the exchequer, was responsible for authoring the Stamp Act by gaining its support from a vast majority in Parliament in 1765. Grenville's law became a "notorious act of taxation without representation," sowing "the seeds of revolution" and sparking "an earthshaking shift in colonial political allegiances."[36]

These legislative measures, sponsored by Parliament, were deemed right and just, an opinion soon shared by most of its members and King George III. All understood the cost of maintaining military defense and civilian administration in the colonies. Under George Grenville's Stamp Act, colonists would pay a tax on almost anything written or printed. It included licenses, mortgages, wills, deeds, newspapers, advertising, calendars, almanacs, dice, and playing cards.

The truth was that the cost of maintaining military defense and civilian administration in the colonies jumped from seventy thousand pounds in 1748 to three hundred fifty thousand in 1764 annually. Additional taxes were required to offset these drastic increases.[37]

The Royal Proclamation

American concerns were growing in the colonies. The Royal Proclamation of 1763, issued at the close of the French and Indian War, tried to limit the settlement of Americans beyond the Appalachians. George Washington initially thought the declaration would only be temporary, but he became more concerned when, after five years, London was still enforcing the tenets of the proclamation.

In the French and Indian War, Indians had most closely allied with the French. Once the French withdrew from North America, British royal authorities became eager to make friends with the Indians surrounding their colonies. Efforts to develop these friendships with the various native groups through appeasement directly led to severe tension with the colonists.

George Washington and his Virginia militia felt they had won the right to expand westward due to the many sacrifices they made fighting alongside the British throughout the French and Indian War.

The Ministry in London feared a massive westward movement. Reluctance was due to their fears that the Indian tribes would rebel. The

British "feared the Indians who hunted the lands of Ohio and the trans-Appalachian territories that today form Kentucky and Tennessee. Chief Pontiac's rebellion in the Ohio Valley in 1763 had been a bloody and expensive affair."[38]

The Stamp Act Crisis

Eventually, revenues from taxes and colonial population growth were at the center of the conflict. These issues changed Americans' initial attitude of remaining British citizens to one of deep resentment and the ultimate desire by many to declare independence.

William J. Bennett, in his book *America: The Last Best Hope*, describes the Stamp Act's immediate result as the colonies catching "fire with stirring talk about equality, the consent of the governed, and the importance of ancient rights and newly asserted liberties."[39]

Relations between Great Britain and the American colonies had begun to deteriorate seriously by the 1760s as a result of the Stamp Act's passage and other legislative actions, such as the Writs of Assistance of 1761, which allowed British authorities to search, seize, and enter a colonist's property without cause or warrant. John Adams later wrote in his memoirs that it was during James Otis's legal challenges to the Writs of Assistance that the origins of the Revolution arose. Otis was Adams's mentor and business partner.[40]

December 1765 was a watershed moment for America. John Adams described his feelings: "The enormous engine fabricated by the British Parliament for battering down all the rights and liberties of America has raised through the whole continent a spirit that will be recorded to our honor with all future generations."[41]

Of the colonies, Massachusetts and Virginia protested first. Massachusetts quickly responded against the Sugar Act and its stricter administration in 1764. At the end of that year, Boston merchants formed a "nonimportation society." They pledged to boycott, refusing to purchase English manufactured goods until Parliament addressed colony grievances. By the end of 1765, the boycott had taken hold. "Who were the leaders? James Otis, John, and Samuel Adams wrote vehement protests and worked to bring the other colonies into the protest/resistance. By December 1765, 250 Boston merchants had joined the effort. New York and Philadelphia soon followed."[42]

The Virginia resistance, caused by their declining economy, proceeded mainly from the individual leadership of one man, Patrick Henry. Thomas Paine quoted him as saying, "Free men have certain fundamental rights . . . and no authority, constitutional or otherwise, can enact any binding law contrary to those rights."[43]

Fortunately, his message fell on very sympathetic ears—a far cry from the accusations of treason that had met an earlier speech of Henry's entitled "Defying King George." Many prominent citizens were unhappy with the British government's actions, whether the Stamp Act or any other parliamentary laws affecting the colonies. George Washington was one of many who "were bitterly incensed at the conduct of the king's troops in the late war [French and Indian War], and everyone was enraged by the condescending treatment accorded to colonials whenever they visited England, or their sons went there for their education."[44]

To reinforce Washington's statements on British feelings of superiority, James A. Williamson credits Benjamin Franklin for stating, "Every man in England seems to consider himself as a piece of a sovereign over Americans seems to jostle himself into the throne with the king, and talks of our subjects in the colonies, with lower social status or inferior."[45]

Pushback continued in Boston that August when a mob destroyed the home of Andrew Oliver, an unpopular royal official. Oliver suffered because a newspaper had erroneously named him as one designated to collect revenue from the stamps.

Resistance flared up throughout the colonies against the Stamp Act. In Charleston, South Carolina, Christopher Gadsden led protests where a mob tore up the homes of two Stamp Act officials. Gadsden captured the sense that public opposition to the Crown was galvanizing, saying, "There ought to be no New England man, no New Yorkers known on this continent, but all of us Americans. It was a cry for independence and the new information of a democratic republic."[46]

Annapolis, Maryland, was "a scene of destruction, where a crowd pulled down a warehouse owned by a tax collector. New York City citizens attacked the royal governor's coach. In Rhode Island, the stamp protesters hanged tax collectors in effigy. In Newport, protest signs accused one collector of being an infamous 'Jacobite,' a charge that meant he was a supporter of the deposed Stuart monarch, James II, a Catholic."[47] Of course, no loyal British subject would want to be accused of Jacobitism for fear they would lose their standing with the British government.

At the end of 1764, Boston merchants formed a non-import society. They intended to boycott by not paying for English manufactured goods until the grievance ended. The Stamp Act "intensified the merchants'" efforts throughout the colonies. By December 1765, two hundred and fifty Boston merchants had joined the effort, followed by those in New York and Philadelphia.

Who were the members that were becoming the core of the rebellion? James Otis, John and Samuel Adams, Paul Revere, and many others. They led the uprising, coordinating protests and working to bring the other colonies to the rebellion. Patrick Henry continued his influence not only in Virginia but throughout the colonies. On one occasion, Patrick Henry stated that defying King George was necessary if freedom was to be attained. In response to these words, the New York merchants defied British authority by organizing a complete boycott of British goods.[48]

Colonial pushback continued to grow. Led by James Otis of Massachusetts, nine colonies agreed to send delegates to the Stamp Act Congress in New York in October 1765. New Hampshire, Georgia, and South Carolina were unrepresented.[49] The Stamp Act Congress issued a Declaration of Rights. Despite their loyalty to the king, delegates took a position against the continued implementation of the Stamp Act. Approved by the Stamp Act Congress held in New York, Patrick Henry's resolution demanded that only colonial legislatures had the authority to tax colonists. He opposed the British Parliament's constitution powerfully as the sole sovereign entity to enact specific legislation on its citizens.

The Stamp Act failed to meet the British objective. People in each of the colonies refused to do business using stamped documents. Officials collecting revenues under the Stamp Act were also intimidated because mobs would physically beat them.

In the spring of 1766, Parliament repealed the Stamp Act due to this intimidation and because the effort was not worth the financial and political objectives established. In response to its repeal, the colonies first celebrated and erected a statue of King George III. Overnight, it seemed like the abolition reduced political pressure on the British government and altered the colonists' view of a continued alliance with Britain. Americans appeared content to live within the British crown—but few believed this would be a long-lasting peace. It was only temporary.

George Grenville, the mastermind behind the Sugar Act and the Stamp Act, was opposed to the repeal of the Stamp Act and protested vigorously. Although George III often disagreed with him, he did share Grenville's resentment on this issue. In response to this resentment, Parliament passed the Declaratory Act. It reasserted the right members of Parliament possessed to create additional taxes on the colonies if they were considered necessary.[50]

Williamson notes that Parliament believed that "His Majesty's subjects in these colonies owe the same allegiance to the Crown of Great Britain that is owing from his subjects born within the realm." Williamson, in the spirit of compromise, described that George Grenville also "amended the Sugar Act by reducing from three pence to one penny the duty on every gallon of molasses taken from the French islands to America and extended the lower impost to the produce of the British West Indies as well. . . Despite the American public's positive reaction to the repeal of the Stamp Act, the amendment to the Sugar Act, and the reduction in the cost of molasses, opposition soon arose once again."[51]

There were other sources of tension between the colonies and the British government that eventually dissuaded Americans from accepting any reconciliation with Britain. Parliament began to enforce the Navigation Acts of 1651 and 1660, which to the British, "represented a lucrative source of wealth and trade."[52] These acts had not been enforced for more than a century and significantly impacted the American colonies, especially New England merchants. War plans recommenced. The colonies believed there were enough restrictions. Any other tax by the British Parliament on the colonies was not to be.

A century earlier, in 1660, King Charles II had ascended to the English throne upon the Restoration of the monarchy following the English Civil War. He had advocated for and received the second 1660 Navigation Act. He wanted this legislation because he sought the profits that would come with the introduction of this act. The act was intended to prevent "fraudulent evasions" and specified that it would increase overall shipping and navigation of the kingdom. The Navigation Act of 1660 specified the following: "Thenceforward, no goods or commodities whatsoever shall be imported into or exported out of any lands, islands, plantations, or territories to his Majesty belonging or in his possession . . . in Asia, Africa, or America, in any other ship or ships, vessel or vessels whatsoever, but in such ships or vessels as do truly and without fraud belong only to the people of England."[53]

The effect was for the British to consolidate control over colonial exports: "Colonial exports [mainly American] had to be transported in English, or colonial ships and . . . colonial imports had to first pass through English ports—whether the goods were for England or another European country . . . the goods were then to be inspected and taxed."[54]

All goods going to or from America had to first stop in England to be taxed. The Navigation Acts of 1673, 1696, and 1773 were all specifically designed to close trade loopholes, increase the list of goods and commodities, increase taxes, and appoint vice-admiralty courts in Colonial America to help enforce the navigation laws.

At the 1773 act in particular, America and all other English trading partners worldwide were angry at Britain's increasingly aggressive trade policies. America pushed back hard because of these taxes and the fact that American shipping and shipbuilding would end. The colonies were united in their opposition, giving "an identical grievance . . . thus, facilitating combined resistance, and they once again provided a simple war cry: no taxation without representation."⁵⁵

In reaction to this and other parliamentary initiatives, Pennsylvania hosted a Continental Congress in Philadelphia between September 5 and October 26, 1774. It indicated that the separate colonies looked toward each other as they sought relief from Britain. Twelve of the thirteen colonies sent representatives who drafted resolutions reflecting the views of the attendees and the settlements they represented. For the first time, most of the thirteen colonies combined with supporting their initiatives.

The Death of General Warren at the Battle of Bunker's Hill⁵⁶

The Battles of Lexington, Concord, and Bunker Hill

By the time the first shots of the American Revolution were fired, the crisis with Great Britain had gone far beyond taxation without representation and the petitioning for tax relief. In 1774, as the congress was once again planning to petition the British government for tax relief, George Washington said, "Taxes take their toll," in his letter to Lord Bryan Fairfax. Washington inserted himself in the middle of the petition process: "I think the Parliament of Great Britain hath no right to put their hands into my pocket without my consent than I have to put my hands into yours for money."[57]

In 1775, the battles of Lexington and Concord proved inevitable. General Gage, Britain's newly assigned commander in North America, ordered Colonel Francis Smith to conduct a "sweep" of the area of Lexington and Concord, intended to destroy the weapon and ammunition magazine, which self-preservation had necessitated the Americans establish. General Gage later confessed that his soldiers made a retreat from Concord. Gage further admitted that the sweep was to capture key rebel leaders, namely Sam Adams and John Hancock, and destroy a "magazine housing American weapons." Regardless, King George III, along with John Montagu, the Earl of Sandwich and also the first lord of the admiralty, and numerous other leaders fully supported General Gage's actions.

Parliament's actions continued to aggravate the public, especially leaders such as Washington. This aggravation included sending troops to capture the weapons of Minutemen at Lexington and Concord. General Gage's efforts resulted in a Minuteman response that attacked his troops, forcing them to retreat to Boston. Once there, twenty thousand American militia surrounded the British troops and inflicted one thousand casualties at Bunker Hill.

Although the British forced the Americans to retreat, their victory was pyrrhic at best. As a result of these actions, the Americans saw this defeat as a moral victory, confirming to them that the "spirit of liberty" could overcome even a professional army such as the British Redcoats.

The direct outcome of this American success was that the Second Continental Congress appointed George Washington as commander in chief of the Continental Army in June 1775. The Americans began to arm themselves, even while negotiating for peace with the British Parliament. Once the American Declaration of Independence was finalized and distributed in the summer of 1776, the king and Parliament's reaction was to prepare for police action to put down the revolt. It was an action that would accomplish nothing except for a long and futile war for Great Britain.

Additional Factors Leading to War

Explaining the sequence of events is necessary to set the stage for Phase I of the war. It is possible to identify the early beginnings of an American national identity from the fourth stage of the Seven Years' War. This final stage, also known as the French and Indian War, was due to the colonies' efforts to defend against threats along the northern and western borders between the colonies and New France. As Brinton Crane wrote in his book *The Americans and the French*, "For New Englanders and New Yorkers, the existence of a French menace on their northern borders was for years a very real thing, more real than any acute danger from a foreign power was to seem to Americans until the Russians acquired their own atomic bomb."

The French and Indian War was not just a series of British actions to defeat an enemy. It was a series of British-American steps to protect the colonies from both the French and its Indian allies. The British colonies in America showed as early as 1753 that they were working together for their common defense. A case in point is when French and Indian raiders plundered Deerfield, Massachusetts. Connecticut sent its militia to Massachusetts to assist its neighbors. This cooperation became common during the eighteenth century and played an essential role in persuading the colonists that they had shared interests, especially regarding the defense of their borders.

The American Colonies Mature

Americans did not create a formal union until much later. They slowly came to realize that they could unify. Both the leaders and the populations of the thirteen colonies were developing this desire and capability to at least work more closely for their common welfare. This desire was not only in war but in political and financial terms.

Representatives from seven colonies gathered at the Albany Congress of 1754 to discuss increased cooperation. At this congress, Benjamin Franklin observed that their "disunited state" encouraged aggression. The French, said Franklin, "may with impunity . . . kill, seize and imprison our traders, and confiscate their effects at pleasure as they have done for several years past, murder and scalp our farmers, with their wives and children, and take an easy possession of such parts of the British territory as they find most convenient for them."[58]

The American Revolution, Phase I

There were three separate and distinct phases to the American Revolutionary War. Phase I, 1775–1776, was characterized by spontaneous resistance versus a police action, such as the battles of Lexington and Concord and the aborted American invasion of Canada.

Great Britain's General Gage was assigned as Britain's commander in chief in North America and stationed in Boston in 1775. He saw the colonial crisis as a law enforcement problem that must end. His first effort as commander was to disarm Minutemen and capture their leaders. Like King George III and most members of Parliament, he failed to understand the depth of American opposition to any taxation, martial law, and a massive British Army and Navy presence in North America. Phase I of the war had begun.

Washington's ascent to commander in chief of the Continental Army and his efforts to train a new army totally lacking in formal military skills began. Professor Karl Friedrich Walling, during a Strategy and Policy Lecture at the Naval War College, commented, "As often happens, neither side understood the nature of the war at the beginning. Who would win depended in large part on which side reassessed and adapted better than the other according to the changing nature of the war—a race before time ran out on Great Britain's will or American resources and will."[59]

King George III's reaction was best captured in his letter from March 1775 to Lord Guilford North, prime minister during the Revolutionary War. His resolute words would inform Parliament about what must end the rebellion: "I have no doubt, but the nation at large sees the conduct in America in its true light, and I am certain any other conduct but compelling obedience would be ruinous, and therefore no consideration could bring me to swerve from the present path which I think myself duty-bound to follow."[60]

In January 1776, the American expedition failed to take Montreal and Quebec as planned. This disaster was a sign of American strategic problems throughout the war. George Washington realized the so-called spirit of liberty was not enough to defeat this world power. Washington began to understand that he needed drastic improvements to his army. He desperately needed excellent, reliable logistics to ensure the survival of his army, which also required better political organization and leadership.

In March 1776, the British evacuated Boston, a moral victory for Americans. Great Britain appointed two brothers, General William Howe and Admiral Richard Howe, to replace General Gage. In July 1776, congress adopted the Declaration of Independence. The declaration was necessary because it was the first statement by the American people clarifying why a complete separation from Great Britain was essential to a liberated future for America. Until 1776, the colonies depended on Great Britain, not each other. Congress had to convince its citizens that they could not ignore reality by burying their heads in the sand. They needed to unite their efforts to oppose a common enemy.

Thomas Jefferson wrote the Declaration of Independence, expressing the mood of at least the "revolutionaries" among them. It dramatically captured the vision and objectives of this statement of rights:

> We hold these Truths to be self-evident, that all Men are created equal, that they are endowed by their Creator with certain unalienable Rights, that among these are Life, Liberty, and the Pursuit of Happiness—That to secure these Rights, Governments are instituted among Men, deriving their just Powers from the Consent of the Governed, that whenever any Form of Government becomes destructive of these Ends, it is the Right of the People to alter or to abolish it, and to institute new Government.[61]

Although equal rights of all Americans have been a continuing process, still incomplete, most citizens overwhelmingly favor meeting this ideal. The commencement of this process began with this declaration.

No less a figure than Abraham Lincoln, who could rival Jefferson in his own way with words, put it most poignantly in 1858: "All honor to Jefferson—to the man who, in the concrete pressure of a struggle for national independence by a single people, had the coolness, forecast, and capacity to introduce into a merely revolutionary document, an abstract truth, applicable to all men and all times, and so to embalm it here, that to-day, and in all coming days, it shall be a rebuke and a stumbling block to the very harbingers of the re-appearing tyranny and oppression."[62]

A strong coalition between all thirteen states was essential but was difficult to implement and did not fully meet expectations until after the successful post-war Constitutional Convention of 1787. The first step in building a strong coalition was the Declaration of Independence. While signing it, Benjamin Franklin said Americans had "to hang together, or surely, they would hang separately." For the rebels, there was no other satisfactory outcome.[63]

George Washington Takes Charge of the Continental Army

After taking command of the Continental Army as commander in chief, Washington began focusing on the day-to-day issues of his army. Considering that this was the first national, locally led army in British North America, understanding the devastation diseases could wreak on all commands was essential. Washington considered it mandatory that he prevent infections. Essential hygiene efforts and drills were the first steps in making this group of volunteers into a professional army that could survive in battle and camp disease-free. In his first general order, Washington directed that "proper necessarys [latrines] were to be convenient to troop barracks. The 'necessarys' should also be filled frequently, and anyone who failed to follow this General Order would be subject to Regimental court-martial."[64]

Ensuring the troops followed Washington's general order, his quartermaster and each of his noncommissioned officers were responsible for executing them within troop living quarters. Washington took from his experience in the French and Indian War, where he had learned that no detail was too small. He knew his soldiers would die of dysentery and other deadly diseases if strict adherence to good hygiene did not occur.

Washington's time and the time of his subordinates was spent training his troops and regulating the requirements of the Continental Army as a whole. He addressed the battlefield by providing advice to his troops regarding battle behavior as well: "Be cool but determined. Do not fire at a distance." He further advised, "If any man attempted to skulk, lay down, or retreat without orders that he be instantly shot down as an example—resolving to conquer or die and trusting to the smiles of heaven."[65]

He did have significant help in altering his army's overall "good order and discipline." Along with his generals and commissioned and noncommissioned officers, Washington enlisted General von Steuben in military training, including military drills, ceremonies, and related military disciplines. Steuben's impact on the Continental Army was essential. He not only provided hours directing drill ceremonies, but he also wrote a complete training manual for the Continental Army focused on the specific needs of the training system he had learned as a member of the Prussian Army. The impact of this material proved to be an essential military document for years after the American Revolution.[66]

The American Revolution, Phase II

During a strategy and policy lecture at Navy War College, Professor Karl Friedrich Walling described Great Britain's greatest strength—its Royal Navy. The Navy provided transportation for the British Army, enabling it to expand its reach in time and distance. Because of this, George Washington understood that he must change the American military strategy. He knew his army would fail without it.

The sheer difference in force size, especially with respect to sea power and the overwhelming number of Redcoats, became evident during the Battle of New York in August of 1776. "The British, led by the Howe brothers, attacked New York City with the largest maritime expedition in history to that date. Ten ships of the line, twenty frigates, one hundred means of transport, ten thousand seamen, and thirty-two thousand soldiers—including twelve thousand Hessian mercenaries."[67]

Washington considered which overall course of action would allow his troops to survive and be victorious. He knew a viable strategy would ensure his army's survival and expand American and foreign confidence in a realistic opportunity for victory. In collaboration with officers and subordinates, Washington figured he could focus his forces on smaller British detachments without significant losses to his regulars and associated militia. His priority was the preservation of his army by keeping it concentrated and by avoiding battles with the enemy's superior numbers. He then could focus on smaller victories that would both preserve America's confidence and discourage the British Army and the British people at home.

He began implementing his new approach during the British invasion and ultimate control of New Jersey, the British occupation of Philadelphia, and the battles of Trenton and Princeton. The American strategy emphasized conventional war in the northern and the middle colonies and included small-unit guerrilla tactics during the summer and fall of 1776. This gradual change was also significant because of the American's defeat in the Battle of New York City and during the long march from the New York disaster through New Jersey.

A week after the catastrophic defeat on Long Island on August 27, 1776, British forces converged on Manhattan, cutting through Washington's lines. Washington had no option but to retreat north to escape British encirclement. The British then pushed Washington across New Jersey and over the Delaware River to Pennsylvania, where the Continental Congress was to establish its capital in Philadelphia, as well as resettle the Continental Army so that they could regroup and prepare for counterattacks. The results of Britain's victories and the subsequent retreat of the American army were described by one historian as the "American Dunkirk." There were just enough boats arriving to evacuate the remains of a defeated Continental Army. George Washington lost a third of his regular force, and the militia melted away. From the time of the signing of the Declaration, Washington's most significant challenge was leading his army through New Jersey to Pennsylvania. His early efforts to prepare his army for the battlefield and subsequent thoughts about proper battle strategy were now critical to survival.

A view of Washington's thinking is evident in his "heartsick" letter to his cousin, who was managing Washington's Mount Vernon estate, dated September 30, 1776. In addition to explaining his current emotional status, his words also demonstrated the way forward as he searched for opportunities for victory against the British forces and Hessian mercenaries. "At present, our numbers fit for duty . . . amount to 14,759 . . . and the enemy within [a] stone's throw of us . . . I should put in my stead . . . and yet I do not know what plan of conduct to pursue. I see the impossibility of serving with reputation or doing any essential service to the cause by continuing in command, and yet I am told that if I quit the command, inevitable ruin will follow from the distraction that will ensue."[68] Fortunately for Washington, the British efforts to overtake the retreating Americans failed when General Howe diverted much of his force to Newport. This division of troops necessarily slowed his pursuit of George Washington. With this decision, Howe lost his opportunity to destroy any organized resistance by the Americans. The direct consequence of Howe's decision to split his forces made it possible for George Washington to complete his long march through New Jersey relatively unharmed. However, even though Washington eluded the pursuit of the British, the Continental Army lost most of its force to desertion during their difficult retreat.

Once the Continental Army safely landed at McConkey's Ferry on the Pennsylvania side of the Delaware River on December 8, 1776, Washington had time to seriously rethink his strategy and complete a plan for his army's survival and ultimate victory Washington then re-formed his troops and marched them back to McConkey's ferry to attempt a brazen attack that will be remembered forever in the annals of American history.

With troops that could withstand tremendous physical abuse from the weather and ground conditions in the face of freezing temperatures, a frozen river, blizzards, and highly hazardous roads, Washington organized his soldiers to attack the British garrison at Trenton, New Jersey. The newly developed strategy enabled him to utilize surprise and proper enemy selection rather than the disastrous policy of frontal assault on any British unit available, large or small.[69]

The Battle of Trenton

The execution of Washington's strategy began on December 25, 1776, as he stood on the banks of the Delaware River looking toward New Jersey. Once again finding himself at McConkey's Ferry, he depended on the cover of darkness to assure himself that the enemy could not mount a counterattack at the planned attack point. Washington knew that to be victorious he had to ensure that his full force would arrive no later than five o'clock in the morning.

Daylight was fast approaching. It took until three o'clock to cross the Delaware River with all the boats. The artillery transport was to be completed by four. Then, troops would have time to form again for the attack.

If they arrived at or near the scheduled time, the troops could mount an attack. Washington knew that if these planned arrivals were significantly late, the British would become aware of the impending attack and his army would be in grave danger. He had to avoid delay at all costs.

He knew safety was in the darkness, but their late arrival forced him to quickly proceed with the attack in daylight or prepare his army for a retreat. He decided a retreat would end in mass casualties. The only viable alternative was to continue a forced march to Trenton and attack the enemy. Even though the army arrived during daylight, the enemy was unaware of their presence. Once they reached the embarkation point, Washington gave orders to split into two divisions and push directly into the city before the enemy could react.

Luckily, the first division reached the city's outskirts on schedule, and the second division was only three minutes later, making it without discovery. The late march by the Continental Army and the subsequent attack resulted in a route of the Hessian units at Trenton.[70]

The Battle of Princeton

Washington knew that after Trenton, he needed another victory to achieve his desired results. Princeton was his chosen target, where British troops were billeted for the winter. However, his army was fast heading for dissolution. Tours were ending for most of his soldiers at the end of the year. He spoke about these realities to his troops, intending to encourage them to reenlist for themselves and their country. "You have done all I have asked of you, but your country and its new-found freedom are at stake."

He continued by further appealing to their patriotism and understanding of the mission—to fight for victories that would ultimately ensure freedom for all Americans. Washington also shared that intention would not be enough to provide the ultimate success of this revolution. Even the success in Trenton would not be enough. Continued fatigues and hardships were required. In Washington's speech, "Armies Cannot Go Home," he stated, "If you consent to stay, you will render that service to the cause of liberty. With their support, they would receive the honor for their valor; that is, an honor not possible under any different circumstance."[71]

The American attack was a phenomenal success, one necessary following their New York defeat. Washington's army had maneuvered to the side of a British detachment, avoiding a confrontation with the British troops sent to entrap Washington's forces. Washington could save his planned attack for Princeton's unaware forces. On the road to Princeton, the Americans unexpectedly faced an additional British unit. Initially, the battle did not go well, so the Patriots strategically withdrew until the main segment of their troops could arrive. The combined American force began shooting in volleys until the British detachment withdrew. Washington yelled, "The day is our own," as victory drew near during the Battle of Princeton in January 1777.[72]

Although Washington would continue to suffer from deteriorating formations throughout the war, on this day, his leadership, based on a commitment to duty and respect for his soldiers, retained the forces necessary to win at Princeton. His success with storms, an ice-filled river, and courageous soldiers ended in victory. These battlefield successes encouraged the Americans to increase their earlier demands.

The British Forage War

Although New Jersey had surrendered to Great Britain, looting by Great Britain's Hessian mercenaries began to alienate even American Loyalists from the British cause. Throughout the New Jersey campaign and the remainder of the war, Great Britain could never convert military success into political success as it lost the fight for the "hearts and minds" of the American people.

Following the Battles of Trenton and Princeton, the so-called Forage War in New Jersey—where Continental small units continuously harassed British and Hessian troops trying to forage for supplies—took a toll on Howe's army, which shrank from thirty-one thousand in August to fourteen thousand "effectives" by February 1777. At least 4,300 British and Hessian soldiers were killed in action, severely wounded, or captured after already losing 1,500 in New York and more than 2,800 in the New Jersey campaign. Many more fell to disease, malnutrition, exposure, and the hazards of the winter campaign.

Using the logic of Carl von Clausewitz, Great Britain had a "policy-strategy" mismatch from the beginning. If the goal was to restore American loyalty, military force was the wrong means to obtain it. Along with this mismatch, the British further weakened themselves by dispersing their troops in New Jersey, partly for easier foraging and partly to control the entire state.[73]

Washington at Valley Forge[74]

The Surrender at Saratoga

In the summer of 1777, British General John Burgoyne marched out of Canada with eight thousand troops. At the beginning of this march, Burgoyne shared the confidence of his superior, British Prime Minister Horace Walpole, who "envisioned a grand and decisive stroke against the Americans. Before the year was out, he intended to seize control of the Hudson River, split the colonies in two, and thereby deliver a potentially fatal blow to the rebellion."[75]

Burgoyne moved his forces forward and met stiff resistance. Local militias destroyed bridges, blocked roads, and harassed his men behind trees. By late summer (a summer of constant surprise attacks from small rebel militia units) the British were beginning to slow down an already slow and cumbersome army seriously weighed down by massive amounts of baggage, camp followers, and the wounded. Burgoyne's supply lines from Canada with ammunition, foodstuffs, and other supplies were almost completely separated from them, forcing his men to halt about forty miles above Albany. After battles on September 19 and October 7, the Americans, under General Horatio Gates, defeated their enemy.

"[Saratoga] was a crushing defeat for Britain and a decisive victory for the cause of American independence. When Burgoyne started south that summer, it was still possible to believe in a decisive British victory and that colonists had spilled their blood at Lexington, Concord, and Bunker Hill for naught."[76]

Burgoyne's success in meeting his goals was not to be. After his defeat and total surrender, along with Trenton and Princeton, America began believing they could win. Equally as important, foreign governments, primarily France, became interested in assisting the Americans once it became evident that the rebels could defeat Great Britain, France's mortal enemy.

Origins of the American-French Alliance

The Treaty of Paris formally ended the French and Indian War in 1763 against Great Britain and the colonies. They had "felt diminished and humiliated," as France's colonial holdings overseas had been significantly reduced, especially in North America.[77]

Instead of dropping its goal of defeating the British—something the French had difficulty doing—it began plans to rebuild its navy and army. Rather than accepting the reality of its decline, it would attack and defeat the country responsible for its misery, Great Britain.

Immediately after its 1763 defeat, France began planning for revenge. It disbursed special agents to gather information on the British colonies in North America. They studied the economy, took soundings in ports and rivers, and drafted military plans for attacking Boston, New York, and Philadelphia.

Throughout the late 1760s and early 1770s, French spies assembled a report on American colonists' unhappiness with British tax policy and their total lack of representation in Parliament. They also reported on their speculation that since the fall of New France in 1763, Americans felt less dependent on British military protection. They summarized that this was France's "grand opportunity" to obtain a new foothold in North America.

France desired to gain revenge on Great Britain for France's earlier defeats. They also wanted American colonists to attain total independence from Great Britain, although Count de Vergennes, the French foreign minister, didn't initially agree. "We do not desire that a new republic shall arise . . . [and] become the exclusive mistress of this immense continent." His view quickly changed to a desire to establish relations with the Americans.[78]

By 1777, indications were that the American war effort might actually succeed. The French became determined to be involved in that success. Vergennes and the French Crown began seeing that this American victory would open the doors to revenge against their hated enemy. With their long-term strengthening of the French Navy, they felt confident that their armed forces could successfully invade Great Britain.

France's intelligence gathered information on Britain's will to continue its war with the colonies. With Britain's decreased budgetary strength, depleted workforce, and waning public support of the war, it became apparent that France could deliver a smashing blow for the Americans.

Once Vergennes heard the news that the American colonies had won at Trenton, Princeton, and Saratoga, he felt assured that Americans were a good bet for success. Before those battles, the evidence had been lacking, and Vergennes avoided speaking with Franklin until he saw that victory was possible. Those victories changed everything for the French and marked the actual turning point of the American Revolution.

The American Revolution, Phase III

Phase III was primarily unconventional and asymmetric warfare in the Southern colonies from 1778 to 1783, which ended in the Battle of Yorktown. In April 1778, the Continental Congress ratified the treaty with France. Washington believed the French had finally saved them: "I believe no event was ever received with more heartfelt joy. America is, at last, protected by a miracle. In ratifying this treaty, America had to shed their colonial prejudices against the French and of a Catholic king."[79]

In June 1778, General Clinton ordered the withdrawal of British forces from Philadelphia to New York City. Clinton had replaced General Howe as commander in North America. As a statement of the changing commitment to the British "civil war" in America, the honorable Charles Britain, the architect of the British logistics miracle of an effort conducted throughout the war, ordered the diversion of ten thousand British troops to defend Florida, the West Indies, and Canada. This logistical accomplishment was nothing short of miraculous due to the remoteness of the colonies nearly three thousand miles away from Britain, the inherent speed limitations of ships of sail, and the dynamic nature of the rebellion. With a force of twenty-five thousand British regulars remaining, after the diversion of troops, General Clinton immediately sent out units to harass and plunder towns in eastern New York, as well as coastal Connecticut.

Although Washington was in no position to attack New York City, he was able to disrupt British outposts at Stony Point on the Hudson and at Paulus Hook, New Jersey, in July 1779. Clinton's response to these raids was to order British forces to evacuate Newport, Rhode Island, in October 1779.

After Clinton's attacks in eastern New York failed, the British understood that they could not control the countryside and were forced to consolidate their forces further within New York City. "In a classic meeting engagement, Mawhood [a British regimental commander] attacked with great gallantry and nearly gained the field. The Americans broke, rallied, and, in a web of tactical decisions by many officers and men, won another victory."[80]

In response to this withdrawal, small groups of Jersey militia began attacking British and Hessian forces throughout the New Jersey countryside. They initiated ongoing skirmishes with small militia units over the next twelve weeks. Washington did not lead this contact, although he supported it and did what he could to assist.

Summary of Battles in the Southern Colonies

On May 12, 1780, the British shifted their military focus to the Southern states. Both British military and civilian leaders in London and North America supported this expansion. They endorsed this policy because the South was said to have large numbers of Loyalists presumed to be willing to join with the British Army in defeating migrating northern rebellious groups led by General Nathaniel Greene, Francis Marion (known as the "Swamp Fox"), and others.

The Continental Congress initially placed General Horatio Gates, the American general during the Battle of Saratoga, in command of the Southern army. They rejected Washington's recommendation for General Nathanael Greene for the post. Gates proved to be a disappointment in this capacity.

On August 16, 1780, during the Battle at Camden, South Carolina, militia units from Virginia and South Carolina were soundly defeated by General Cornwallis's troops. By October, Gates was relieved of his command, partly due to the dramatic defeat but also because he retreated well before his army did. Alexander Hamilton commented, "Was there ever such an instance of a general running away . . . from his whole army? The rout was shameful, the worst American defeat of the war." It was also the catalyst for promoting General Greene to Gates's command position.[81]

Early British leadership changes included the appointment of Colonel Banastre Tarleton to conduct raids on villages wherever the enemy appeared. Tarleton was a twenty-six-year-old cavalry officer who had provided active raids of colonists along the coast. Tarleton also developed quite a reputation for taking no prisoners during his attacks.

In his new capacity, and with General Cornwallis's instructions, Tarleton nearly captured Governor Thomas Jefferson, Patrick Henry, and other leaders within the Virginia government. Only a warning from Captain Jack Jouett after he rode overnight through fifty miles of dense forests and dangerous Indian trails saved the day. He reached Monticello before Tarleton's arrival, preventing the capture of Jefferson and the others.[82]

Washington continued to make essential changes to American strategy as he reacted to Great Britain's move to expand its influence over the Southern colonies. He communicated American policy changes to his generals and his close friend, the Marquis de Lafayette, to counter Britain's perceived control over the Loyalists in the region. In a letter to Lafayette on July 30, 1781, Washington explained his intention to change tactics for victory: "It is more than probable that we shall . . . entirely change our plan of operations . . . Our views must now turn toward endeavoring to expel [the enemy] states if we find ourselves incompetent to the siege of New York."[83]

The Loyalists fought elements of the American militias for two deadly years. The guerrilla leader, Francis Marion, operating under Washington's orders, effectively harassed the British and Loyalist forces in South Carolina, earning him the nickname "Swamp Fox" from the British for his slippery tactics. Marion's continuous raids on these units prevented British forces from overrunning the Americans within the state. Washington's overall strategy for victory over the British and their ultimate withdrawal from the colonies had finally reached the realm of possibility.

In October 1780, General Greene's appointment to head the southern branch of the American army proved popular with the soldiers. His direct leadership working with various small military units in guerrilla warfare also proved helpful throughout the Southern campaign. His leadership and trust in his subordinates to work independently as they harassed the enemy was especially helpful. This was exemplified by his use of Dan Morgan, who then won a critical victory over British Major Patrick Ferguson and his American Loyalists at King's Mountain in North Carolina. To promote his leadership abilities, Ferguson told his troops that he could defend against "God almighty and all the rebels out of hell." Seven rifle shots would mortally wound him in the battle against the colonials.[84]

General Greene's defeat of the British and their Loyalists during the battles at Guilford Court House, near Greensboro, North Carolina, was the final skirmish until Yorktown. General Cornwallis's letter to Sir Henry Clinton said it best: "I am quite tired of marching about the country. If we mean an offensive war in America, we must abandon New York and bring our whole force into Virginia."

Greene fought Cornwallis's forces but was initially defeated at Guilford. His forces refused to retreat, ultimately forcing Cornwallis's army to regroup and fall back for supplies. General Greene was described as never winning any major battles but did force Cornwallis to "exhaust himself and his army, marching more than five hundred miles through the Virginia and North Carolina countryside. The British forces' wearing down in the South led them to Yorktown. Nathanael Greene, Dan Morgan, and the guerrilla leaders Francis Marion and Thomas Sumter achieved this result."[85]

Washington and his newfound ally, France, sought one "knockout blow" to end the war, although Washington and both military and civilian leaders in France had different views on how to proceed. France desired "campaigns on the margins" of Georgia and Canada; Washington preferred to attack the British in New York. They ultimately agreed to disrupt British plans in the South. Their available joint military resources for a successful mission included two French fleets, one French army, and two American armies. By the summer of 1781, their final plans were complete to fight the enemy in the South. These forces were to join in late September at Yorktown, Virginia.

On September 26, 1781, Washington's combined American and French forces totaled seventeen thousand, including the Comte de Rochambeau's regulars, Lafayette and Anthony Wayne's Virginians, and reinforcements. On October 19, 1781, General Charles Cornwallis, plus 7,250 men, surrendered, and the war ended ingloriously.[86]

Surrender of Lord Cornwallis at Yorktown[87]

The USS *Constitution* defeats the HMS Guerriere during the War of 1812.[88]

CHAPTER THREE

THE WAR OF 1812

Initially, the War of 1812 was not a quarrel between the British and Americans. The primary problem was between the British and the French. However, issues between the British and Americans created conditions predisposed to conflict. The Americans had long-standing grievances against Britain, including freedom of navigation on the seas for trade ships, freedom from impressment of US sailors by the British navy, and Britain's long-standing opposition to the American westward movement to attain land occupied by the American Indians for centuries. The British and their Canadian subjects wanted to protect those lands from the Americans.

Jefferson's Embargo of 1807

President Thomas Jefferson feared that a war with the British Empire would require him to change goals from reducing taxes and addressing the national debt to building an expensive army and navy; therefore, he opposed the war. Instead, the president worked toward a comfortable diplomatic victory. And he hoped to scare the British imperial lords into giving it to him.

On June 22, 1807, the HMS *Leopard* attacked the American naval frigate *Chesapeake*, resulting in American casualties and injuries. The British navy, in urgent need of personnel for their war against France, boarded the *Chesapeake* and detained four sailors on charges of desertion. This incident prompted Jefferson and Madison to demand reparations for the affected families and the return of the impressed sailors. The US also sought the removal of Admiral Sir George Cranfield Berkeley, who oversaw the operation.

More importantly, they wanted Great Britain to cease the impressment of American sailors and harassment of American ships. These were sailors that were aboard military vessels, as well as merchant vessels. The United States and President Jefferson needed more leverage over Britain to gain their commitment to American freedom of the seas. They needed more soldiers, fortifications, cannon, and seaports. They were especially vulnerable to attacks by British warships.[89]

The United States Navy had warships "tied up for repairs," and "none of the American frigates were fit for sea" against the largest navy in the world.[90] Not able to mount a significant military resistance, the Americans could not defeat Britain or venture into Canada to confront them there through an invasion.

After the Treaty of Paris formally ended the Revolutionary War in 1783, the United States was caught between the self-serving trade policies of two warring nations, Great Britain and France, both attempting to bully the United States into taking a side. The US tried to solve these challenges by pursuing a policy of trade embargoes to attempt to establish leverage, though these attempts predominantly backfired during the embargoes. Phineas Bond, the consul general of Great Britain in the United States, concluded that "the consequences of a rupture would be serious to us, but ruinous to the United States . . . Their commerce, now so extensive and lucrative, would be annihilated, and with these her Revenue would fail, for they are the Sources from which her Coffers are filled."[91]

In 1807, two actions by the British government would make this attempt to maintain neutrality more difficult for the US. First came a proclamation that "reiterated a perpetual claim to all natural-born subjects"[92] that they encountered from the American merchant fleet on the high seas. Orders in Council, orders from the crown that dictate policies for the British government to follow, were used to mandate that all shipping bound for mainland Europe first "visit Britain, pay duties, and take a license before proceeding to the continent."[93]

On the other hand, Napoleon and his regime vowed that they would seize any ship that had visited Britain. Consequently, the Americans became trapped between the British and the French. "They would have to pick their poison—to risk British seizure by sailing directly to French-dominated Europe or follow British regulations at the risk of French confiscation."[94]

Despite the tensions, British authorities were not inclined towards war with the United States, their attention being largely consumed by the conflict with Napoleon. They consented to provide compensation for the impressment and the casualties from the *Chesapeake* incident. A number of sailors seized from the *Chesapeake* were returned, except for one who perished in captivity. In the following autumn, the British recalled Admiral Berkeley and Captain Salusbury P. Humphreys of the HMS *Leopard* to Britain. Nonetheless, the British maintained their stance on the right to intercept and inspect neutral merchant vessels, control trade, and reclaim deserters.[95]

"Despite the British hard line on core policy," Americans, who had promoted a war with Great Britain, temporarily backed off.[96] In late 1807, Congress limited military outlays to provide for a common defense: one million dollars to upgrade seaport fortifications and expand the US Army to around ten thousand. Even these numbers of men were too few to defend a nation rapidly growing by geography and population against a superpower such as Great Britain.[97]

The American leadership intended to build more frigates, but they were too big and costly for their current budget. Instead, "Congress authorized more small, cheap, and virtually useless gunboats. Most Republicans were against building a more reliable fleet for fear that it could never compete with the British and would only invite a preemptive strike like that recently inflicted by the Royal Navy on neutral Denmark."[98]

An Alternative to War

The Americans were faced with a difficult situation and wanted to avoid war, which would have required an increase in tax revenue, to which Republicans were opposed. The government decided their best option was to create an embargo of merchant shipping and to somehow build a stronger navy and army for self-defense.[99]

The Republicans were convinced that factory workers in Britain and slaves in the West Indies would "starve" without American trade. According to Jefferson, "If the Americans stopped exporting their wheat, flour, fish, pork, and cattle," Britain would have to relent. In December 1807, Jefferson proposed an embargo on "all maritime commerce by American ships," effectively halting our foreign trade.[100]

According to Alan Taylor, the intention was to protect "idled American merchant ships from French and British seizure," and at the same time, "the embargo would pressure the belligerents to accept the American position on neutral shipping and sailors."[101]

The Republicans in Congress passed the Embargo Act on December 22, 1807, "relieved to avoid declaring war."[102] John Quincy Adams, future president of the United States and representative to Holland and Germany, doubted it would affect the belligerents, stating, "Nations which sacrifice men by the hundreds of thousands, and treasures by the hundreds of millions in war, for nothing, or worse than nothing, pay little attention to their real interests. In vain, the Federalists opposition protested a measure that they saw as self-destructive and for a bad cause to retain British subjects on American ships."[103]

The plan would, however, backfire, as the effect of the Embargo on Great Britain was not as intended. Through the embargo, the absence of American goods removed competition with British and Canadian goods, and Great Britain was able to find "alternative sources of food" where necessary. Ironically, according to Taylor, many "British-born sailors" were discharged from the American Navy to find work in Great Britain.[104]

Americans were also heavily reliant on foreign trade, more so than Jefferson had anticipated. The market for wheat, for example, crashed as "the price of wheat fell from two dollars per bushel before the embargo to seventy-five cents a year later."[105]

Smuggling also became a problem for the United States as "along the border with Canada, the embargo encouraged smugglers to push American products into Canada in exchange for British manufacturers."[106] There was an earnest effort from the administration to stop the smuggling, utilizing militiamen to enforce the embargo. However, the smugglers "took up arms to defy the militia," and several reports of violence were reported against the militias by the smugglers.[107] Albert Gallatin, now secretary of state, stated that federal authority had ended along the border.

The Federalist Party, in the wake of the failing trade policies of the Republicans, was able to grow its support in the Northeast, which was heavily dependent on foreign maritime trade.[108] "Federalists insisted that Jefferson's supposed cure was far worse than the British disease of meddling with ships and sailors." Federalist merchants had accepted the loss of these sailors to impressment because "transatlantic trade had been so profitable."

The gains for Federalists in political support continued to pile on, as accusations that Jefferson and his Southern-state party loyalists had intended to favor Napoleon, and "impoverish" New England through the embargo.[109]

To further exacerbate the situation, the British, according to Taylor, understood that his political party was losing support to the Federalists and "balked at making diplomatic concessions to Jefferson's faltering administration," so in essence, the embargo was proving to be a strategic failure.[110]

Even though the embargo was hurting the Republicans politically, however, the Republicans were able to paint the Federalists as loyalists to the Crown, and Madison was voted in as president in 1808, where the Federalists were only able to win all of New England except for Vermont.[111]

By the end of Jefferson's second term in 1809, the embargo's results had demonstrated that it had significantly "weakened the United States," especially economically. Politically, it further divided the nation between the New England Federalists and the Republicans, who were spread throughout the central and southern United States. On March 4, 1809 on Jefferson's last day in office, the embargo was ended by the Republicans in Congress.[112]

The Embargo's Effect on Canada

Although the United States intended the Embargo of 1807 to coerce the

British into respecting the sovereignty of the newly formed country, the unintended consequences were both the British resolve to increase their support of Canada at the United States' expense and the economic impact it had on international trade.[113]

According to Taylor, "because duties on foreign trade primarily funded the federal government, the restriction depleted the [national] treasury. The prohibition also trained people along the border to defy their own government."[114] This made an invasion of Canada far more challenging to accomplish, as support along the border for an invasion decreased significantly.[115]

Also, while the US trade was negatively affected by the embargo, Canada received a boost to its economy through the increase in trade. Canada was able to dominate the markets of the West Indies, as the US was no longer available to export these goods. This made Canada the main exporter of "grain, fish, livestock, and lumber," which the US erroneously believed prior to the embargo that the West Indies would have to do without.[116]

According to Taylor, "British officers and magistrates offered a toast to Thomas Jefferson and his embargo at a dinner in Upper Canada. They explained to a British traveler that the embargo had 'done more for Canada than fifty ordinary years would have affected.' The traveler concluded, 'It has taught Great Britain the value of these provinces, which I sincerely hope will prove a brighter gem in her Crown than even the States.' The embargo was to coerce the British. The prohibition instead increased their resolve to defend Canada as necessary to the empire."[117]

The Struggle for Sovereignty

After the embargo was ended by Jefferson as his last act as president in 1809 with the passing of the Non-Intercourse Act, US merchants were now allowed to trade with anyone—except for its two most fruitful trade partners, Britain and France. This was another attempt by the US to coerce the two largest European powers into respecting the United States as a sovereign nation on the high seas.

The Non-Intercourse Act, however, proved just as ineffective as the

Embargo Act, and so Macon's Bill Number 2 was passed in 1810 to allow trade with all countries, including Britain and France. Subsequent to this bill becoming law, Napoleon had promised to lift restrictions on US trade, as declared in the Berlin and Milan decrees of 1806 and 1807, respectively, though these promises to lift trade restrictions were not kept.

In believing Napoleon and choosing to direct aggression toward Britain, President Madison acted to counter the country's dependence on Britain and ultimately renew the people's concept of freedom in America as a sovereign nation. He would begin the fight to prevent one powerful nation from asserting its sovereignty over the US on the seas. It would require the development of an American navy and naval officers of distinction to succeed.

The war was bound to occur. The British were using their naval power to belligerently assert their dominance on the high seas, and America insisted on maintaining their trading neutrality. America was caught between two nations with powerful navies who insisted that all trade go through them. It was impossible to fight both the British and French navies, with America possessing a fledgling navy of its own. America would soon declare war against Great Britain, despite an internal conflict between Federalists, merchant New Englanders, and the Republican Congress with their War Hawk leaders.

The Louisiana Purchase: Another Complication

The Treaty of Amiens, signed on March 25, 1802, brought peace between France and Great Britain, however fleeting. Joseph Bonaparte and Marquess Cornwallis signed the "Definitive Treaty of Peace." However, the treaty only lasted a little over a year, until May 18, 1803, when the first of the Napoleonic wars was declared. Under the settlement, Britain recognized the new French republic.[118] Being in debt from war with Britain, Napoleon was keen to generate revenue for France's ailing treasury.

Also, for the French, the Louisiana territory was indefensible against Britain. Selling rather than occupying the Louisiana territory was a more tenable solution. Great Britain had eliminated France's ability to populate and defend the Louisiana territory by destroying the French Navy at the Battle of Trafalgar. Napoleon countered Britain's desire to fill the Louisiana territory by selling it to America in a calculated effort. The French believed that the sale would reduce Great Britain's footprint in North America, eventually leading to America's dominance, with Canada soon to follow in terms of its importance. Ironically, Thomas Jefferson found the funds to purchase this vast land through the British banking system as the US government's official banking agent at the time was the Baring Company of London. It doubled the size of the United States and helped thousands of Americans find cheap property to meet their need to move westward.

Phase I: Westward Movement, Tecumseh, and the Indian Confederacy

Another cause for the War of 1812 was the American westward movement, with pioneers looking for cheap land. While the British were in charge of the colonies, they had restricted movement west to maintain peace with their Indian tribe allies. After the Americans declared independence, the British could no longer restrict this movement. However, Britain's continuing relationships with many of the Indian tribes within American territories caused constant fear and irritation in the American mind as they began to move west.[119]

Only one direction was possible—the defeat of Britain and its Indian allies, regardless of the internal American opposition from the Federalists in New England. They called attention to neglected phenomena such as freedom of the seas and respect for US neutrality. The American Indians attempted to form a confederacy of tribes, which would increase their success in stopping the United States and its aggressive movement westward.

Within the Northwest frontier, an astonishing leader appeared among the Indians, a powerful orator named Tecumseh. He sternly told the Indians to give up the White man's ways and especially to avoid alcohol. He had observed his fellow chiefs, supplied with whiskey, signing away millions of acres during peace negotiations since the 1790s.[120]

Tecumseh and the Shawnee Tribe attempted to settle in present-day

Indiana: "Like the European Americans, the Shawnee and other tribes also had their dreams of a separate and independent Indian nation east of the Mississippi and on the Great Lakes. Americans saw the Indian reaction as both 'insulting and hostile.' Native Americans were outraged with settlers, land speculators, politicians. [They believed] armed thugs were stealing their land. Indian raids, deadly, often brutal, though successful in short-term, gave better armed white men an excuse to kill Indians indiscriminately."[121]

To assist in reaching their goal, Tecumseh allied his people with the British. This alliance ultimately helped Britain and especially Canada but did not help the American Indians. And the Americans would not forget that the native tribes had allied with Britain against them. The result would end the Indian Confederacy and the British presence in North America. Canada, thanks to intelligent military leadership, survived the American onslaught.

The Inevitable Conflict With Native America

Numerous accounts exist of American expeditions into territories occupied by Native Americans. The mere prospect of an ambush in a valley was enough to unsettle even the most courageous American soldiers. General James Wilkinson once noted that marching through such territory could provoke "more anxiety than half a dozen well-fought battles the world produces." This fear was palpable as troops ventured into the northern woodlands for combat. It was primarily a profound animosity towards Native Americans that spurred Americans to engage in the war despite the harrowing experiences of Indian attacks on US settlers.

In addition to describing the sentiment of the Americans at the time, however, we must not forget that Americans were responsible for Native American genocide. During the American westward movement of the nineteenth century, a centuries-old native society was destroyed.[122]

Playing on the shaky nerves of their enemy, smart Indians focused on the intimidation of White Americans. The Indians falsely promised William Hamilton Merritt, a Canadian officer, that they would not kill or torture the prisoners, but once the British officer departed, the captives suffered untold torture and death. Merritt recalled that "the poor devils were crying and imploring me to save their lives, as I was the only 'white' they saw."[123]

Merritt also described White Americans' fear of the Indians and the British reliance on the Indians as allies. British officers believed the Indians had the right to live in their lands without American aggression.

John Askin, a fur trader, interpreter, and militia officer for the Canadians held this opinion as well, that England and the United States had distinct approaches to the Native population, counting on them as allies against the Americans. "You may rely on it that without the Indians [the British] could never keep this country."[124]

He also commented on the utility of this relationship, as the Native warriors were in their element in the terrain out west. "The Americans never will take the upper posts . . . for in the woods, where the Americans must pass, one Indian is equal to three white men."[125]

Britain wanted to use Native warriors because Americans were afraid of them. One British agent explained that "The Americans . . . are constantly in alarm either by an Indian war or at least the shadow of bands of Indians. They imagine their heads in danger of being scalped. A war with England has no terror compared with those arising from their savage allies."[126]

Tecumseh traveled throughout the Indian Territory, urging them to form a confederation to resist pressure from the Americans. However, his hold on Indian behavior was precarious. By 1811, things began to change significantly. Tribes bordering the Ohio River united under the highly regarded and honored British and Canadians. Tecumseh also provided outstanding leadership within the various Indian groups until his death fighting the White Americans in 1813.

Even though he respected Tecumseh, his brother, Prophet, refused to be held back. Tecumseh was more prudent, seeking alliances with other tribes and the British before they attacked, but Prophet was more impulsive. Instead, while Tecumseh was away traveling, Prophet attacked the American militia while they were encamped at a place called Tippecanoe in modern-day Indiana. "In November 1811, the governor of the Indiana Territory, William Henry Harrison, set out with an army of about one thousand in an attempt to put an end to the growing Indian Confederacy that was struggling to prevent American expansion into Indian Territory."[127]

General Harrison was able to repulse the Indian attackers on November 7, 1811. The Indian attack was at night—it was rare for the Indians to launch a night attack. In retaliation, Harrison waged an attack a few days later, on November 11, on Prophetstown, and though the Americans suffered more casualties, the Shawnee, led by Prophet, failed to defeat the Americans and their superior firepower. The remaining Indians abandoned the town, retreated to Canada, and Harrison ordered the town destroyed.

The destruction of the town, coming so late in the year, created severe hardships for most of the Indians—warriors, women, and children who had made it their home. It did nothing to add to American prestige. It would also be a significant issue in the war that lay just a few months ahead. It gave Canadians and Britons enough reason to want to defeat the hostile American forces, who were supported by the War Hawks in Congress. Thanks to General Harrison, the Americans did gain revenge for American settlers and previous Indian massacres. Harrison ultimately benefited from this victory in his presidential bid in 1840, with the legend of the *Battle of Tippecanoe*.[128]

The Americans on the frontier blamed the British for stirring up the Indians. The War Hawks in the United States Congress also heavily supported this blame. In opposition, Congressman John Randolph ridiculed the war fever of the new members. He "compared his new colleagues to a 'whipper will' [sic] that calls but one monotonous tune: Canada! Canada! Canada!"[129]

It was true that the frontiersmen and the congressional War Hawks wanted to invade Canada. They also wanted to remove the British threat once and for all. The War Hawks and Republicans installed Henry Clay of Kentucky as Speaker of the House. John C. Calhoun joined the group and would go on to shape America's destiny for forty years. Thomas Jefferson cheered on the War Hawks. He believed Canada's defeat would be "a mere matter of marching." Jefferson was a brilliant political philosopher and statesman, but he was not blessed to be a military strategist. He would rue the day when he had uttered those words.[130]

Phase II: The Canadian Invasion

Contrary to Jefferson and the War Hawks' belief in an effortless conquest of Canada, Joseph Ellicott, an influential figure as a city planner, land office agent, lawyer, politician, and Erie Canal supporter, expressed a contrary view. He stated, "from the manner the war is conducted, there is much more probability of [northern New York state] being conquered by and added to Canada than Canada be conquered by the United States."[131] The expectation that Canadians would greet American forces as liberators was met with astonishment when the opposite proved true. Many Canadians were descendants of Loyalists who had left the United States during the American Revolution, identifying proudly as "United Empire Loyalists" with no desire for American "liberation."

In return for their allegiance, Britain had assured the French Canadians of their rights to use the French language and to freely practice Catholicism. Consequently, they held no grievances against England. On June 25, 1812, James Vosburgh headed west to the Niagara River, bearing crucial news of the American declaration of war. Bypassing American Fort Niagara, he crossed over to Queenstown in Canada and informed Thomas Clark, a local merchant. Clark then notified General Isaac Brock, the British commander, of the impending American advance. After delivering the message, "The Americans are coming," Vosburgh returned to the United States only to be arrested and imprisoned by his compatriots, who accused him of treason for his role in forewarning the enemy.[132]

Vosburgh acted on behalf of John Jacob Astor, a prominent fur trader allied with the Republican Party and notably close to Treasury Secretary Albert Gallatin. His journey to Canada aimed to secure Astor's fur assets in the region. Vosburgh avoided imprisonment as his mission pertained to a commercial matter rather than an act of subterfuge. However, his actions inadvertently proved detrimental, as they furnished the Canadians with intelligence that afforded them additional time to fortify against an American offensive.[133]

The majority of the war's Canadian engagements took place near the border shared with the United States, spanning from Lake Champlain to Detroit, throughout the Niagara Peninsula in Upper Canada (now Ontario), and in the maritime provinces of Nova Scotia and Prince Edward Island. These regions were vital to Britain as key suppliers of raw materials, particularly lumber, which would become a significant concern for England should America gain control over these resources.[134]

In 1810, prior to the declaration of war, the United States inadvertently weakened its military position. Republican members of Congress "renewed their threat by slashing appropriations of the Army and Navy,"[135] deeming these forces both perilous and cost-prohibitive. Their strategy was to depend on the militia instead.

The aim was to incite hostility within America towards Britain. Americans harbored the belief that going to war could open the door to annexing Canada, the vast and sparsely settled land lying to the north. Yet, Canadians would have taken satisfaction in witnessing the defeat of any aggressors, much like their ancestors did in the French and Indian War. Both the British and French Canadian populations held deep-rooted allegiances to Great Britain.[136]

Growing Anger Between Belligerents

The American War Hawks had five primary goals associated with the invasion of Canada, namely, to punish Britain for its "endless arrogance,"[137] put an end to Britain insulting them, stop the illegal handling of American shipping and American sailors, stop British incitement of Indians in the Ohio Valley (what was then the Northwest), and open the door to American expansion into the West.

The most important objective was to gain the prize of pushing the British out of Canada and taking possession of its vast territory for the United States. The quality of its senior Canadian generals, such as General (Sir) Isaac Brock, and the weaknesses inherent in the top American officers would make the difference between victory and defeat. Brock's career preparation as a general was driven by his desire to someday fight Napoleon. He had gained war experience in the war against the Netherlands in 1799 and with Lord Nelson at Copenhagen in 1801. He now expected to earn his stripes by stopping the American invasion. To do this, he would have to form a credible army that would include Canadian regulars, the militia, and a large contingent of Indians. His superior, Governor-General (Sir) George Prevost, shied away from using Indians; General Brock pushed hard until Prevost agreed with his plan regarding them. Brock knew that Americans were afraid of the Indians, so he viewed their use in battle as a strategic advantage.[138]

Governor-General Prevost was a respected French-Canadian leader who had won support for defending the colony against invasion. As General Brock's superior, General Prevost was required to approve General Brock's effort to supplement his regulars with a reliable militia made up of men sixteen to sixty years old. Brock's preference was to gain some of the regulars currently defending the governor-general. Prevost would not release them, although he had 5,600 regulars at his disposal in Quebec. Ultimately, Brock received only 1,200 regulars and Indians to defend seven forts situated from the St. Lawrence River to Lake Huron.[139]

It was a challenge for such a small group of regulars. But the Indians would provide their skills of fighting and scaring the Americans. Battles and skirmishes continued throughout Lower Canada, Quebec. If the Canadians and the British were defeated, it would be a disaster for both. However, with strategic military planning, there would be no conquest.

The First Land Battle of the War

Although Congress declared war on Great Britain on June 17, 1812, it was the engagement on July 17, at the American Fort on Mackinac Island in the straits between Lake Huron and Lake Michigan that began the War of 1812. The first problem was that the fort's commander, Lieutenant Porter Hanks, was not aware of America's declaration of war against Britain. The government had failed to inform him of this fact.

General Brock arrived at the fort with around 1,300 men, half of them Indian warriors. Brock marched the forces around in a manner that appeared to multiply their numbers and used the war cries of the Indian forces to further intimidate the small contingent of Americans stationed at the base.[140]

Faced with a sizable attacking force, including the Indians, who had a reputation for savagery in battle, Hanks had to fight or surrender, and wisely, he chose to quit. He feared his small garrison, including women and children, might be tortured by Britain's Indian contingency.[141]

The British took over the fort, and the first battle of 1812 was over. Not a drop of blood had been spilled, but the humiliating surrender did not sit well with America. Military leaders no doubt began feeling the conquest of Canada might be slightly more difficult than the War Hawks and Jefferson had suggested. It was called a *bloodless surrender*. The surrender also convinced Britain's Indian allies that America was a weak nation and provided the Indians with substantial loot they gathered from the fort's surrender. It showed them that the rewards for fighting against Americans could be significant. Their alliance with the British and Canadians would be a critical factor over the coming months and years.[142]

The Battle of Lake Erie[143]

Thwarted Plans to Invade Canada

Brigadier General William Hull, governor of Michigan Territory, set out to launch America's invasion of Canada. The initial goal was to capture Amherstburg, a British fort on the Detroit River, which emptied into Lake Erie.[144]

In July 1812, the American schooner *Cuyahoga Packet* sailed into Lake Erie and to Detroit. Its captain and crew were unaware they had been at war for two weeks. Some of William Hull's army members, thirty men too sick to march with the rest of the army, were aboard *Cuyahoga Packet*, which approached the fort at Amherstburg. The HMS *General Hunter* launched a Canadian longboat with six heavily armed provincial marines commanded by the General Hunter's captain, Lieutenant Frederic Rolette. Rolette, a French-Canadian, pulled alongside the *Cuyahoga Packet* and boarded the American Schooner.[145]

Canadians, usually polite with Americans, drew their muskets and ordered the captain to lower his sails. Confusion broke out among the American crew, especially when Rolette fired a shot directly at the schooner. Although the Americans outnumbered the Canadians five to one, the Canadians overtook the vessel and searched *Cuyahoga Packet's* baggage, seizing two large trunks.[146]

The Canadians soon realized they had captured a prize far more valuable than just a minor schooner. The two trunks belonged to Brigadier General Hull and contained documents detailing the strategy for the upcoming campaigns. The American failure to secure their war plans proved to be a disaster. The *Cuyahoga Packet's* trunks contained American troop strengths, war plans, and Hull's correspondence with the secretary of war, William Eustis. It was an unprecedented act of stupidity. The aide-de-camp, Hull's son, was responsible for delivering the trunks. British Major General Isaac Brock was soon given the documents to review. Two weeks prior, General Hull and his forces had entered Canada across the Detroit River, intending to capture Fort Amherstburg. Hull believed he was in an excellent position to deal with the outnumbered British garrison.[147]

General Hull had an additional problem with the documents that were now in the hands of General Brock. Brock now knew Hull's strategy for attack. Brock had not intended to be in the area where the invasion was to take place, but this newly captured intelligence changed those plans.[148] General Brock went on the offensive and deceived General Hull, again with the aid of Indian warriors, into believing they were hopelessly outnumbered. Hull capitulated and surrendered the fort. This surrender ceded control of Fort Detroit and, thereby, the entire Michigan territory to the Canadians. Hull then decided to halt his invasion of Canada in light of the surrender of Fort Detroit, the surrender of Fort Dearborn just a day earlier, and the Canadians' successful siege of Fort Mackinac a month prior.[149]

Hull's failure during the bloodless surrender of Fort Detroit on August 16, 1812, led to his eventual court-martial for cowardice and dereliction of duty, for which he was convicted and sentenced to die. President Madison would later, however, give Hull a reprieve from his death sentence due to his heroism during the Revolutionary War.[150]

Unlike the bloodless battles at Fort Detroit and Fort Mackinac, the small American Fort Dearborn, near Chicago, set an example of brutality and horror that colored the entire war in the north and shaped relations between Indians and the Americans for years to come. Occupants of the fort abandoned the indefensible position and marched toward Fort Wayne, Indiana. However, Potawatomi Indians attacked, and more than half of the ninety-three men, women, and children died in the attack, while the rest were taken captive. The massacre was only fifteen minutes in duration. Members of the Miami tribe were present and, by some accounts, fought bravely, but according to other accounts, did not defend the Americans. President William Henry Harrison would later use the reports of the tribe's alleged abstention during the attack as a justification for the assault of the Miami tribe's villages, though they were not present during the attack on Fort Dearborn. This drove the Miamis from their neutrality into the waiting arms of the British.[151], Even after the war ended, White Americans would remember this massacre and lay the blame on all Native Americans everywhere.

Canadian Patriotism and the Battle of Beaver Dams

The Americans continued through 1813 to attempt to conquer Canada, focusing on invasions across the Great Lakes and the critical St. Lawrence River. By May, they finally captured Fort George and the city of York (now Toronto) in Upper Canada. They burned a government building, which set the stage for the British burning of Washington DC in August of 1814 as an act of revenge.

On June 21, 1813, Laura Secord embarked on a perilous twenty-mile trek from Queenstown to Thorold Township, navigating through an ominous black swamp to deliver a critical message to the Canadian militia. Her feat immortalized her as a heroine. At thirty-eight, this wife of an injured Canadian informed Lieutenant James Fitzgibbons and his "Bloody Boys" of an impending American advance. Along her journey, she met with Mohawk warriors allied with the British and Canadians, who helped her complete her mission. Secord's courageous act ignited the Canadian spirit and became a rallying point for patriotism.[152]

On June 24, the American forces launched an offensive, pushing the British and Canadian defenders through Queenstown. However, thanks to Secord's prior warning, the Canadians had fortified their positions. Major General van Rensselaer, leading the Canadian and British troops, strengthened Queenstown's defenses, culminating in a triumph at the Battle of Beaver Dams on the same day. Lieutenant Colonel Winfield Scott led the American troops. The tide turned with the British and Canadian reinforcements' arrival and the artillery bombardment on the boats attempting to cross the river, rapidly deteriorating the American position. "With the arrival of the British and Canadian reinforcements and an artillery bombardment on the boats still trying to cross the river, it was soon the Americans' turn to find their situation becoming untenable." The American militia, intimidated by the three hundred Mohawks whose war cries gave the impression of a much larger force, lost their resolve to fight within three hours.[153]

British triumphs at Stony Creek and Beaver Dams in June dampened the briefly renewed American aspirations to gain a foothold in Upper

Canada. The pivotal effort to conquer Canada involved a strategic push led by Major General James Wilkinson, who was appointed to the St. Lawrence Theater towards the end of 1813, with the goal of capturing Montreal.[154]

The plan involved a simultaneous attack along the Richelieu River from Lake Champlain, which could have potentially split the Canadian forces. However, the American offensive stalled following decisive British victories in October and November. A British contingent, comprising over 1,600 French-Canadian regulars and Indigenous allies, repelled an American force of about 4,000 at Chateauguay on October 26, 1813, and again at Crysler's Farm in present-day Quebec on November 11, 1813. The campaign was ultimately abandoned by Major General James Wilkinson upon learning that American Major General Wade Hampton had retreated from his segment of the campaign.

The humiliating capitulation of Fort Detroit, the prior American loss at Mackinac Island, the Canadian triumph at Queenstown Heights, the unsuccessful American campaign to seize Montreal, and the defeat at Crysler's Farm were all pivotal episodes for both America and Canada. Eliot Cohen, a Johns Hopkins University professor and senior adviser to former US Secretary of State Condoleezza Rice, noted in his book *Conquered into Liberty* that "The attack on Canada was an American defeat." He also concluded that "ultimately, Canada and Canadians won the War of 1812."[155]

It's significant to acknowledge that only a minority of American historians have conceded this particular point. Eliot Cohen elaborated that the aspiring American invaders were defeated in engagements like Queenstown Heights in Upper Canada and Chateauguay in Lower Canada, failing to surpass the strategic acumen of Canadian military leaders.[156]

The French Invasion of Russia

The American strategy was partly based on the assumption that Britain's engagement with Napoleon would aid their own military efforts. In June 1812, coinciding with America's declaration of war on Britain, Napoleon began his catastrophic invasion of Russia. His formidable army of 650,000 "never lost a battle against Russians themselves, but the vast distances and the Russian tactic of abandoning and burning their towns and cities and destroying their crops as they retreated, drew the French deeper and deeper into that unforgiving land."[157] These scorched earth tactics "denied the French the food and shelter they needed and significantly prolonged their campaign."[158]

In September, the French forces clashed with the Russians near Moscow. After a day of fighting, the Russian troops retreated, leaving the path open for the French to enter the capital. Napoleon's expectations of triumph were quickly dashed; upon entering Moscow, the French troops discovered alcohol but scant provisions. Their departure from the city was marred by the onset of snowfall, which proved to be a more formidable adversary than the Russian military itself.[159]

By late October, Napoleon's army was in a precipitous retreat, ravaged by typhus, dysentery, the cold, starvation, and widespread desertion, reduced to a mere 100,000 men. Their defeat mirrored that of a far larger and more vicious force over a century later, succumbing to the unforgiving Russian landscape rather than the force of its inhabitants alone.[160]

Phase III: Great Britain

As the campaigns against the Native Americans and the invasion of Canada deviated from their intended course, American leaders recognized the critical need to avoid defeat at the hands of Great Britain. The downturn of Napoleon's fortunes in Russia in late 1812 and his eventual defeat by a European alliance, leading to his exile to Elba in early 1814, incrementally relieved the British forces to redirect their attention towards North America. Although Napoleon's influence would resurface in the months to follow, for the moment, the British could intensify their military efforts against the United States.

In the lead-up to the War of 1812, President Madison and his advisors sought to avert conflict with Britain. They reintroduced the Non-Intercourse Act with Macon's Bill Number 2 in March 1810, hoping economic leverage would compel the British to end their blockade on

American ships. This strategy nearly succeeded due to Britain's poor harvests and ongoing need for American goods. Even the British Parliament withdrew the Orders in Council related to impressment, addressing a major American complaint. But by the time the news arrived in the United States, war had already been declared, and there was little appetite to reverse the decision. Thus, on June 18, 1812, the war began, later characterized as "probably one of the most unnecessary wars in history."[161]

The War of 1812 is often cited as one of the least necessary conflicts in North American history, yet it played a significant role in shaping the national identities of the countries involved. Just two days before the US declaration of war, on June 16, 1812, the British Parliament had annulled the Orders in Council that rendered any ship heading to a French port vulnerable to capture. Nonetheless, on June 18, 1812, unaware of Britain's conciliatory step, the US Congress passed a resolution to wage war against Great Britain. The slow pace of transatlantic communication meant that the US was making decisions based on outdated information regarding British policies. Had there been more efficient means of communication, both nations might have evaded the conflict.[162]

England's policy decisions led President Madison to lose his grip on the unfolding events early in his tenure. Specifically, he faced the diplomatic challenges inherited from Jefferson's presidency, chiefly the issue of maintaining American neutrality amid the hostilities between France and England. America's stance was to engage in commerce with the nation that would first acknowledge its neutrality and maritime rights. Consequently, when France accepted American neutrality, under international law, trade with Britain would be compelled to cease.

Tensions with Britain were escalating, underpinned by their persistent belief in their dominion over the former colonies. Madison, striving for peace, and the British minister in Washington, DC, had come to an agreement to revoke the orders punishing neutral shipping, a move that could have forestalled war. Yet, this potential resolution was thwarted when the British foreign minister rejected the treaty, effectively "turning thumbs down on the treaty."[163]

March on Washington

The conflict between Britain and America began with the initial skirmish at Fort Mackinac in 1812, and hostilities expanded to areas close to the Canadian border. The British then escalated the war to the East Coast with an offensive at the Battle of Bladensburg, Maryland, in August of 1812. The United States' feeble efforts to repel the British at Bladensburg soon backfired. In August 1814, the British forces landed at Chesapeake Bay and progressed towards Washington, DC. The American militia, trying to block their path, was unsuccessful. Consequently, the British advanced towards Washington unimpeded.[164]

As news of the approaching British spread, government officials and residents hastily evacuated the capital on August 24, 1814. The war, derisively called "Madison's War," was particularly detested in New England, where many state governments declined to contribute militia forces to the war effort. Opposition was so strong among some Federalists that they were accused of signaling British warships with lights along the shorelines, an act that would stain them with the label of "blue light Federalists" and brand them as traitors for years to come.[165]

By 1814, America was grappling with naval threats on three fronts: in the north at Niagara-Lake Champlain, in the south at New Orleans, and at Chesapeake Bay near Washington, DC. Despite the declaration of war in 1812, Congress concluded their session without expanding the Navy, significantly constraining the nation's defensive capabilities at sea. The Navy's assets were limited to a handful of frigates and an array of gunboats.[166]

On September 11, 1814, a formidable British fleet attempted to take control over Lake Champlain. The American forces, led by Captain Thomas McDonough aboard the USS *Saratoga*, engaged the British and achieved an unexpected triumph, compelling the surrender of HMS *Confiance* along with three other British vessels. This marked a remarkable success for the then-fledgling American Navy.[167]

The American naval presence in the Chesapeake Bay was abysmal, comprising only a handful of gunboats and armed barges. During the Battle of Bladensburg, a formidable British force under Vice Admiral Sir

Alexander Cochrane disembarked, featuring veteran soldiers who had just concluded service in the Napoleonic wars, commanded by Major General Robert Ross. Their march towards Washington, DC, commenced with a stop at the American flotilla on the Patuxent River, a tributary of the Chesapeake, intending to annihilate the nascent American fleet. Faced with this threat, American fleet Commodore Joshua Barney made the decisive choice to scuttle his own fleet rather than let it fall into British hands.[168]

After the destruction of the flotilla, British commander Ross was presented with the strategic decision to advance towards either Baltimore or Washington. He had several days to deliberate and multiple routes to consider for his march. Opting to head northwest to Bladensburg, Ross encountered a quickly gathered local militia totaling about 6,500 men. Despite his forces being numerically inferior with only 4,500 soldiers, their superior tactical skills and combat experience gave them the edge. Coupled with American Brigadier General Winder's inexperience and the absence of a contingency plan, the American troops were easily dispersed, leaving the pathway to Washington undefended and clear for the British.[169]

Post-Bladensburg, Ross and his officers marched to Washington, where they entered the White House and dined on the meals abandoned by American officials. The destruction of Washington followed, with the White House, the unfinished Capitol, the Library of Congress, and the House of Representatives suffering significant damage. The scope of the destruction could have been greater if not for the intervention of severe weather, including heavy rainfall and tornadoes, which curtailed the flames.

As word of the approaching British spread, members of Congress, government officials, and residents hastily gathered their belongings and fled the capital. President Madison and First Lady Dolly Madison lingered until the very last moment before the British invasion of the town, managing to save invaluable American artifacts. Among the treasures they preserved were the portrait of General Washington, the original US Constitution, and other emblems of the fledgling republic.

The British Burning Washington[170]

The Star-Spangled Banner: Francis Scott Key
O say, can you see, by the dawn's early light,
What so proudly we hailed at the twilight's last gleaming?
Whose broad stripes and bright stars through the perilous fight,
O'er the ramparts we watched were so gallantly streaming;
And the rocket's red glare, the bombs bursting in air,
Gave proof through the night that our flag was still there;
O say, does that star-spangled banner yet wave
O'er the land of the free, and the home of the brave?
 —Francis Scott Key, *The Star-Spangled Banner*

During the autumn of 1814, Britain targeted a resilient fortification, and America's identity was enriched by the words of a poet. The British set their sights on Baltimore and Fort McHenry, the bastion with a distinctive star shape that defended the city's harbor. On September 13 and 14, Francis Scott Key, a young lawyer and poet, went aboard a British vessel to secure the freedom of an older American physician, Dr. William Beanes, who had been captured by the British for detaining their soldiers after the devastation of Washington. As Key negotiated for Dr. Beanes's release, the bombardment of Fort McHenry began. During the siege, Dr. Beanes inquired whether the American flag still flew over the fort, a question that spurred Key to compose his poem, which would later become the National Anthem of the United States.

Lieutenant Colonel George Armistead, the commanding officer at Fort McHenry, was well aware that the British had come with a formidable assault force, intent on the fort's destruction. If this had been earlier in the war, and if Armistead had shared the same defeatist attitude as the discredited General Hull, Fort McHenry might have capitulated without resistance. However, Armistead was made of tougher mettle. Additionally, during this engagement, the British could not rely on the support of their once-allied Native American forces.

"On Tuesday morning about sunrise, the enemy commenced the attack from his five bomb vessels, at a distance of about two miles, when finding that his shells reached us, he anchored and kept a continuous and well-directed bombardment," Armistead said. "We immediately opened our guns and mortars, but unfortunately, our shots and shells fell considerably short of him. It left us exposed to constant and tremendous show of shells, without the remote possibility of our doing him the slightest injury. It affords me the highest gratification to state, that although we were left exposed and thus inactive, not a man shrunk from the conflict. The bombardment continued until 7 a.m."[171] Britain had thrown its best shells at the fort without effect for twenty-five hours of continuous bombardment. Wednesday morning, nine of its ships got underway and sailed down the river.[172]

The British were halted in their advance on Baltimore by the formidable resistance of Fort McHenry. Unable to breach its defenses, the British invasion force withdrew to Jamaica to regroup and prepare for a subsequent offensive in America, with their sights now set on New Orleans.

Additional Indian Problems: The Battle at Horseshoe Bend

Another Indian uprising by the Upper Creeks, known as the Red Sticks faction, had overwhelmed Fort Mims, forty miles from present-day

Mobile, Alabama, on August 30, 1813. The Creeks, led by Chief Red Eagle, massacred nearly two hundred fifty settlers.[173]

Upon hearing about the massacre while recovering from wounds in Tennessee, Andrew Jackson rose from convalescence to command militia troops against the Creeks. During the campaign, six of his soldiers who attempted to desert were executed under Jackson's orders as a stern measure to maintain discipline and morale among his troops. His rigid and uncompromising leadership earned him the moniker "Old Hickory," while the Native Americans who endured his severe tactics referred to him as "Sharp Knife." Jackson's forces decisively defeated the Creeks at the Battle of Horseshoe Bend on March 27, 1814, resulting in the deaths of 900 Creek warriors. Subsequently, Jackson imposed a treaty that stripped the Creeks of twenty-three million acres of their land.[174]

Andrew Jackson during the Battle of New Orleans.[175]

The Battle of New Orleans

The War of 1812 lasted three and a half years, ending with the Treaty of Ghent in December of 1814, which wouldn't be ratified until two months later.

General Edward Pakenham was related to the famous Duke of Wellington, "England's greatest soldier," who would go on to defeat Napoleon at Waterloo in the same year. Sir Edward and seventy-five hundred Redcoats, many veterans of Wellington's previous successful campaigns against France, arrived in New Orleans to fight Andrew Jackson and his primarily Tennessean militia.

The British embarked on the Louisiana campaign on December 14, 1814, with the objective of capturing New Orleans and seizing as much of Louisiana as they could. Unbeknownst to either side, the Treaty of Ghent would be agreed upon just ten days later after six months of discussions—a delay resulting from the slow communication across the Atlantic. Britain proceeded with its campaign, considering control of Louisiana as a potential leverage in the ongoing peace talks at Ghent. In an effort to win over the local population, the British suggested that the residents of the newly formed state of Louisiana secede and align with either Britain or Spain. Meanwhile, the Americans were concerned that the territories acquired in the Louisiana Purchase, which had since become several new states, might be wrested from them.[176]

General Jackson established stringent martial law in New Orleans. He formed an alliance with the notorious Barataria Pirates, under the command of Jean Lafitte, who, though they pledged allegiance to none, were adept in combat. At the urging of his officers, Jackson requested Lafitte's assistance, which was granted.[177]

The British advance remained unnoticed until December 23, 1814, when they reached the plantation of Major Gabriele Villeré. Narrowly avoiding capture, Villeré managed to elude the British and informed General Jackson of their presence and that they were seeking him. As the Cajun son of a wealthy Louisiana planter, Villeré provided critical intelligence on the British maneuvers. This intelligence enabled Jackson to solidify his defenses in the thickets surrounding New Orleans. He strategically positioned his troops along the Rodriguez Canal, forming a line perpendicular to the Mississippi River, with the river anchoring his right flank and a dense cypress swamp securing his left. This setup gave

Jackson a formidable defensive stance.[178]

Jackson had successfully assembled a force of approximately five thousand individuals. His ranks were diverse, comprising volunteers from New Orleans, Creole gentry, business owners, laborers, militiamen from Tennessee and Kentucky, along with freed slaves and members of the Lafitte pirate band. He positioned these troops within the woods, rendering them difficult to detect by the enemy.[179]

The attack on January 8, 1815, started with British General (Sir) Edward Michael Pakenham ordering rockets to be fired. Jackson told his forces the rockets were "mere toys to amuse children." Jackson's "calm courage inspired his men."[180] The famed Ninety-Third Highland Regiment and the fierce Kilted Scots performed a frontal assault on the Americans. In return, the Americans took dead aim at the advancing Redcoats, merely mowing them down individually. The outcome was more a massacre than a battle.[181]

British casualties mounted in just a few minutes, with 291 dead, 1,162 wounded, and 484 captured or missing. The battle also killed the British commander, General Pakenham. The American toll was thirteen dead and eighty-nine wounded. The Americans won with "murderously accurate rifles" of the militiamen, in particular those of the militia from Tennessee.[182]

The defeat was a "bitter blow to British pride." Who could have imagined the Americans, the "dirty shirts," could inflict such destruction on His Majesty's army?[183] Most would later be responsible for Napoleon's defeat at Waterloo. News of this great American victory came to Washington, DC, at the right time. The people were still depressed about the burning of their own capital. The incredible victory at the Battle of New Orleans helped to reduce their depression and gave them a reason to rejoice.

The Signing of the Treaty of Ghent. Christmas Eve, 1814[184]

On Christmas Eve, 1814, the British and American representatives signed the Treaty of Ghent. Although its settlement proved popular to European Americans, for Native Americans, the Treaty of Ghent was the first step in the destruction of the Indian nations and the disastrous impact on all their people. Many American Indians have yet to recover from the destruction of their societies. Although President George Washington and many other American leaders worried about the survival of the Indian tribes, they also supported the massive westward movement of European Americans.[185]

The Aftereffects of the War of 1812

After the Battle of New Orleans, the failed attempt to conquer Canada and the failure to obtain maritime concessions became an afterthought. It became known as the myth of the glorious war. Although Jackson and the American troops had a sensational victory near New Orleans, the *Federalist* newspaper, among others, complained, "It is attempted to make us believe that all the objects of the war have been obtained, when everything for which it was declared has been abandoned. It was a redefined national victory."[186]

The victory primarily belonged to the artillery of the regular army and the celebrated riflemen from the frontier. A different legend dismissed the battle as inconsequential because it was waged two weeks after the signing of the peace treaty. The peace did not become official until the exchange of ratifications on February 17, more than a month after the Battle of New Orleans.

According to an American prisoner of war from Massachusetts, Benjamin Waterhouse, "nothing now is thought of or talked of, but New Orleans and Jackson, and Jackson and New Orleans. We already perceive that we are respected, and our country is spoken of honorably. Now we are all one of the same people. You have all English blood in your veins, and it is no wonder you fight bravely."[187]

The Battle of New Orleans decisively forced the British to accept peace as an option. It empowered the United States to transform the previously unclear settlement into a strategic upper hand in all future negotiations with the British. Furthermore, it significantly boosted the Federalists' political standing in each election up until James Monroe's resounding victory over the Federalist nominee in the presidential race of 1816.

Post-War Summary

In the Indian treaty councils, the Treaty of Ghent committed over half of the Indian domain to the American government. At Ghent, the Native Americans were not allowed at the negotiating table because the United States would not allow it. As a result, and because of the agreement between the US and Great Britain to revert to pre-war boundaries, the Indians were just as vulnerable to American expansion westward as before the war.

In the Great Lakes country, American officers held new treaty councils with most of the native nations during the summer of 1815. Many Indians attended the councils just to "get the presents."[188] The council adhered to the letter, if not the spirit of Ghent. But, the commissioners did pressure the Indians to ratify land cessations they had disputed before the war. Commissioners for the American government clung to a controversial prewar suspension of two million acres of designated Indian land in southeastern Michigan alone. In the South, during Andrew Jackson's campaign of 1814 against the Creek Indians of Alabama, he forced them to "surrender nearly 20 million acres of land—over half of their domain."[189] Although the Treaty, again, mandated prewar boundaries to be restored after the war, the Creek Indians never recovered this land.

The complex and brutal acts the United States government committed against the American Indians are well documented. However, the commissioners of the time warned that natives faced destruction if they resisted. It would get far worse during the infamous Trail of Tears forced migration and in the decades beyond. The United States, even with its successes, is still tainted by its abuse of the North American Indians.[190]

CHAPTER FOUR

THE ANGLO-IRISH WAR

Certainly, the solution to avoiding the Anglo-Irish War of 1919–1921, also known as the Irish War of Independence, was to have resolved the issues that drove it before it ever began. The means by which Great Britain could have accomplished that was through Home Rule, where Ireland would have had internal control of domestic politics and British Parliament would have overseen Irish foreign trade, foreign military, and political relations. In fact, this solution was contemplated and held in abeyance until after the First World War.

The rebellions that characterized the history prior to the Irish Revolution didn't begin appearing out of the ether. Century after century of British control led to significant economic hardships (such as the potato famines) that in turn led to open rebellions that were viciously put down by the British. Britain largely viewed Irish land and assets as their own resources to exploit. As a result of exploitative policies, resentment accumulated over time, giving each new effort by the Irish nationalists to rid themselves of the British a renewed energy.

Prior to the Dublin Uprising of 1916, known popularly as the Easter Rising, there were a series of rebellions led by a number of underground organizations, such as the Society of United Irishmen and the Fenian Brotherhood. The Easter Rising proved to be a turning point in Irish history because of the brutal executions of sixteen rebel leaders, carried out in public by British leadership to make an example of them. The Irish people, as a result, began to change their allegiance from England to that of the Irish

Republican cause, overcoming centuries of Irish history. That rebellion, combined with the failure of both sides to implement Home Rule over time, had spelled defeat for Great Britain's future of ruling Ireland.

Once British force against the rebellion became intense with the addition of the English police force known as the Black and Tans and Irish Republicans increased violent activity, the Irish public became progressively more supportive of the insurrection. The British public became more appalled by the violence as the war progressed, ultimately calling for an end to British rule in Ireland. The object that became less valuable to them was the cost of continuing the war. This case could have been resolved politically, but the British civilian and military leadership did not understand that the use of military force through limited war could not achieve what peaceful negotiation at an earlier date could. They soon learned that the counterproductive political effects of their strategies would lead to a fully independent Irish Republic.

The failure of Britain's civilian leaders to comprehend what could and could not be achieved by force in this limited war cost Great Britain an important geographic region and several million subjects, not to mention the lives lost on both sides during the war.

In matching strategy and policy, it is important to ask two questions: is the policy an objective that can best be accomplished by military means, and is the military's capability understood by civilian leadership?

In the case of Vietnam, the Johnson administration did not understand the enemy's military capability and what it would take to win the war. In the Anglo-Irish War, the British government did not understand that the best solution to the Irish problem was through peaceful means. The British had faced a similar question in the American War for Independence. These were important examples of the failure of civilian leaders to comprehend what could and could not be achieved by force. These failures proved to be fatal to the conduct of these limited wars, as the British leaders believed that they would ultimately succeed if more troops and ordinances were added on.[191]

The Republican Tradition

Wolfe Tone, a leader of the Society of United Irishmen and the Irish Rebellion of 1798, is regarded as the founding father of the Republican Tradition. He stated that from the time of his youth, he "regarded the connection between Ireland and England as the curse of the Irish nation." The tradition that grew from this belief evolved into the movement's conviction that ultimately the use of armed force would be necessary to break this curse.

Through the evolution of this movement, Republican leaders came to view British soldiers and civilian leaders as never having brought anything but deception, suffering, starvation, and misery to the Irish people. The belief was that only after the British departed from the island of Ireland would things ever change for the good of all Irishmen. There was an "emotional core" to Republicanism, as reflected in the quotation by Tone, above.

This was considered the root of the effect of British, or more specifically, English control. Author M. L. R Smith said, "The notion of colonial subjugation is the strongest theme in Irish republican nationalism. The contention that Ireland remains at the mercy of an exploitative foreign power, with all the attendant suffering it causes, forms the central hypothesis of republican political analysis."[192]

Smith continues that Wolfe Tone believed that "the bane of Irish prosperity is the influence of England,"[193] a strong opinion that was not widely held in the late eighteenth century. Tone further believed "that [Britain's] influence will be ever extended while the connection between the countries continues."[194]

In the 1797 constitution of the United Irishmen, the group's leaders emphasized that Ireland would continue to be exploited for the selfish goals of the British government as long as the link between the two nations existed: "We have no National Government; we are ruled by Englishmen and the Servants of Englishmen, whose Object is the Interest of another country, whose Instrument is corruption and whose Strength is the Weakness of Ireland."[195]

Battle of Ballynahinch. In the center, Captain Henry Evatt of Ireland's Colonel Charles Leslie's Monaghan Militia lies mortally wounded.[196]

Developing from early Irish history to the outbreak of the Anglo-Irish War, the Irish Republican mind and its strategies reflected the belief that the British were the cause of their problems, and being the common element in these problems, they needed to be removed from Irish life.[197]

Reflecting on the words of Wolfe Tone, M. L. R. Smith described "the plague" of British influence in Ireland: "The history of British involvement in Irish affairs is seen in terms of Britain's attempts to use its power systematically to drain Ireland of its human and material resources through underdevelopment, restricted markets, famine and emigration, and the imposition of alien institutions. Republicans see the province's existence as an artificially manufactured political arrangement to preserve British domination of the whole island."[198]

According to this belief, any presence of the British in Northern Ireland greatly divided the Irish people, and the development of a "mature class-based polity" slowed economic progress and distorted social values. In other words, by maintaining control over Northern Ireland, Great Britain is viewed as having maintained their control over all of Ireland, not just their province in the north. That suggests that the Irish Revolution will remain unfinished as long as Great Britain is present at all.

The Rebellion of 1641

The Irish Confederate Wars of 1641–1653, also known as the Eleven Years' War, were one part of the civil wars in Ireland, England, and Scotland that broke out midcentury. All three countries were ruled by one king, Charles I of England.

The rebellion in Ireland was focused on Irish Catholics versus English and Scottish Protestants living in Ireland. The war ended with Irish Catholics and Scottish Presbyterians fighting the ultimate winners, the English Parliament. The fight was over who would govern Ireland—the Irish, English, or Scots. With England's victory, the religious Protestant group ended up owning most of the land in Ireland. They would dominate Ireland for years. Some consider this war the most devastating war in Irish history.[199]

The Irish plot to rebel against foreign elements living in Ireland began in October 1641 with initial preparations for a rebellion that lasted until 1642. The formation of small cells of Irishmen, recruited by the local Irish lords, was organized. Their first targets were large numbers of civilians from opposition ethnic and religious groups, primarily Protestants. The Irish objective was to force out Protestant settlers who now occupied Irish land previously owned by the Irish gentry. These lands were known as the "plantations of Ireland."

The British government forces in Ireland were comprised of English civilian officials, soldiers, and Irish members of the Royal Irish Constabulary (RIC). Their intent was to punish all Catholics for their attacks on English Protestant settlers concentrated around Cork, Dublin, Carrick, and Derry. To support local Protestants, English troops were sent from Great Britain. Only limited numbers of British soldiers were in Ireland during the civil wars. Once the British military arrived, the insurrection was put down. The massacre of Catholic civilians occurred at Rathlin Island and elsewhere. All sides displayed "extreme cruelty in this phase of the war.... Casualties included 4,000 Protestants killed—12,000 may have died of privation after being driven from their homes."[200]

The response by Catholics focused on the English-Irish government in Dublin. They mobilized in Dublin, Wicklow, and Ulster with targets of public buildings, such as Dublin Castle, the seat of the Irish government. It is important to note that the Irish Catholic plot was similar to the Irish efforts in the Easter Rising of 1916, with a similar outcome: defeat.

Like every other Irish rebellion against the British up to the Anglo-Irish War, the Irish rebels' ability to gain the support of the Irish Catholic population was largely unsuccessful. Until that changed, these rebellions would not be successful.

The Confederate War, 1642–48

This war immediately followed the end of the 1641 rebellion. The Association of The Confederate Catholics of Ireland was established to plan and manage the Catholic war effort. Since Irish Catholics controlled roughly two-thirds of Ireland, it was essentially an independent state and was a coalition of all Irish Catholic societies. The Confederates ruled much of Ireland until 1649.

In Ireland, the Protestant forces were split into three main factions: the English Royalists, English Parliamentarians, and Scottish Covenanters. King Charles I sent a large army to Ireland in 1642 to put down the Irish rebellion. Initially, Catholic Confederates controlled important port towns, such as Waterford and Wexford. Due to their relative strength in Ireland, the Confederation received assistance such as money and supplies from other Catholic powers in Europe, including Portugal, Spain, and the Papacy. The Confederation's capital was Kilkenny, where they raised their armies.

The Irish Confederation avoided defeat primarily because of the English Civil War, where most elements of the English military were required. The Confederation filled the vacuum until the English Civil War ended. Perhaps with quicker action the Irish Confederation could have developed a strong enough army to keep control of Ireland. They kept control by attacking English and Scottish garrisons. Irish forces did succeed in overthrowing Galway, forcing the surrender of the English garrison in 1643. However, the British maintained control of Ulster, Dublin, and Cork. Those cities remained in Scottish and English control throughout the rebellion.

The English Civil War ended, giving England the opportunity to transfer forces to Ireland. Unfortunately for the Irish, the Confederates never completed the task of conquering and reorganizing all of Ireland.

"The wars following the 1641 revolt caused massive loss of life in Ireland, comparable in the country's history only with the Great Famine of the 1840s. The ultimate winner, the English Parliament, arranged for the mass confiscation of land owned by Irish Catholics as punishment for the rebellion and to pay for the war."[201]

With this defeat, the Irish would have to rebel once again if they were to set themselves free of English bondage. They would ultimately succeed, but not for two hundred and fifty years. There would be several other rebellions before freedom and independence were ultimately accomplished. During these rebellions, the Irish leadership would learn how to energize their people to fight for independence and how to remove this "foreign" nation, England.

The Rebellions of 1868–1870

From 1868–1870, the Catholic population was again rising. At this time there was widespread questioning on whether they should remain within the British empire or separate and become independent. The possibility of Irish Home Rule again became an issue for the Irish. Though the people had differing views about it, those in favor of rebellion no longer thought of Home Rule; they thought only of complete separation from the British.

After failing to realize a free and independent Ireland, William Gladstone, the prime minister of Great Britain from 1868 until his final retirement at eighty-six years old in 1894, proposed a specific plan for Ireland unlike any plan previously established during this period or before. He possessed his "own natural inclination to do justice to Ireland."[202] Gladstone believed that he could solve the problem of Ireland "forever" by taking two measures: disestablishing the Irish Protestant Church throughout Ireland and supporting legislation to compensate a tenant financially upon eviction. Gladstone "thought that the grievance of the Established Church lay at the root of all other issues and would allow the

Government to intervene in the relationship between landlord and tenant on behalf of the tenant was at that time itself a revolution."[203]

Gladstone's "radical" economic and political plans were bitterly contested by Conservatives within the British Parliament. Ironically, these reforms were fully implemented by those same Conservatives some years after Gladstone's death. They would also be the ones to end the plan for an independent Irish Republic.

The Conservatives then "passed a resolution that a national legislature would mean neither revolution nor weakening of the power of the Empire. On the contrary, it would do more to conciliate the empire by restoring Ireland's nationality. To engineer this revolution, a new practical nationwide organization arose."[204]

This organization was made up of both former Gladstone aids and Conservative members of Parliament. For the Irish citizenry, this organization contributed to the failure of the cause of reform anticipated by Gladstone. Parliament was also able to end any radical desire to free Ireland from England while allowing the Irish population representation by establishing a local Irish Parliament, an entity Conservatives could then control.

Once again, the fundamental reason for failure was a lack of widespread support by the Irish people, a failure that would persist until after the Easter Rising of 1916. At this point, the Conservatives in Parliament held the day despite Gladstone's wishes.

The Fenian Influence

The Fenians were a transatlantic association made up of the Irish Republican Brotherhood, which had been founded in Dublin by James Stephens in 1858, and the United States arm of the Fenians, referred to as the Fenian Brotherhood, also founded in 1858, which was led by John O'Mahony and Michael Doheny. The Fenians on both sides of the ocean advocated rebellion against British rule in Ireland. This collaboration culminated in the Fenian uprising of 1867, which failed but also laid the groundwork for the Irish Revolution.

The main organizer of this rebellion was the Irish Republican Brotherhood (IRB), led by James Stephens. Widespread unrest in the Irish people due to the British effort to control free speech was illustrated by the British attacks on *The Irish People* newspaper. In anticipation of an Irish rebellion during the previous year, 1866, James Stephens began making efforts to gain support from the United States to gain financial assistance for a rebellion.

The Irish uprising of 1867 began in February in County Kerry, followed by a nationwide insurrection. There was also an attempt to take Dublin in early March 1867 that ultimately failed. In addition to poor planning on the part of the radicals, the British successfully infiltrated the Irish Republican Brotherhood leaders within the IRB ranks. The rebellion was also a failure because rebel leaders were unable to enlist the Irish people in their efforts. A small group of radicals financed by the United States claimed they would rise again, advocating "militant republican separatism and contributed to . . . general radical national activity, but they failed to recruit the general Irish population—a failure which would be repeated numerous times leading up to the 1916 Uprising."[205]

Despite their failure, because of the transatlantic nature of the Fenians, they became a unique radical group. Their intentions were to establish an independent Irish Republic by force of arms. By 1865, the Fenians began preparing for a rebellion. Part of the plan was to recruit Irish soldiers in the United States, soldiers who had been caught up in the American Civil War. Of the fifty thousand men willing to fight, six thousand were veterans of the American Civil War and already battle-seasoned.

In September 1865, the British began plans to curtail free speech as it related to the radical Fenians. Their first attack was to close the Fenian newspaper *The Irish People*. In doing so, most of the Fenian leaders were arrested. There were follow-on actions by the Fenians, including the attempted rescue of Richard O'Sullivan Burke as he sat in Clerkenwell Prison awaiting trial in London in December 1867. An explosion caused by Michael Barret occurred while attempting to rescue Burke. The attempt ended with the death of twelve people and the wounding of one hundred and twenty others. Barret was given the death penalty for his efforts.

On another occasion, three Fenians failed in their attack on a prison van containing two other Fenians, Captains T. J. Kelly and Timothy Deasy. One police sergeant, Charles Brett, was shot by Peter Rice, a Fenian, as he sat inside the van. Rice intended to shoot the lock to set the captives free, but the bullet passed into the interior of the van and killed Brett.[206]

As Irishmen were rounded up, five were decided to be the culprits, and though four of these men were involved in some way with the escape attempt, one man, a marine on leave named Maguire, was completely innocent. These five were executed by hanging and were known as the Manchester Martyrs. The man who pulled the trigger, Rice, escaped to the United States with Kelly and Deasy.[207]

The man whom the court decided, in error, fired the shot, William Allen, rightfully denied killing Brett but gave these words upon his condemnation: "I want no mercy—I'll have no mercy . . . I'll die as many thousands have died, for the sake of their beloved land in defence[sic] of it. I will die proudly and triumphantly in defence[sic] of republican principles, and the liberty of an oppressed and enslaved people."[208]

Beyond Fenianism, "something much more than a mere return of the status quo was required."[209] A meeting at the George Hotel in Limerick obtained the signatures of 198 Roman Catholic clergymen for the Repeal Declaration to restore Ireland's nationality, which the authors believed would do more to conciliate the empire.

Cardinal Paul Cullen of Dublin stated, "Our poor country has been reduced to a state of the greatest misery and destitution. Our towns and cities are filled with poor men, women, and children, half-starved, without shoes, stockings, or proper clothing to preserve them from the snows and frosts of winter. More squalor of this kind is to be seen in Dublin alone than in the great cities in France, Austria, or Spain."[210]

Because of these conditions over the two famines that occurred from 1845 to 1852 and later, 1879, millions of Irish inhabitants emigrated to the United States. Facing starvation, they traveled across the Atlantic in the hopes of saving themselves and their families. Four hundred thousand cottages of the poor were later leveled to the ground. This emigration was followed by a strong condemnation of Fenianism in a pastoral letter from the ultraconservative archbishop. He instructed this pastoral letter to be read to all churches and chapels of his diocese. The letter advocated for electing leaders to Parliament that were sympathetic to the plight of Irishmen and to turn away from violence. For all intents and purposes, the 1868 Rising and Fenian movements ended.

Gladstone's Impact on Irish Freedom

In the 1880s, Irish Nationalists once again demanded Home Rule, or self-government. These demands brought significant opposition from the British Parliament and contradicted Gladstone's ideas for Ireland. Gladstone believed that several measures could be forwarded to placate the nationalists, including the disestablishment of the Protestant Church in Ireland.

While this measure was being debated in the British Parliament, conservative opponents demanded that Gladstone read from the Act of Union aloud. This conservative opposition group warned him not to do anything against it. According to Robert Kee, the establishment of the Protestant church in Ireland was fundamental to this Irish Constitution, stating explicitly that "the doctrine worship, discipline, and government of the said United Church . . . shall be and shall remain in full force forever." The conservatives of the time believed removing the Protestant church in Ireland would be "the most violent shock to the constitution since the Reformation."[211]

Through Gladstone's action against the Protestants, which made up only one-sixth of the country's population, Gladstone was determined to outlaw the Protestant religion from Ireland forever for the sake of the Irish Catholic majority. With the loss of their church, the question arose: where would the newly disenfranchised Protestants go to worship their chosen religion?

The reality was that with this Catholic majority in Ireland, nothing was going to satisfy them until they had a total separation from Protestants in their country and full independence from Britain. According to this plan, the process should begin with the removal of the established Irish Protestant church.[212]

Ironically, the pushback from this decision was both enormous and not foreseen by Gladstone or his staff. The truth was that England would never willingly accept Irish independence.

Member of Parliament John Arthur Roebuck felt strongly that Irish independence would not benefit England. "Cut off Ireland from England and you cut off her right arm."[213] An English radical, Roebuck announced, "I have a voice in this great assembly [Parliament], that voice shall be raised in the maintenance of Imperial rule. No sentimental talk about oppression to Ireland, and indeed nothing on earth shall move me from that position."[214]

During the debates on whether the government should play into the Irish population's wishes, the government sensed the beginning of the end of Imperial rule if they allowed such a separation. Debates within the government refused to "willfully shut their eyes to the advantages of the incorporation of the two countries."[215] A question then arose, especially with the Catholic Irish: were Ireland and England two separate countries, or one country and one colony? Ireland and England took diametrically opposing views. The Irish Catholic population sided with one country and one colony; the English chose to feel they were two countries—one Ireland and one England.

Another member of Parliament gave the opinion, "It is a mistake to suppose that when there arose symptoms of nationality, they must either succeed in suppressing them or else they must give them full sway and allow them to lead to absolute separation and independence."[216]

Gladstone had no intention of overturning the Union; it was only to make it work. He, too, worked to see the Union as two nations, not a colony of Ireland. Gladstone succeeded in "disestablishing the Protestant Church over the whole of Ireland [which] became law in 1869." Gladstone "hailed it as the greatest victory ever won in the British Parliament."[217]

This "greatest victory" also gave rise to Conservative opposition in Britain, ensuring that Gladstone would ultimately fail in his plan to help Ireland become an equal partner within the empire. According to Kee, only half of the sixty-seven years since the joining of Britain and Ireland through the Acts of Union of 1800 had been anywhere near beneficial for Ireland. The other half of the time, the Conservative movement continued to grow, which sought to limit Irish autonomy. First they gained support in authoring the Coercion Acts, several pieces of parliamentary legislation over a few decades which limited ordinary liberties for the Irish population. These were "Coercion Acts of every style, all restricting the ordinary liberties of the subject of the Peace Preservation Acts, and Arms and Insurrection Acts proclaiming Martial Law, and the suspension of Habeas Corpus."[218]

At this time as well, a million Irish died from starvation, and a million more emigrated from the country. Also, one of the major pillars of the Acts of Union, the establishment of the Protestant church, had just been removed, which destabilized the relationship between the two nations further.[219]

Leading up to the Schism

After the failed Fenian revolt of 1867, the Irish in Dublin were dissatisfied with the status quo. The issue of religion had seemingly been resolved, though the issues of tenant-landlord relations and Irish autonomy had not.

Charles Stewart Parnell was a member of the British Parliament from County Meath in Ireland who would prove to be an advocate for the Irish poor and a catalyst for the movement toward Irish independence. Parnell would publish *Nationalist Politics* by March 1899 and for years to come.

Arthur Griffith, the eventual founder of the Sinn Féin political party in 1905, published the *United Irishman* newspaper as a media platform for Republican politics. By March 1899, Griffith became known for writing fiery editorials. George Morton Griffith, no relation to Arthur, had an article published on September 16, 1899, that detailed what would become the strategy for forming the Sinn Féin party. Arthur, and his paper, also promoted solidarity with the Boers during the British-Boer wars in Africa. The Boers were a group of French, German, and Dutch settlers in South Africa, mainly farmers. In fact, the word *Boer* means "farmer" in

Afrikaner. It was deemed necessary by Griffith and his friends to support the underdog Boers who had a fighting spirit but fewer resources, and to oppose the British Empire in this African war.[220]

Arthur Griffith also voiced opposition to Irish men joining the British Army as the British solicited Irish support for their side in the Boer Wars. Griffith, Gonne, and James Connolly "were instrumental in the foundation of the Irish Transvaal Committee." In March, "a crowd of twenty thousand gathered in front of Customs House in Dublin" to protest conscription.[221]

This became a forerunner to the protests against British conscription of Irishmen throughout World War I. The conscription issue, and the Boer War itself, showed the solidarity of the Irish protesters for the Boer cause. Griffith was elected to represent South Mayo, and when he eventually resigned his seat in the House of Commons leading up to the Irish revolution, he stated, "I have been some five years in the House, and the conclusion with which I leave it is that no cause, however just, will find support, no wrong, however pressing or apparent, will find redress here unless backed up by force."[222]

The Schisms

The story of Ireland's participation in the Boer War of 1899 was a foreshadowing of the Irish revolution to come. The events in Ireland and in Africa seemed to predict possible attacks against the British by Dublin Irishmen nearly two decades later. By 1897, the Irish Republicans formed elements of an Irish Brigade. By October 20, 1899, the Irish Brigade became the vanguard of the Boer forces. Between British and Boer forces near Ladysmith, South Africa, the Irish Brigade played an important part in the Boer victory. News of the brigade's successes fighting the British reached Ireland newspapers, and the Irish people were thrilled to hear of Irish heroism.

Colonel John MacBride and his men on the front line quickly became heroes in the hearts of the Irish at home. From Ireland, Arthur Griffith and Maude Gonne sent their heartfelt congratulations for the Irish Brigade's successes and valor, along with a flag representing the Irish nationalist spirit. The Transvaal Irish Brigade received this flag for their valor, and before Christmas, the flag was raised above the Irish Brigade camp.[223]

What was learned by those present during the conflict with British forces in Africa was that the brigade had gained valuable war-fighting experience that could be used during any future conflicts with the British.

The Home Rule Movement

Irish nationalists had demanded Home Rule (or self-government) from the British at least since the 1880s. Arthur Griffith's Sinn Féin, initially a newspaper and fringe group that evolved into a political party, wanted some form of Irish independence. Although Home Rule was finally approved in 1912, the intention of the act was to keep Britain and Ireland together. Once passed, however, Northern Ireland immediately set up the Ulster Volunteers, an opposition group in favor of British rule, to prevent any implementation of Home Rule, and prevent any agreement with the Irish nationalists in Southern Ireland. Instead, the Ulsters wanted to preserve the status quo of British rule.

Despite Northern Ireland's stance against Home Rule, the British Parliament passed the third Home Rule Act on September 18, 1914—which was immediately postponed by the Suspensory Act because of the commencement of World War I. Even with the Suspensory Act, the Home Rule Act would be revisited by Parliament due to pushback from the Ulsters. The growing dispute between Southern and Northern Ireland would eventually cause a civil war once the Anglo-Irish War ended. Home rule would have to wait until after the Great War, which was erroneously expected to end within the year.[224]

The Easter Rising of 1916: Plans for the Rebellion Take Form

The Easter Rising was the final stage before the commencement of the Anglo-Irish War. With British preparations for the First World War, the next action by Parliament was to recruit an Irish regiment in the new

British Army. Most in Ireland, led by John Redmond's call, supported the conscription of Irish men in support of the British war effort. Not all had this opinion.

There is extensive information on the Easter Rising of 1916 and its significance for ultimate Irish freedom. The Irish political leadership began to feel the only possible basis for successful revolutionary action was the popular discontent of the Irish people. However, only small groups of Irish leaders and their volunteers were focused on the "evils of the English Government in Ireland." Citizens were only focused on the losses of their children on the battlefields of France.[225]

As plans for a rebellion began to mature, Patrick Pearse, then a member of the Irish Republican Brotherhood, became concerned with his personal safety and ultimately being found out by the British government. For his own safety and the safety of his colleagues, he felt obligated to officially deny that he was planning an insurrection. By February 5, 1916, Pearse notified John Devoy in America and passed information that they were planning an insurrection on to the Germans as well. The rebels had appealed to sympathetic groups in both America and Germany for material assistance. They also provided information regarding the rebellion commencing by the designated date of Easter Sunday, 1916.[226]

Regarding assistance from Germany, they were promised twenty thousand rifles, several machine guns, and five million rounds of ammunition. This military assistance was loaded on a ship, the SS *Libau*, but was intercepted by the British navy off the coast of County Kerry prior to the uprising and never reached the rebels. Because the British had intercepted communications between Germany and their diplomatic contingent in the United States, they knew not only the planned date of the insurrection but also when and where the weapons were being delivered.[227]

In Pearse's view, there was a pressing need for rebellion before the end of the First World War, which many believed would come quickly. Protests within the Irish community were becoming louder and more frequent as the recruiting campaign to raise one hundred thousand new Irish men to send to the war in France was well underway. Irish Republican leaders felt it was time for action. "The British were convinced that the rebellion would be very soon, despite claims of the Irish volunteers."[228]

On April 19, 1916, Irish Volunteers, also known as Sinn Féin Volunteers, during a meeting of the Dublin Corporation (the former Dublin municipal government), learned that detailed instructions for the arrest of the Volunteer leaders and other national figures were ordered. As this information from Dublin Castle became known, Volunteers were in a state of considerable turmoil. They understood that the government was poised to disarm them. The Sinn Féin leaders responded by ordering the volunteers to prepare themselves against suppression by the British government.

The Easter Rising rebels' plan was ambitious for a general uprising, including an intricate and mobile occupation of Dublin. Its overall planning and execution resulted in a misunderstanding that illustrated that its planning was limited and ultimately ineffective. The rising was supposed to include other areas of Ireland and this extensive takeover of Dublin. It barely covered Dublin and just a few locations throughout Ireland.[229]

Actions to Arrest Sinn Féin Leaders

Rebels from the Irish Volunteers and the Irish Citizen Army finally began working together. They surrounded government military barracks and occupied railway stations and other key approaches to Dublin. They also controlled prominent public streets and formed a joint Irish Republican Army contingent occupying the Dublin main post office.

Thomas MacDonagh, a poet and University of England lecturer, led the occupation of Jacob's Biscuit Factory just behind Dublin Castle, the headquarters for the British government and its local Irish contingency. Others led by Edward Daly fortified the Four Courts area, all in preparation for the expected British government military attacks, which occurred soon after and included significant artillery shelling.[230]

As Irish prisoners of the Easter Rebellion accumulated, the British and their loyalist-Irish collaborators were treated with hostility by the Dublin people and many throughout Ireland. That hostility reflected growing support of rebellion by the people. This support was also understood to be only the beginning of a long road to the important support of the Irish people. They would also develop widespread public support for independence. Britain's propensity for acting against its own goals and the reality that Sinn Féin was not seen as responsible for the rebellion would prove difficult.

Eoin (pronounced "Owen") MacNeill, an Irish leader who established the Irish Volunteers and had been arrested despite not having taken part in the rebellion, commented that the Easter Rebellion was terribly mismanaged. The rebels proclaimed the Republic, occupied government buildings in Dublin, and held out bravely for a week until the Royal Irish Constabulary and the Irish loyalists fighting with them brought in their artillery.

Éamon De Valera, formerly a university math professor, had become part of the rebel leadership, thus making himself known to the leaders of the Easter Rising, and would subsequently become a key leader of Sinn Féin and the eventual post-rebellion governing body. But in late 1916, he was already planning for the next rebellion.

The Irish Volunteers remained in most of the positions they had occupied on Easter Monday—their mission of causing as many enemy casualties as possible was at least partially successful. Pearse, Clarke, Plunkett, and Connoly sent out propaganda dispatches that tended to exaggerate the circumstances, such as "Ireland is rising, and Germany's help is on the way." It was irrelevant whether they had won or lost. But it was the act that would start old slumbering fires of fierce nationalism within both the leadership and the Irish people.[231]

Whatever support they were able to elicit from their Irish countrymen was based primarily on Britain's reaction to the uprising. This reaction was anything but gentle. In contrast to the Irish Volunteer's organization and execution, the British opposition was well organized, lethal, and, within a short time, relatively successful. The British response to the Irish defeat included a series of public executions of rebel leaders by firing squad that were spread out over a ten-day period in May for maximum effect. This list included the aforementioned Pearse, MacDonagh, and MacBride. In addition to the executions, the British arrested thousands of nationalist activists, imprisoning many. An eventual benefit from the rebellion resulted from the names of previously unknown rebels becoming known and admired by the Irish people. They became martyrs to the Republican cause—the "national cause." This notoriety began to replace earlier feelings of general apathy and almost a slight aversion toward the rebels and the Easter Rebellion.

Richard Bennett in *The Black and Tans* quotes the poet Yeats and his summation of the Easter Rebellion, Britain's awkward approach to punishing the key rebels, and the impact on the Irish people. As Yeats wrote:

> A terrible beauty is born. The men who died became pictured in postcard photos, thus becoming household heroes throughout Ireland. Those who survived the street firing squads became prisoners who were released in 1917. These British actions against the rebels of the Easter Rebellion, dramatically illustrated the failings of the English vis-à-vis the English Administration in Ireland. They always seemed to do the wrong thing in Ireland. John Bull does things in a week that disgrace him for a century."[232]

The public outcry began because of the mass arrests and the impact during the public executions of the primary leaders. This action was designed to emphasize that the British were in control of their colony and that those involved in the insurrection would receive proper justice. However, these actions had the opposite effect. The reality was that the population was increasingly shocked and outraged by these mass arrests and brutal executions.

The Irish population during wartime martial law was also a factor that reversed public sentiment. The immediate impact of the rising was a proclamation of independence that had been announced by the Irish Republic during the Easter Rising. These events were certainly precursors to the ultimate conflict of 1919–1921 and the subsequent Irish Civil War between North and South Ireland. All were made in defense of a new Irish Republic.

The Aftereffects of the Easter Rising

Not being associated with the Easter Rebellion of 1916 by the Irish public, the next generation of Sinn Féin leadership, General Maxwell De Valera and others had successfully established Sinn Féin in the minds of Irish people as the political arm of the rebellion. Sinn Féin seized the opportunity to keep the momentum of the rebellion by scoring a number of political victories.

Although the Easter Rising was a significant event on the way to the Irish Revolution, leaders such as De Valera recognized that public sentiment was only gradually gaining acceptance of an independent republic. Many in present-day Northern Ireland, in what were known as Ulster counties, would never accept an Irish Republic as their solution. What helped the Republicans in the south was a series of missteps by the British government, producing martyrs, which pushed the Southern Irish public closer to declaring independence. Britain created these martyrs, including political prisoners such as Thomas Ashe, who was killed in prison on September 23rd, 1917. He and other prisoners had chosen to go on a hunger strike, and he was killed during a force-feeding session.[233]

The rise of Sinn Féin as a political force would only continue due to Great Britain's political mistakes. The British forces were becoming seriously depleted on the war front, and reinforcements were needed. On April 16, 1918, the British authorities imposed massive conscription obligations on the Irish people by requesting one hundred thousand recruits in an effort to replenish their troops on the Western Front quickly. Ireland was identified to be a major contributor, in addition to the other member nations of Great Britain.

The Irish resistance described it as a replenishment of "cannon fodder." British Prime Minister Lloyd George pushed Parliament to find potential recruits at the nearest available source. Lloyd George immediately got the Irish Conscription Bill on the Statute Books to facilitate this recruitment.

The Roman Catholic hierarchy opposed using Irish men to make up the British quota. For the first time, the whole of Ireland pushed back on the British. Government Catholic leaders released the Bishop's Manifesto, telling the Irish people they had a right to resist "by every means that are consonant with the law of God." The British government ignored this Ireland-wide resistance until Lord French became governor-general in Ireland, specifically to implement the Conscription Bill.

On April 23, 1918, protests on Saint George's Day for Englishmen commenced. Sinn Féin leadership pronouncements included a statement that the Irish population preferred to live in Ireland than die in France. Sinn Féin leadership called for a general strike with support from the Irish Trade Union Congress and Labor Party. They closed all shops and factories in Southern Ireland. Belfast, not intending to rebel against the British, did not take part.

In another potential boost to the Irish Republican movement, Sir Henry Wilson, the British chief of the Imperial General Staff, declared the discovery, from his intelligence services in May of 1918, of a possible German plot to provide weapons and ammunition to the Irish rebels. Although evidence of the plot was weak at best, on Prime Minister Lloyd George's directions, this fictitious plot was used as an excuse to sweep hundreds of Sinn Féin members and key leaders into prison without charge or trial, including De Valera and Arthur Griffith. The intention was to reduce the momentum of the movement for Irish independence. They likely hoped, because of strong anti-German sentiment, to gain additional support among the Irish for the war effort.[234]

With the more peacefully minded Sinn Féin leaders in prison, Michael Collins and other Irish Volunteer leaders were left to conduct a terror campaign against the RIC, British troops, and loyalists. In early July 1918, the first armed attack on the RIC occurred since the Easter Rising. Volunteers ambushed two RIC men who were there to stop any attacks. They intended to obtain police carbines and ammunition. One man was shot in the neck, the other beaten. Severe rioting, including raids by Irish Volunteers to secure arms and ammunition from armories, farms, and private citizens. One such riot occurred in Dublin on Armistice Day, 1918, where one hundred British soldiers were injured.[235]

In December 1918, Éamon De Valera won a Sinn Féin election victory at East Mayo on an openly Republican platform. He would have refused to take his seat in the British Parliament in accordance with the Sinn Féin policy of abstention, but he was still imprisoned in London. De Valera eventually escaped from the London Gaol in February 1919. Other prisoners were released in March 1919.

Collins, at this time, continued to organize and make speeches, though the British authorities were not pleased with his efforts. He gave a speech on January 6, 1919, at a "prohibited protest meeting at Dunmanway in County Cork. Police and soldiers charged the crowds with batons and fixed bayonets, but Collins escaped."[236] On the next day, he and other Irish Parliament members called for a meeting of an Irish National Assembly, known in Gaelic as the Dail Eireann. This meeting was to take place on January 21, 1919, at the Mansion House in Dublin.

Sinn Féin recruited those who attended this First Dail. Again, they were not initially threatening violence via the military, though complete independence from Great Britain was the goal. Unbeknownst to the Dail, an attack was planned by the Irish Republican Army, previously known as the Irish Volunteers, at Soloheadbeg, County Tipperary. Two RIC constables were killed during these attacks as they were transporting explosives. The IRA leaders coordinating the attack were most notably Sean Treacy, Seamus Robinson, Sean Hogan, and Dan Breen. Even though the attack was not authorized by the Dail, it is regarded as the beginning of the war.

The British government quickly responded to this attack. Dan Breen, one of the men who made the attack, told of how they were wanted men after the ambush at Soloheadbeg. "South Tipperary . . . had been proclaimed a special military area"[237] under the Defense of the Realm Act, and a bounty had been placed on their heads. Regarding the incident, Breen recalled later that they had "discussed the proposal for a long time. Finally [they] decided to disarm the guard and seize the explosives, for, as Sean said, there was nothing we needed more at that time than guns and explosives."[238]

The Anglo-Irish War Begins

Irish independence was declared on January 21, 1919, during the meeting of the First Dail. In his speech to the Dail, Dr. Richard Francis Hayes, a member from East Limerick said, "As regards the Republican prisoners, we must always remember that this country is at war with England and so we must in a sense regard them as necessary casualties in the great fight."[239] It was not clear to members of the First Dail or to the Irish people in 1919 how the war would begin or whether the Dail would even pursue independence by way of force.

On March 29, 1919, the first political killing of the war took place with the shooting of British resident magistrate John C. Milling at Westport, County Mayo. He was targeted because he had sent volunteers to prison for unlawful assembly, which was a common occurrence at the time.[240]

Burning of Cork, St. Patrick's Street, December 14, 1920[241]

The main Irish players in the new effort to attain freedom from the British and to ultimately construct a new republic were, predictably, the previous leaders of Sinn Féin, the Irish Republican Brotherhood, and the Irish Volunteers: De Valera, Arthur Griffith, Cathal Brugha, Michael Collins, and Charles Burgess. These were the new leaders of the rebellion seeking full independence. They were no longer willing to settle for Home Rule.²⁴²

The British were threatening to shoot ministers responsible for the new rebellion, but the end of the First World War changed everything. The Irish quickly diverted their efforts to another task, building the IRA from the ranks of the Irish Volunteers. These volunteer recruits had never really wanted to fight the British; they had only wanted to avoid conscription.

Sinn Féin's leadership, the new leaders of the rebellion, forced these Irishmen into accepting this new strategy, an expansion of the rebellion as they knew it.

The Dail organization, led by De Valera, their president, and Michael Collins, their minister of finance and director of the organization, established ministries and conducted open meetings. They also raised a public loan to finance their campaign for international recognition. Along with these plans, leadership assaulted the British administration. They called for citizens to boycott the RIC as agents of a foreign power. Ireland had large amounts of its population still in small villages and hamlets (of two hundred or less), making it difficult to recruit them for the political cause. There were few large centers of population.

The Black and Tan constables were mainly made of World War I veterans and were acting as reinforcements for the RIC constables, who were trying to restore law and order. In their efforts to end the revolt, the Black and Tan units brutally murdered members of the Irish population. Their recruitment started in January of 1920 and continued throughout the war. This violence ultimately created dramatic changes within the Irish population, swinging public opinion to the Republican cause.

Worshipers at Catholic mass stayed separate from the police in attendance. Tradesmen became afraid to deal with the police, and girls who fraternized with the British police were punished by members of the Irish population by removing their hair. Irish mobs would remove the notable wives and children of the community out of their houses as they burned them down.²⁴³

In the spring of 1919, volunteers of the Young IRA began focused attacks. Castle Intelligence Officers eventually began to understand the patterns of the Irish guerillas and their targets. Their military barracks were raided for arms, and policemen were ambushed and shot down in public. This was designed to intimidate the British authorities in any way they could. Under these circumstances, efforts to recruit for the RIC essentially ended. To say the least, Ireland was in an ugly mood that was moving its support away from the British, despite the First World War and its initial support of it.

Ireland's chief export had for years been thousands of young men. Initially, potential emigrants were not permitted to leave due to the First World War. Those who remained in Ireland during and after the Great War became displaced persons in their own country, saddled with high unemployment and low wages. Consequently, agrarian unrest became common in many areas. This unrest originated from the initial battles with the police. The Sinn Féin's countrywide boycotts also proved effective.

The development of the Sinn Féin "squad" led to the terrorizing of the detectives of the "G" division in the Castle's Intelligence Agency in the Irish capital. The English agents did not fully appreciate the full extent of the threat to their authority. This would lead to major losses in English personnel at the agency.[244]

British leaders thought that order could be restored by hitting the Irish in the pocketbook. The local police developed the idea to make local Irish councils liable for the violence in their districts. This did not stop the troublemakers, as they did not have the funds to pay for such a penalty in any case. An official at Dublin Castle, Sir John Taylor, the assistant undersecretary, then became concerned that he would be targeted for assassination by those who had appointed him to keep peace with the church and Home Rulers. He had been selected because he was Catholic with Nationalist sympathies, operating within Castle's Intelligence Agency.[245]

Taylor could not understand the aims of the Sinn Féin. Because of this ignorance, he misinterpreted their intentions and "disastrously misinformed his masters at Westminster."[246] Sinn Féin and various unionist employers launched coordinated strikes that would further confuse Taylor and the local administration. In addition to reacting against the strikes, the police began reporting terrorism, cattle rustling, and highway robbery spreading over the countryside.

These events suggested that farmers and shopkeepers might be agreeing to collaborate with Sinn Féin. Erroneously, Taylor and the police still viewed the Irish rebellion as easily crushed. They would rue the day they so underestimated this enemy.

But Sinn Féin had their difficulties as well. De Valera, the Dail president, understood they needed American support and traveled there to obtain it. Their first stop, prior to reaching America, was to meet with President Woodrow Wilson at the First World War Peace Conference at Versailles, France. During their meeting, President Woodrow Wilson seemed sympathetic, stating, "Every people should choose its own master." He made these comments without fully appreciating Sinn Féin's actual purpose.[247] However, once Wilson fully grasped the situation, he stated, "When I gave utterance to these words, I said them without the knowledge of Sinn Féin's' full intentions."[248]

President Woodrow Wilson, like many others—Irishmen included—thought that the country was as much a part of the United Kingdom as Wales or Scotland. In hearing these words, Sinn Féin's leaders realized that they stood alone. This epiphany spurred them into additional violence. The delegation returned to reality as they arrived home, forgoing a trip to America.[249]

The rebels continued their guerrilla tactics in Ireland. "In Dublin, soldiers in steel helmets, volunteers to the Irish Republican Army, patrolled the streets with fixed bayonets. Searches by military raiding parties reminded newspaper correspondents of the German occupation of Belgium . . . tanks, armored cars, lorries, guns (other military stores). The expeditionary force was being equipped against some formidable enemy. But the British Army was not at war with the few hundred poorly armed shop assistants and farm boys of the IRA, who began to raid police barracks more boldly."[250]

IRA Attacks Continue with Increased Force

The IRA's objective was to take arms and ammunition and proceed with the war. The barracks were attacked or set on fire. In response, the British government, supported by Irish volunteers, "proclaimed the whole of the Irish nation as an illegal assembly."

The Black and Tans and their auxiliaries established a pattern of attack and reprisal that was to become all too familiar. As a case in point, two hundred soldiers invaded a town in the evening and destroyed the shops of the tradesmen, who were understood to have served on a trip, freeing rebels. Damage was thought to be at least three thousand pounds. In response, IRA soldiers killed one soldier, wounded four, and apprehended the remainder of their weapons before escaping. The follow-up court jury supported no verdict of murder.

In August 1919, the IRA responded to the Black and Tans by attacking police barracks in County Cork and County Claire. Two constables were killed, and one was wounded. As a result of these changes in Irish strategy, the RIC withdrew their forces from outlying areas and concentrated them in larger and more defensible units.[251]

The process of law seemed to be collapsing, especially within the County of Cork. Witnesses refused to give evidence for fear of reprisals from IRA gunmen. In County Claire, the Sinn Féin set up their own law councils to establish their own definition of law and order. It became clear to both belligerents that the Castle Administration was beginning to crumble as well. It would get worse.

The Irish Revolutionary War 1920–1921

Beginning in the early 1920s, there was a period where Irish-Anglo relations were less violent, at least for a short period of time. This relative peace gave time for Sinn Féin leaders, such as De Valera, to bring greater opposition to the British government by rallying against them in both Ireland and abroad.

While on a visit to the United States, De Valera had time to develop his strategy for Ireland's continued war with Britain. In short, Ireland was only requesting that Britain "take one of your hands off my throat and the other out of my pocket."[252]

Archbishop Mannix Pays a Visit

Archbishop Daniel Patrick Mannix, a Catholic and a native of Cork, was appointed and served as the Archbishop of Melbourne, Australia before the Irish Revolution began. He was an outspoken critic of Great Britain's handling of Irish matters following the Easter Rising. Mannix related the current conflict with Britain to that between Britain and the American colonies over a century earlier. He viewed these conflicts as parallel, saying, "Ireland has the same grievance against England which the American revolutionaries had, only ten times greater."[253]

Archbishop Mannix announced he was visiting Ireland to see his mother and would sail on the first of August 1920. Prime Minister Lloyd George spoke to the House of Commons regarding Mannix, indicating that due to his recent public comments, he could not go to Ireland. On August 8, an English destroyer stopped the SS *Baltic*, carrying Archbishop Mannix, near Queenstown, Ireland, where they knew Mannix planned to arrive. The English presented Mannix with "a document stating he was free to go anywhere except Ireland, Liverpool, Manchester, and Glasgow."[254] At this point, Mannix observed, "The English government are making themselves look very silly."[255]

Much of the Irish and English press agreed it was an awkward attempt to ban Archbishop Mannix from entering Ireland and parts of England. The English leadership disagreed with that analysis.[256]

Catholics everywhere were enraged. With this great indignity to the "Great Archbishop," they generally believed that Lloyd George's decision to keep Mannix from landing in Ireland, as well as much of England, was "an invasion of the rights of citizenship and as a procedure that was provocative—inciting further unrest in the local Catholic community, as well as to Catholics throughout the world. The Irish Catholic hierarchy protested mightily against the indignity to the archbishop—who was highly revered by them."[257]

Mannix was happy with Lloyd George's decision to prevent him from landing in Ireland, as it demonstrated the complex and volatile relations between Ireland and England.

The Black and Tans Take the Offensive

Because the Black and Tans had become such a negative influence on the Irish protesters and the general population, they were both feared and hated. To control attacks, they divided up into small detachments and disbursed. They were also confined to their small barracks—out of sight whenever off duty to avoid retribution.

They were developing a reputation for causing more stress and maintaining less control than the military. The Black and Tan's view was that they would not hesitate to do their duty to end Irish Republican resistance.

In August, the Black and Tans "wrecked and burned buildings in Roscommon, Galway, Cork, Tipperary, Kerry, and Limerick,"[258] clearly efforts to punish those who had previously attacked them. Rather than continuing to control the Black and Tans, on August 13, 1920, police leadership at Dublin Castle attempted to portray a more positive picture of the Black and Tans' actions by issuing the first edition of *The Weekly Summary*, a four-page news publication meant to compete with the local newspaper's critical account of the Black and Tans. They would include "staccato editorials"[259] in an attempt to keep up morale and spin the presence of the Black and Tans as positive:

> They did not wait for the usual uniform
> They came at once.
> They were wanted badly, and the RIC
> Welcome them.
> They know what the danger is.
> They have looked Death in the eyes before and did not flinch.
> They will not flinch now
> They will go on with the job—the job of making Ireland once again safe for the law-abiding.

AND AN APPROPRIATE HELL FOR THOSE WHOSE TRADE IS AGITATION AND WHOSE METHOD IS MURDER.[260]

The British authorities knew the reputation of the Black and Tans was growing ever more negative. However, they believed their contributions were critical if the rebellion was to end in their victory. The RIC welcomed them to the battle despite their unfavorable reputation.

After the violence of August, military courts pushed for an inquest into the deaths of members of the RIC. The authorities became fully apprised of these deaths and that Black and Tans were major players in those deaths. Calling their methods "distasteful," and after coming to grips with the truth, the local British Magistrate in Dublin resigned, saying, "I hope my colleagues will follow my example so that the wrecking of Irish towns and the ruin of Irish industry may be proceeded without any camouflage or appearance of approval by Irishmen of the sabotage of their country, which retention of office without function would imply."[261]

The Restoration of Order in Ireland Act

The Restoration of Order in Ireland Act became law on August 9 but had a "stormy passage through the House of Commons" before reaching the king for final approval. This bill was designed to allow for martial law and changes in law with respect to individual liberty in Ireland. It effectively abolished trial by jury, though author Richard Bennett argues that standards in jury trials had diminished significantly up to this point in Ireland. It also established that military courts-martial were permitted for all crimes. Witnesses and jury members did not dare to attend trials for fear of becoming victims of reprisals. Participation would probably bring violence from the IRA if they did. In capital cases, one member of the court would be certified by either the lord chancellor of England or the lord chancellor of Ireland.[262]

Carl von Clausewitz explained the importance of the people, the government, and the military working together to continue the war or withdraw from the war. The results of these loosely run judicial proceedings were making their way back to England and were met with significant disapproval.²⁶³ The time came when the public became concerned that their government was heading toward widespread disaster rather than successfully bringing the Irish back into the fold. With deteriorating public support from the people, a key element of Clausewitz's triangle of support (the people, the military, and the government) failed; that is, public opinion in Ireland and Great Britain was quickly turning in support of Irish independence.²⁶⁴

In addition to the severely deteriorated image of Great Britain in Ireland, public support in England was now also looking for an end to this destructive war. The cruel killing on both sides, as well as the constant brutality of the Black and Tans, was having the greatest impact.

Restoration of Order Delayed

Terence MacSwiney, lord mayor of Cork, was one of the earliest victims of the newly signed law. MacSwiney, also a member of the First Dail and member of the IRA, had presided over a meeting of IRA members and was arrested, with the RIC mistakenly believing the meeting was a "Republican court."²⁶⁵ Though his mother was English, MacSwiney possessed a "fanatical zeal for Irish nationalism" and was a fierce fighter for the cause.²⁶⁶ After he was sent to prison, he vowed to go on hunger strike for the duration of his incarceration, and the British authorities would soon discover the resolve with which he made his vow.

As part of a worldwide protest of MacSwiney's arrest, conviction, and imprisonment, the mayor of New York City vigorously appealed for his immediate release. The papal secretary of state of Rome reported that there were three hundred thousand Brazilian Catholics demanding the pope intervene on MacSwiney's behalf. The British Labor Party demanded his release as well.²⁶⁷

MacSwiney noted during his trial that "facing [the] enemy we must declare an attitude simply. We see in [Great Britain's] regime a thing of evil incarnate."²⁶⁸ He was then sentenced to two years without hard labor.

In addressing the court after his guilty verdict, he said, "I have decided that I shall be free alive or dead within the month, as I will take no food for the period of my sentence."[269] These statements focused the world on Ireland in ways never imagined.

Amidst the escalation of violence on both sides, a peace conference had been planned for August of 1920, to be held in Dublin. Given the circumstances, the victory of Sinn Féin during regional elections in August 1920, the treatment of Archbishop Mannix, the arrest of the MacSwiney, and a "burst" of murders and reprisals, the conference was facing significant challenges before deliberations began. It convened on August 24, and among the accepted proposals were the release of MacSwiney to "abate forthwith the stringency of the policy of repression and adopt a policy of amnesty" and the grant of "full nationalist self-government," though as a part of Great Britain, with no partition to exclude the Ulster counties in the north.[270]

MacSwiney's death came as he planned, in Brixton Prison, seventy-three days after his initial internment. His Irish comrades quickly labeled him as the "uncompromising" MacSwiney.[271] Since MacSwiney's arrest, the violence in Ireland had increased significantly; fifteen RIC men were burned to death without a chance to defend themselves.[272] The violence continued. This did not, however, shake the British government's resolve. The king stated, in no uncertain terms, that he would not back down, saying, "MacSwiney was determined to make himself a martyr, and I am determined to prevent it."[273]

H. H. Asquith, former British prime minister, would later recall that "the decision to allow the Lord Mayor of Cork to die in prison was a political blunder of the first magnitude."[274] MacSwiney, who was aware of the political consequences of choosing martyrdom, said, "I am confident that my death will do more to smash the British Empire than my release."[275]

In Cork, eleven prisoners began a hunger strike of their own, which lasted two days longer than MacSwiney's. On the twenty-eighth day of their strike, on September 7, the English government sent a telegram to the Trade Union Congress that eleven prisoners were on hunger strike and were perishing. Of the eleven prisoners, ten of them had not been tried and had no charge against them. The other had spent twelve months in prison without a conviction.[276]

Meanwhile, the Black and Tans continued to leave their mark on Ireland, targeting Irish Republicans in particular. In response to this violence, a RIC constable was shot in Limerick. Because of this, several dozen Black and Tans, in a drunken rage, "smashed the windows of houses, as people were sitting down for Sunday dinner."[277] They then entered homes, destroying family ornaments and pictures, including, ironically, "a portrait of King George."[278] With a motor vehicle loaded with gas, a Black and Tan group attempted to set the entire O'Connell Street on fire. The result of this attack reduced two homes to rubble.

Things had changed for the Irish as well. The streets of Limerick were full of protesters against British violence. The RIC district inspector was killed in Templemore, Tipperary, following the counterdemonstration. In response, the Black and Tans set fire to the town hall, the marketplace, and the urban district council offices. Terrified residents escaped the violence by running into the fields outside the town. These attacks terrified the locals.

In the minds of Black and Tans, the Irish were considered traitors to Britain, and with the heavy use of alcohol before and while carrying out the attacks, the violence became more severe.[279] Both sides were guilty of the destruction of property and death, but the Black and Tans and their violent attacks on the population were especially destructive because they did not discriminate. They killed, looted, and burned anyone in their way. The English people's support of the war effort was also significantly lessened with each act of the Black and Tans. Public opinion in Great Britain and throughout the world began widespread support of a peace settlement that would end the death and destruction.

As the violence spread throughout Ireland, the O'Conor Don, a unionist landowner, in reacting to the violence, stated, "If the Government doesn't turn these damned Black and Tans out of the country, we'll soon all be damned republicans." Many other leaders at the time held this same view. Government support of the Black and Tans, plus some members of the RIC itself, had become unacceptable, even to the "moderates."[280]

The goal of achieving a peaceful settlement was looking less likely in the week following the peace conference after the IRA made nearly a thousand raids for weapons throughout the country. The IRA was clearly not ready to negotiate under the current circumstances.[281]

Troubles between the Catholics and the Protestants were also reaching a head. According to Richard Bennett, "There was rioting in Belfast, and the outlines of a deliberately fostered campaign to drive the Catholic population out of Northeast Ulster was clearly discernable."[282]

The most violent of the two sides, without question, was Great Britain because of the hated and feared Black and Tans. According to Bennett, "They were the most effective fighting force on either side. They were ruthless, arrogant, and often drunken and violent."[283] These attributes existed throughout their time in Ireland.

The recently assembled companies of the Black and Tans were geared up for additional reprisal raids. In Balbriggan, a village twenty miles north of Dublin, the IRA assassinated head constable Burke of the RIC and wounded his brother. The Black and Tans responded by looting and burning several public houses, "shooting and bayoneting two citizens to death in their nightshirts"[284] who were suspected IRA men, burning an English-owned stocking factory, and destroying thirty homes. These acts of violence, such as the "Sack of Balbriggan," were easy to execute without hesitation, as the Black and Tans "regarded all Irishmen as murderers and 'Shinners,'"[285] a derogatory term for Sinn Féin members.

Another reprisal from the IRA occurred in Dublin, where unarmed British soldiers were killed during a ration party as they were trying to obtain bread. Four men with revolvers shouted for soldiers to put up their hands and surrender their weapons and then, at the same time, fired, "killing one soldier and mortally wounding two others." Kevin Barry was an eighteen-year-old medical student who was found beneath a car with a pistol. He was then arrested, found guilty of murder, and hanged.[286] The subsequent Black and Tan attacks served to inflame Irish emotions further; the same can be said for the reprisals of the IRA.

In England, those who were sympathetic to the Irish plight were justifiably outraged by the Black and Tan reprisal raids, and this sentiment was shared even more intensely in Ireland. The *Times* of London said, "It is difficult to believe that the occurrences at Balbriggan [could] have been entirely the result of a spontaneous outburst of resentment on the part of the incensed policemen" within the Black and Tan's organization. The *Times* continued, "There seems to have been behind it a directing influence."[287]

The IRA was also not innocent, though. They were using tremendously destructive ammunition, dumdum bullets, at the time of the Black and Tan reprisal raids. These bullets were banned by the Hague Convention because they were flat-faced and caused more damage when they entered the body. Ultimately, the indignation from both opposing parties was directed toward England. According to M. L. R. Smith, "The truth was that for many, the British position in Ireland had become morally indefensible."[288]

Efforts for Compromise

Although the Unionists called for the establishment of self-government in Ireland, they also "expressed unilateral repugnance to any form of partition of Ireland."[289] This could have become the basis for negotiation, but other plans would negate that possibility. Those supporting the members of the IRA would only consider a unified Ireland but under Republican control. Once the British withdrew from Ireland under an armistice, Ireland continued their civil war between Ulster Northern Ireland, and Republicans primarily in the south, but also Republicans in Northern Ireland. That war had long-lasting implications, with continual acts of terrorism by the IRA and Northern Ireland. But before the organization within the Emerald Isle could be determined, peace with England had to be accomplished.[290]

Sean Hogan's IRA Flying Column[291]

The Truce at Last

A truce was reached on July 11, 1921, and negotiations began on October 11, 1921 in London.[292] A hard truth was soon realized by the British about the end of hostilities: pursuing the goal of maintaining control over Ireland as a resolution to the conflict was not feasible due to the public's unwillingness to continue fighting. Also, according to Smith, "The British capacity for physical resistance had not been eliminated, therefore the republicans could not be expected to prescribe the terms of a settlement."[293] Thus, both sides decided a compromise was necessary. The Irish wanted, above all else, to ensure the revolution's major goal of the British government's departure from the affairs of the newly forming Republic of Ireland.

One part of this compromise was allowing Northern Ireland to self-determine their fate, either to be under Britain's control or to become a part of the Republic. The leaders hoped the association with the Crown would dissolve if enough of Ulster decided to become a part of the Republic, but they had underestimated that nearly two-thirds of that population would choose to stay with the Crown.[294]

The outcome of the war, and the treaty that was signed, was the formation of the Irish Free State, which would keep the Irish attached to the Crown but give them, for all other purposes, an internationally recognized nation status. This continued association with Great Britain would cause a further civil war between the National Army and the Anti-Treaty IRA. Many leaders of Sinn Féin, including De Valera, would stay in opposition to the new government simply because it required a pledge of allegiance to the Crown. The establishment of a true republic would have to wait until a new constitution was formed in 1927.[295]

CHAPTER FIVE

THE KOREAN WAR

There were issues under dispute between President Harry S. Truman and General Douglas MacArthur during the Korean War. As theater commander, MacArthur disagreed with Truman's political objective for victory during part of the war. President Truman's objective was to maintain South Korean independence by pushing back North Korean military forces above the thirty-eighth parallel. MacArthur demanded an alternate course of action.

Although theater commanders and presidents have differed in the past, MacArthur committed a cardinal sin for a military commander at the time: he went public on what he determined was Truman's strategy for defeat and his own strategy for victory, openly contradicting his commander in chief.

According to MacArthur's testimony to the Senate, he alleged that his plan called only for "bombing Manchurian airfields, blockading the coast of China, and employing Chinese Nationalist troops in Korea and South China; but he proposed these measures only on the grounds that they would achieve the UN's limited political objective more quickly, with fewer casualties, and with more chance of avoiding a third world war."[296] MacArthur also wanted to be the decision-maker regarding the possible use of atomic weapons.[297] In contrast, Truman advocated for the administration and Joint Chiefs of Staff's alternative—a more limited military strategy of avoiding spreading hostilities to mainland China—because Truman felt it would achieve the objectives of the conflict without necessarily risking an escalation in hostilities. According to Robert Osgood, the "decisive difference between MacArthur and the administration [regarding strategy in Korea] arose from divergent estimates of [the MacArthur plan's] military advantage and of the risk of total war and overcommitment which they entailed."[298]

In other words, the Truman administration believed MacArthur's approach and potential actions would have the opposite effect that was intended and would draw China directly into the conflict, possibly starting a third world war. It was MacArthur's view that China would enter the war in any event. MacArthur was also willing to go it alone or without the United Nations' concurrence, if necessary.

The Truman administration's policy in Korea and throughout the world was not to destroy Communism—at least in the short term—but to contain it and halt its expansion. The Truman Doctrine, introduced in 1947, promised American support for democracies around the world facing authoritarian threats but was characterized by limited political objectives. The onset of the Korean War would put that strategy to a long and bitter test.

MacArthur disagreed publicly with these aims and was relieved of his command as a result. In that instance, the failure of the military to comprehend or agree with the political objective may have prolonged the war, as American and other members of the United Nations forces went beyond the thirty-eighth parallel. This strategy resulted in the Chinese entry into the war. However, Truman's policies did not result in World War III, and China may have entered the war regardless of Truman's in-theater decisions.

MacArthur's decisions may have prolonged the settlement of this limited war, but they were not allowed to alter its ultimate outcome because MacArthur was removed. The military strategy did not supersede the civilian conception of victory.[299]

Prelude to the Korean War

Within a year of the end of World War II, European Communist forces supported by Bulgaria, Yugoslavia, and Albania were carrying out a full-scale war against Greece. The Communists also demanded that they have the right to establish bases in eastern Turkey and the eastern end of the Black Sea. Through 1946, these forces carried on a full-scale war against the Greek government. Soviet expansion also threatened Mediterranean nations and the Middle East.

On February 21, 1947, Great Britain cabled the British Embassy in Washington, DC, and notified the US State Department that it could no longer support Greek Royalists in its civil war against the Communists. Great Britain was slowly becoming bankrupt due to the financial and human costs of the Second World War. Over a weekend of discussion, Dean Acheson, secretary of state, deliberated with a small team and reported on the following Monday that Greece, and to a lesser extent, Turkey, were important, strategic pieces to US policy abroad. The United States was coming to the realization that Greece might fall to the Communists, so America quickly decided to provide aid on the order of a quarter of a billion dollars for the remainder of the year. Truman also decided to commit the United States to the defense of Greece and Turkey by providing American troops and civilians with certain needed skills.[300]

During a joint session of Congress, Truman proposed the so-called Truman Doctrine. It represented a policy reversal from cooperation with the Soviet Union to the containment of Soviet power. There arose strong opposition within Congress to this reversal, many fearing the possibility of all-out war with the Soviets. On March 12, 1947, despite pushback from Congress, Truman decided to commit the United States to resist aggressive Soviet policies. American aid was then immediately provided. According to David McCullough, "During a joint session of Congress, Truman said that the gravity of the situation facing the world necessitated his appearance before Congress. He felt America's foreign policy concerns, as well as the national security of the United States, were involved."[301]

In this speech that outlined the problem and defined the Truman Doctrine, he described Greece as an "industrious and peace-loving country that [had] suffered invasion, four years of cruel [Nazi] occupation, and bitter internal strife."[302] Truman continued, that "all the railways, roads, port facilities, communications, and merchant marines" were destroyed during the occupation. Thousands of villages were razed, and the vast majority of Greek children had poor health due to outbreaks of tuberculosis.[303]

The Truman administration reacted quickly to the Greek government's requests for assistance by committing to the restoration of internal order and security that was so essential to Greece's economic and political recovery. Truman further assured Americans that he was fully aware of the implications involved if the United States extended assistance to Greece and Turkey. Beyond everything else, Truman was convinced the United States must support the freedom of people resisting attempted subjugation; the Cold War had begun.[304]

Truman stated during the joint congressional hearings that the United States and other members of the United Nations must assist Greece and Turkey, as well as other European nations coming under attack. Truman's view was that the United States must provide all the assistance necessary to maintain the "integrity of the Greek Nation."[305] If the United States failed to assist Greece, Truman believed there would be a serious effect on the Middle East and Turkey. This was the genesis of the concept of *falling dominoes*.

This aid effort became known as the Marshall Plan and was passed by Congress and signed into law by Truman as the Economic Cooperation Act of 1948. Truman had initially planned a request to Congress for $16.5 billion, but in the end, $13.3 billion was appropriated for European assistance over the next four years.[306] In addition to funding, Congress authorized the support of American civilian and military personnel to provide for the on-site execution of their financial and material assistance to Greece and Turkey. It also provided the authority for instruction and training for specific Greek and Turkish military personnel.

In Truman's view, the alternative to this assistance would be much worse. "The world's free peoples look to us for support in maintaining their freedoms."[307] At this stage of the Cold War, he was speaking about our support of European nations. Very soon, Truman's comment would be expanded to include Asia.[308] Truman also justified the cost of the Marshall Plan by arguing that it would be used for peace, not for war, which he reasoned in any given year could cost upwards of $100 billion, a ten-fold increase in financial cost, not to mention the cost in American lives.[309]

Another post-Second World War initiative by the United States that thwarted Soviet aggression in Western Europe served to reinforce Truman's willingness to meet Soviet Communist aggression with economic and military strength. The aggressive separation of West Berlin from Western Europe by the Soviets provoked Truman to respond by providing food, clothing, and other assistance during the Berlin Airlift from June 1948 to September 1949.

In studying the history of the Cold War and America's resistance to Soviet aggression, the Berlin Airlift is considered the single most significant event in the post-war strategy prior to the Korean War. It was a significant influence on the newly established Truman Doctrine, which would also protect countries in Europe and Asia.

These American successes in Europe set the stage for the Soviets to make the decision to channel their aggression eastward. They did not feel militarily strong enough to confront the United States in Europe directly. At the end of World War II, the United States and the Soviet Union agreed on dividing Korea into two occupation zones separated by the thirty-eighth parallel. Japan had occupied Korea from 1910 until 1945, when the occupation zones were established. Japan's colonial rule of Korea was largely oppressive, with the Japanese occupiers seeking to erase Korean history and culture.[310] The Soviets became confident that America would not physically support South Korea, and their confidence was reinforced when Americans removed their two remaining divisions from Korea in 1949. This removal created a political vacuum in Korea that eventually would have to be filled by the United States and its allies.

At the time, America had a serious shortage of military manpower. Military leaders initially took the position that the two American divisions in Korea could be better used elsewhere, such as in Europe. "The American government's low estimate of Korea's strategic importance was reflected in the words of high military and political authorities as well as in the disposition of forces."[311]

In the spring of 1949, acting under the advice of the National Security Council (NSC), Truman decided "to withdraw American troops from South Korea and to base the protection of the new country on the development of [the Republic of Korea Army (ROKA)]." As a result of the immense drawdown of troops after the Second World War, there was no American army, a small naval presence, and only a small, but effective, air force left in Korea.[312]

In viewing the removal of the two American army divisions from Korea, the Soviets had decided to support a North Korean invasion of the South. To Joseph Stalin, it was a clear indication that the United States did not have sufficient interest in defending South Korea and, therefore, would not interfere with the coming North Korean invasion. The Soviets also announced Russian troop withdrawals from North Korea because of America's withdrawal.[313]

Once "the North Korean Army poured across the thirty-eighth parallel in June 1950,"[314] the United States military totally reversed its previous strategy. Based on the availability of Marine and Army Reserve troops, they put together an attacking force led by General Douglas MacArthur, a celebrated WWII hero of the Pacific war, and sent it into Korea.

To get a full picture of the decisions made by the United States, Soviet Russia, and China, the dangers each had to face must be understood. The path to peace, the potential death toll, war fatigue, internal changes within each country, and the need to deal with the overall effects of the Cold War on them are necessary points of discussion.

What about the people of each country? How willing were they to support the immense financial costs, the huge toll on lives, and the inability to also develop their own countries after the end of the Second World War? The subsequent destruction of the Korean War would seriously hinder North Korean economic progress.

Early American government assessments of the invasion by North Korea into South Korea were seriously underestimated by the Truman administration. In reversing its decision to protect South Korea, the question suddenly became, "Would it be enough to hold the line in

Korea?" No one would know for several years.[315]

In retaliation for North Korea's invasion of the south, MacArthur introduced ground combat troops to the Korean peninsula in early July 1950, and began the defense of South Korea. As UN forces gained territory, they *slowly* realized the existence of at least one hundred thousand Chinese troops near the 8th Army in the north and another hundred thousand in reserve across the border in Manchuria. The result was that United Nations forces were unable to withstand the enemy attacks within their lines. Chinese troops viciously attacked both the front flank and rear flank of the 8th Army lines. The war for the United Nations forces led by the US 8th Army had begun.

The United States' Decision to Invade the Korean Peninsula

Truman had seen a pattern developing, and Korea, in his mind, was their next focus. Truman observed that "Korea . . . is the Greece of the Far East. If we are tough enough now, if we stand up to them like we did in Greece three years ago, they won't take any next steps. But if we just stand by, they'll move into Iran and they'll take over the whole Middle East. There's no telling what they'll do, if we don't put up a fight now."[316]

Though Truman wanted to keep the decision to intervene in Korea quiet, he allowed Dean Acheson, his secretary of state, to bring a few important congressional leaders into private strategic discussions with the administration. Alex Wiley, a senator from Wisconsin, was not a supporter of the Democrat Party but was an important leader within Congress. Wiley's first question was about what General MacArthur was doing with the conflict. Acheson responded that MacArthur had the situation under control and that the president was heavily relying on MacArthur's advice. Senator Wiley asked if the administration would send troops into the chaos of South Korea. Acheson was purposely vague with his response by saying that the president was considering that possibility, but no troops had yet been committed. That response would have to do until more was known.[317] A conversation with Democrat (Judge) John Kee of West

Virginia, chairman of the House Committee on Foreign Affairs, agreed with Acheson's thought that "South Korea could defend itself unless outside forces—Soviet or Chinese, presumably—entered the war."[318]

Truman's message to the attendees was that he had directed MacArthur to provide all necessary ammunition and equipment to the South Korean Army. They, supposedly, were already trained in its use, though in reality they were not.[319] Information coming from the front soon altered this overly optimistic position that the South Koreans could defend themselves from North Korea. The South Korean collapse in the face of the North Korean military was still unknown or doubted. Once the facts were known, it provided what America and its allies needed to do. The president continued to assert that help was on the way, but it would take time. It was critical that the South Koreans survive the crisis until American forces arrived.[320]

Dean Acheson then requested that American air power be assigned to support South Korean formations. Truman quickly directed that such assistance could only happen south of the thirty-eighth parallel, thus limiting any potential expansion of the war. He also said that his directive might end at some point, but not at that moment. A limited war approach was quickly becoming his strategy.[321]

Adjacent to Korean security, the preservation of an independent, republican Taiwan also concerned the United States. Truman was concerned, primarily, with the war spilling over into Taiwan, and widening the conflict. However, Acheson believed that Taiwan and its defense requirements should be kept separate from the Korean War. Truman made this possible by ordering the US Navy's 7th Fleet to defend the Taiwan Straits. This would prevent any Chinese invasion of the island.[322]

Joe Collins, the Army chief of staff, was asked during Pentagon sessions on Korea to schedule a team to analyze South Korea's chances of survival. Before the meeting ended, attendees determined that the situation in South Korea was bad. The Republic of Korea Army (ROKA) was close to total surrender. Collins further claimed that the South Korean chief of staff was at the point of surrender, that he had "no fight left in him."[323]

Secretary Acheson and President Truman maintained that even if the ROKA was on the verge of defeat, the United States needed to enter the war, regardless of the cost. Truman asked General Omar Bradley if he could call up the National Guard. Bradley said that mobilizing the National Guard "might be necessary."[324]

Truman continued to hang on to the hope that South Korea would find a way to defend itself if the United States supplied the necessary resources. Congress shared Truman's reluctance to fight the war with American troops. However, Truman was not leaving it up to Congress to decide the next step. He did want to keep Congress apprised of current events in Korea, but the decision to use American armed forces there would be his decision alone.

In the subsequent United Nations Security Council meeting, President Truman summarized the events in South Korea for the attendees. The Soviets' absence from the meeting ultimately helped the members commit to supporting South Korea without controversy. Truman's comments covered the current circumstances in Korea and then mentioned he had ordered United States air and sea forces to provide South Korean troops cover and support. Without air and sea support, ROKA would be unable to retreat to fight another day. Truman also told members present that he had approved orders directing General MacArthur to execute the elements of the resolution to support South Korea.[325]

Truman brought up the central issue of war: there would be a domino effect if South Korea surrendered. It could spill over to all of Asia and beyond. This dynamic was to greatly affect the United States as it would soon help justify their strategy to enter the Vietnam War by repeating the fear that the United States must prevent the Communists from controlling Asia: Taiwan, Japan, Korea, Indochina, Malaysia, Indonesia, and perhaps even the Philippines. This domino effect stayed within the United States' reasons for its strategy in South Korea and its approach in Vietnam.

A question that should be asked was why exactly the Communists decided to attack South Korea at the time. Why, also, did the United States decide to intervene? According to Robert Endicott Osgood in his book

Limited War: The Challenge to American Strategy, the simple answer to both questions is that the Soviet Union shifted its attention to Asia because they feared Western strength in Europe and because they believed it was a low priority for the United States. Through this approach, the Soviet Union could minimize the chances of total war and preserve resources. Also, we gave them little reason to doubt their approach would work because "in September 1947, the Joint Chiefs of Staff decided that on purely military grounds the two American divisions stationed in South Korea should be withdrawn."[326]

From beginning to end, Truman was dedicated to limiting the war in Korea out of a fear of provoking Russian intervention and bringing about a third world war. He believed that America should not do anything that would provide an excuse for the Soviets to intervene and plunge free nations into all-out war.

In *On War*, Clausewitz discusses how "the ends and means of warfare must be in line."[327] The end related to pushing North Korean troops out of South Korean territory, while the means were through military force. "Truman acted in Korea on the premise that the reason for the North Korean invasion was the result of a Russian maneuver that largely operated on the assumption that the Kremlin was testing the West's positions on the Communist periphery to discover and exploit weaknesses." Both assumptions would prove to be correct.[328]

One major weakness for the United States and its allies was Korea itself. Truman believed the Soviets intended to attack the non-Communist world. Truman concluded they should not provoke such an event by crossing the thirty-eighth parallel or the Yalu River into China, which might appeal to the USSR for help. He believed the Soviets entering the war would clearly result in pulling Western Europe into another worldwide conflict.

Siding with the Central Intelligence Agency's findings, Truman also believed that the Soviets wanted us to commit solely to a war in Asia so that the Soviets, as he stated in his memoirs, "might gain a free hand in Europe."[329] Truman's implementation of a limited war strategy in

Asia avoided the loss of influence in Europe, which also conflicted with MacArthur's strategy.[330]

The Korean War: Explained

The North Korean decision to invade South Korea constituted a massive offensive from July 1 to September 15, 1950. Kim Il-Sung, the North Korean dictator, won a national election in early June 1950. On June 11, three North Korean diplomats brought south a peace overture, which Syngman Rhee, the South Korean president, quickly rejected. Once Kim Il-Sung's overture had been rejected, he completed his war plans for invading South Korea across the thirty-eighth parallel by June 21, 1950. It was not to be a limited operation, as Kim Il-Sung had first proclaimed.

Although Rhee was aware of these plans, he strengthened his defenses to thwart the attack. Rhee still believed his forces could defeat any invasion by North Korea. Once Joseph Stalin agreed to Kim's plans, the invasion proceeded.

In South Korea's defense, there were months of false alarms about major North Korean movements into their territory. Due to these false alarms, the South Korean military and civilian population, as well as the United States and the United Nations, were not prepared to respond to what would soon be a major invasion by nine hundred thousand North Korean troops and a hundred fifty T-34 Russian-built tanks, each loaded with an 85-mm cannon and two 7.62-mm machine guns.

The ROKA had supposedly been trained by the United States military within the Korean Military Advisory Group (KMAG). They were erroneously judged to be as good as the North Koreans by the KMAG. In fact, General William Lyn Roberts's report to a member of the JCS staff, Lieutenant General Charles Bolte, detailed that he had less than total confidence in the South Korean Army. To the press, Roberts, who subsequently retired, had painted a rosy picture of the South Korean capabilities, though in a Senate Armed Services Committee hearing Ambassador to South Korea John Muccio reported more realistically that the "undeniable material superiority of the North Korean forces would provide North Korea with the margin of victory in the event of a full-scale invasion of South Korea, particularly in the matter of heavy infantry support weapons, tanks, and combat aircraft which the USSR has supplied and continues to supply."[331]

Syngman Rhee repeatedly declared that any North Korean invasion would merely provide an opportunity to destroy them. These estimations by Rhee proved to give the ROKA false hopes they would be unable to realize. The quick destruction of the ROKA would soon clarify reality.[332]

The more reasonable assessment was that "the ROKA had inferior firepower, little artillery, limited tanks, and poor troop and officer training overall. The ROKA's ability to prevent an invasion of this magnitude would not be possible until much later, after the North Koreans controlled most of South Korea. Without direct involvement of the US and UN, the Korean Peninsula would fall to the Communists."[333]

Despite the many delays and false alarms designed to confuse South Korea, North Korea planned their invasion by first escalating "civil conflict" and blaming the ROKA for invading first. Prior to the North Korean invasion south, "the South Korean Army, after months of false alert, had relaxed for a weekend of vacation."[334] Provocations occurred on both sides and had been occurring since 1949. This was frequent enough for Rhee to believe there would not be a hot war between them unless he initiated it.

The invasion by North Korea began with an artillery barrage of the ROKA lines on June 25. Observers explained that there was a hellish artillery attack and explosions all around them. An American journalist, Jim Hak Kui, later informed the UN Joint Command Group that artillery fire occurred as early as 5:00 a.m. The invading North Korean forces would quickly overrun the entire area.

The effect was devastating to the ROKA front line, as "South Korean soldiers and civilians quickly found themselves in the middle of a bloody attack, which ended in the collapse of the South Korean line. This caused a chaotic retreat away from the North Korean line of attack into temporary safety."[335] What proved immediately critical to the South Korean forces was the small but effective contingent of US Air Forces still present in the country.

From the American perspective, the Korean War began on the Ongjin Peninsula, northwest of the South Korean capital of Seoul, on June 24 and 25, 1950. The peninsula was remote and inaccessible. MacArthur's intelligence identified around 74,000 North Korean People's Army (KPA) soldiers in South Korea, 20,000 on the border between North Korea and South Korea. The ROKA had a total of 87,500 soldiers, with 32,500 at the border and another 35,000 within thirty-five miles of the thirty-eighth parallel. With superior battle forces, however, the KPA proved to be far superior to the ROKA. The North also had 150 Soviet T-34 tanks and a small but useful air force of 70 fighters and 65 light bombers from a Russian stockpile left over when they departed North Korea.[336]

Once ready, the KPA then redeployed southward in May and June 1950. They were augmented by thousands of well-trained North Korean troops left over from the Chinese Civil War that had run from 1927 through 1949 and officially established Communist rule. From that moment forward, the Americans would have to decide to enter the war or leave with the idea that there would be one Korea ruled by the Communists.[337]

Ongjin fighting began around 4:00 a.m. on June 25, 1950. The KPA assaulted the 1st Regiment, 7th Division, who took heavy casualties. As a result of this attack, a gaping hole was created in the ROKA 7th Division lines. Part of the ROKA's failure to stop the attack was their lack of commitment to meet the enemy force until late in the KPA attack.

The North Korean forces poured through the hole in the ROKA 7th Division lines. At this point, the entire South Korean line collapsed, and their troops panicked. "An American official on the scene later wrote that the failure of the 2nd Division to fight was the main reason for the rapid loss of the South Korean capital, Seoul. This would be the first of two successful North Korean takeovers of that city. ROKA units fled from the oncoming KPA troops out of fear, lack of firepower, and poor training. These weaknesses led to the entire South Korean front totally collapsing."[338]

A retreat south of Seoul commenced, with both the military and civilians fleeing for their lives. In addition to the overpowering force of the

North Korean military, the retreat was in disarray for a variety of reasons, including poor decision-making by the South Korean military leadership. The Han River bridge was destroyed by South Korea's General "Fatty" Chae during the retreat, which further resulted in the death of hundreds of both military and civilians fleeing to the south. President Rhee, as he departed south on a special train, gave commands that his army continue the battle of Taejon, demanding they fight the enemy to the death. He then escaped the battle and made his way to southwestern Korea, where he would be safer.

As a result of the battle and the collapse of their defenses, the South Korean military and civilians remained in total panic. As the defense of Seoul collapsed, over thirty-seven thousand troops fell to the northern invasion. By the end of the month, 50 percent of the ROKA were dead, captured, or missing. About 70 percent of the two ROKA divisions collapsed after they lost their equipment and weapons. The United States would replace the material at a great cost.

Secretary Acheson, upon hearing of this defeat, ordered American air and ground forces into battle. In South Korea, Truman ordered the repositioning of the US 7th Fleet between mainland China and Taiwan. Acheson then spoke before the United Nations on June 24, asking in Truman's name for additional military aid to the ROKA. The US Air Force was directed to cover the ROKA retreat.[339]

According to General Matthew Ridgway, the ROKA needed intense training, new equipment, and instruction at all levels. ROKA officers had degenerated to the extent that they fell into beating their soldiers, especially when their commands were totally unsuccessful. Senior leadership also needed training if they were to continue leading the war effort. By contrast, both the Chinese and the North Koreans had benefitted from the Chinese Civil War experience, evolving into a true fighting force.

The American Response to the Collapse of the ROKA

Acheson and the president gave their approval to actively support South Korea. It was not only because of the Korean Peninsula's strategic value. American credibility around the world was at stake. They also felt South

Korea was essential to Japan's industrial rebuilding. The ROKA's ultimate loss would include the domino effect where first Korea, then surrounding nations such as Japan, would fall under Communist control.[340]

Full UN approval was necessary to establish a UN command in South Korea. This became a reality because the Soviets were absent and not included in the vote. They were absent presumably because the United Nations had refused to admit China as a full UN member. When Joseph Stalin's subordinates asked whether they should attend or not, Stalin responded, "Nyet." Do not attend.

The sheer number of troops committed to the war by mid-1950 was staggering. Regardless of how the United States became involved in their invasion of Korea, the results of that, and decisions by North Korea, China, and Russia, turned highly lethal. The war would include 593,167 US Army soldiers and over 75,370 US Marines, as well as over 200,000 North Korean soldiers, who would become involved by the summer of 1950. The "immense manpower reserve of the Chinese People's Liberation Army (PLA)" would soon enter the war in support of North Korea. Throughout the summer of 1950, the ROKA had mostly stopped fighting.[341]

Once re-equipped with weapons, military matériel, and troops, the ROKA would slowly reassemble and participate in joint offensive and defensive actions with American and other United Nations troops. It would be a slow reversal. Without initial ROKA support, the United Nations command had the responsibility of militarily sending the North Koreans back to North Korea.[342]

The Initial American Offensive in Korea

The initial American offensive began on July 1, 1950, and ended on September 15, 1950. It was believed by the president, the theater commander, and their support staff, as well as members of Congress, that their direct involvement was an action that would end the war in Korea. However, its actual result was to create a totally new war with China.

Vought F4U-4B Corsair from Fighter Squadron 113 during the Inchon Landing. September 15, 1950[343]

The United States, its United Nations allies, and South Korean forces devised a strategy of a "massive compression envelope" against the North Korean Army. The strategy included a pincers movement of two American formations. A prompt withdrawal by the North Korean Army was then hoped for to establish the unity of all of Korea under South Korean control.

"General MacArthur, convinced of victory, made the wild promise that American soldiers would be home by Christmas. In the meantime, the North Korean Army, by November 24, was sure their victory would end the war, restore peace, and establish Korean Peninsula unity under Communist control. Neither side would accomplish their goal."[344]

Convinced of victory, John Muccio, the United States ambassador to South Korea, reported MacArthur would easily complete a clean-up operation with no problem. These hopes ended with the large-scale Chinese intervention of at least two hundred thousand Chinese

Communist soldiers. Once MacArthur belatedly learned of this surprise attack, he mistakenly estimated no more than thirty thousand Chinese troops were passing over the Yalu River into Korea.

MacArthur believed his seven divisions, combining 8th Army and ROKA troop strength and the availability of B-29 bombers, were enough to halt the Chinese movement toward Korean territory. The target was to clear the enemy from all American 8th Army locations. MacArthur predicted that his losses would be low and logistics would provide a sustained offensive operation. MacArthur's intelligence information proved inaccurate.

The attack resulted in heavy casualties on both sides. After fighting valiantly, Generals Walker and Almond immediately retreated, fighting their way back to South Korea as quickly as they could. It was now the case that the war had changed dramatically from "mere warnings" of a Chinese invasion to an all-out invasion. The Chinese had infiltrated the American lines by traveling through the mountains at night and using other stealth-oriented troop actions.

All hopes of localization of the Korean conflict against North Korean and Chinese forces would have to be completely abandoned. By this point, MacArthur's forces were in full retreat. This retreat was partly slowed due to low visibility inhibiting the US Air Force. They could not stop the Chinese onslaught of forces crossing the frozen Yalu River. MacArthur's troops were now faced with conditions well beyond their control.

China's Decision to Enter the War

As conditions deteriorated for MacArthur, eighteen European nations also committed their support via the United Nations in the defense of South Korea via three resolutions passed between June and July of 1950. These member nations were affected by North Korean troops illegally invading South Korea, an established sovereign nation, earlier in the summer. Truman had committed the United States to their defense, as well as that of Taiwan, with the presence of the United States' and United Nations' ground and air forces and through a naval blockade in the Taiwan Straits.

Beijing's first response to this American commitment had been to criticize the United States' intervention anywhere around the world, but especially in Asia, where China considered that they were the dominant power. On August 20, 1950, Premier Zhou Enlai warned the United Nations that since Korea was China's neighbor, they would defend them.[345] Chinese forces would eventually cross the Yalu River in response to this American and United Nations invasion. They would not stand by and watch the destruction of their ally by these foreign invaders.[346] The Chinese people were also concerned about a solution to the Korean question. China further warned that in safeguarding Chinese national security, they would intervene against the United Nation's command in Korea.

Once Truman heard of these threats, he made the mistake of interpreting the communication as an attempt to blackmail the United Nations. He dismissed the threat, perhaps making a "rookie" mistake.

Sending Troops to Korea: A Historical Record of the Resistance to America and Assistance to Korea explains that beginning in July 1949 through early 1950, high-level consultations were conducted with the Chinese, the Soviets, and the North Koreans about the potential entry of the United States. During these consultations, concerns began to grow, especially after the Inchon landings in mid-September and General MacArthur's rapid push north. This created panic in Pyongyang, Beijing, and Moscow.[347]

In deciding to intervene, Mao and the Chinese political and military hierarchy went through a complicated decision process. It became evident during the process that there would be pushback from those who did not want a war with the United States. They seemed to favor using limited budget resources to free themselves from Nationalist Chinese conspirators still remaining in China after the Chinese Civil War and to address economic development.

China's decision to intervene militarily was the next logical step and was planned well in advance. According to Michael Hunt, author of *Beijing and the Korean Crisis,* "Mao had announced his intentions to invade even before Kim Il Jung's desperate requests for China's direct support. As early as October 2, Mao told Joseph Stalin his desire to attack. His decision even predated his Zhou Enlai visit with Joseph Stalin in Russia on October 8. Ambassador Wang Jiaxiang also traveled to Sochi, on the Black Sea, to meet with him."[348] Supportive of China's plans, Mao's decision was made, detailing the possibility of US retaliatory strikes on the Chinese homeland. It was not an easy decision, judging from America's superiority in air power and naval presence and his understanding that it would take away from the economic, military, and political issues remaining from the Chinese Civil War. In Mao's words:

> Since Chinese troops will fight American troops in Korea (even though they will be using the title Volunteer Army), we must be prepared for the United States to declare and enter a state of war with China; we must be prepared [for the fact] that the United States may, at a minimum, use its air force to bomb many major cities and industrial centers in China, and use its navy to assault the coastal region.[349]

China's plan was to make the attack appear defensive in nature by stationing its divisions in North Korea, though "not necessarily all the way to the 38th parallel," and fighting small skirmishes with an aggressive enemy that "dare[d] to advance and attack north of the 38th parallel."[350] He then planned for these "Volunteer Army"[351] fighters to "await the arrival of Soviet weapons and the equipping of [the Chinese] Army; and then coordinate with the Korean comrades a counter-attack, destroying the invading American army."[352] The request for armaments from the Soviets was expected to be provided prior to any movement south. Chinese forces would commence their attack prior to these commitments being honored.

The second issue had to do with the pushback by internal Chinese Communist military and civilian leaders. Mao's views that China must attack brought on significant protests from ranking members of the Chinese Politburo.[353] According to Mao, they were afraid of the possibility of the US forces not being fully destroyed, and with the US "having already entered an open state of war with China," the result would be the "destruction of the economic construction plan [the Chinese had] already begun, and moreover, arousing dissatisfaction toward [Mao's administration] among the national bourgeoisie and other segments of the people."[354]

There was much discussion between North Korea, the Soviet Union, and China about the consolidation of support and military action against the United Nations forces. Ninety percent of those military forces were American. Not only would China attack these forces, but it would also protect the Chinese homeland from direct invasion.[355]

Once Mao decided to invade, he immediately began preparations. After scrutinizing several generals from the Chinese Civil War, Mao selected Peng Dehuai to command the attack. He was selected because he had experience commanding large units during the Chinese Civil War.

Their first action before proceeding over the Yalu River into North Korea was to broadcast public warnings directed against the advance of the United Nation's forces. These warnings were ultimately ignored by key leaders in Washington and in the theater.

After warning the United States not to head north from Inchon, Mao directed General Peng to deploy his forces and presented the United States with an additional message of letting the enemy forces know that they faced a new situation.[356]

Soviet leaders were more cautious, with a growing reluctance about a protracted, escalating conflict. Existing records indicate Mao, too, had a reluctance to proceed, telling Stalin that "attacking Chinese troops might fail to destroy American forces in Korea and become entangled in a Sino-American military stand-off." Mao also described that the Chinese people were still most unsettled about the invasion. Military risks and the possibility of direct attacks on China continued to be voiced by those who wanted the delay.[357]

Research began to emphasize Beijing supporting North Korean leader Kim Il-Sung's plan to execute an invasion of South Korea. Mao and Stalin discussed the possibility of the United States intervening on the Korean peninsula of South Korea by Kim Il-Sung during a summit meeting in

Moscow from December 1949 to February 1950, where the Sino-Soviet Treaty of Friendship, Alliance, and Mutual Assistance was signed.

In a telegram between Mao and Liu Shaoqi from December 18, 1949, at the start of the two-month-long meeting, Mao detailed that according to Stalin, the "Americans are afraid of fighting a war" and that "it is unlikely that a war will break out, and we agree with his opinions."[358] In establishing these joint opinions, however, Mao and Stalin kept open the possibility of reuniting Korea through military action of their own, of course, with the help of North Korea. The fact that the US had withdrawn two divisions from the Korean peninsula the prior summer only reinforced the belief that the US would no longer be a threat. According to Joseph Goulden, "The last American troops sailed as scheduled on June 30 [1950]. The only soldiers remaining in South Korea were a corporal's guard of advisers."[359]

This meeting was followed up by Mao speaking with Kim Il-Sung during a later meeting between the two. After the American landing at Inchon, "the Military Affairs Committee dispatched Chinese officers to Korea to lay the groundwork for possible intervention." China had raised a "growing alarm" about American and United Nations intervention in Korea. This fear "was reinforced by Soviet and Korean calls for assistance. It gave rise to efforts to coordinate policy among the three countries."[360]

Although the Soviets had a common interest with China in seeing less American influence in Asia, the Soviets had their own reasons for supporting a defeat of the United States in Korea. The Soviets were more concerned with the United States' impact on European politics, so a weakened United States in Asia meant a weaker United States in Europe.

Mao knew Stalin was being cautious regarding the Soviets' part in the war. In fact, Stalin was growing reluctant to assist as he feared a protracted and ever-escalating conflict. Stalin's obvious dilemma was that Mao was not prepared to take the offensive without his assurances that the Russians would support him with weaponry as well as financial aid. It would then be China's role to enter the war in Korea in support of Communist North Korea. Joseph Stalin had initially wanted China to commit six divisions to the invasion. The number grew to fifteen divisions plus support units as troops and equipment became available from China.

Ultimately, Chinese forces would cross the Yalu River in response to this American and UN invasion of the Korean Peninsula, as well as their plan to invade Taiwan to finally unify all Chinese citizens into one nation. And they would continue their internal efforts to destroy the Nationalist Chinese troops and their supporters within their borders.

China Enters the War—Phase I of the Chinese Offensive

The Chinese decided to move south without the guarantee of Soviet air support. On October 19, 1950, they crossed the Yalu River and continued south, moving only at night and resting during the day. They also were ordered to remain completely still when American reconnaissance aircraft appeared overhead so as to not give away troop movements. One day earlier, these same reconnaissance aircraft had "spotted 75 to 100 aircraft on the ground at the airfield near Antung, Manchuria, just across the Yalu from North Korea." The report most likely startled "both [General] Willoughby [US Far East command's chief of intelligence], and the Far East air commander, Lieutenant George E. Stratemeyer," as more reconnaissance was conducted the next day. These aircraft, however, were not present at the same location the next day. Willoughby rationalized that "It would be a sound, reasonable tactic for the Chinese Communist air forces to conduct mass long-distance flights, stopping briefly at selected airfields, as an integral part of their training program."[361]

First Contact with Chinese Forces

The first encounter with Chinese forces occurred in the far north-central territory, along the border with China. On the morning of October 25, 1950, a ROKA battalion, part of the ROKA 6th Division, moved forward, totally unaware of the Chinese arrival in North Korea. The ROKA proceeded northwest from the small village of Onjong during a planned forty-mile push to Pyoktong, along the Yalu River. It was planned to be an easy travel for the first eight miles until they became aware of what they thought was a small contingent of North Korean troops. The attackers were a large group of Communist Chinese soldiers, not North Koreans. Within a few minutes, the South Korean battalion was decimated. From a total of 750 soldiers, the battalion lost 350 killed, wounded, or captured. They were now in full flight for their lives."[362]

"A second South Korean battalion, on the same road, could not push back the Chinese. However, they did take two Chinese prisoners during the chaos of battle. The captured admitted after interrogation they were two Chinese soldiers freshly arrived from Manchuria with a large contingency of troops. The interrogators said these Chinese forces had been waiting in the mountains since October 17 in preparation to ambush the advancing ROKA forces."[363]

The American position on this information was that small amounts of Chinese regulars were being mixed in with the North Korean Army. Willoughby concluded that these "Chinese were incorporated... into North Korean units to assist in the defense of border areas."[364] This explanation was to be a major, incorrect assumption that delayed their addressing the real danger of a large army of battle-hardened Chinese moving south.[365]

The United Nations forces continued to believe this incorrect intelligence, thinking the Chinese had not invaded. That confusion remained for the Americans until the Chinese invaders forced the South Korean and United Nations armies out of North Korea and deep into South Korea.

"By October 28, 1950, the ROKA brought up still another regiment to the area. However, they survived only because of American air support. When the air support ended during the hours of darkness, the regiment took astonishing losses. In a regiment of 3,552, only 875 escaped. In total, an entire South Korean corps was able to evacuate the area. By October 29, 1950, the ROKA, 1st Division was in full flight."[366]

The Battle of the Chosin Reservoir

The Marines of the 1st Marine Division, led by General Oliver Smith, had been trying a more cautious approach to moving north. He was assisted by US Army elements under Colonel Alan MacLean (Task Force MacLean) and Lt. Colonel Don Faith (Task Force Faith), who commanded Regimental Combat Team 31. In several instances Smith's decisions to move slowly, and to consolidate strength around makeshift bases south of the reservoir, proved crucial in preventing total disaster. These consolidations, made of Regimental Combat Teams (RCT) to the east and to the west of the reservoir, irked the X Corps commander, General Edward "Ned" Almond, as he did not believe they were moving north to the Yalu River border fast enough. The Chinese forces in their attack were well aware of these troop positions and would attack all positions simultaneously.[367]

On November 27, 1950, the Chinese began by attacking in small units, picking off American soldiers. In the Battle of Chosin Reservoir, part of the Chinese Army's intent was to surround the Americans on the western end of the reservoir at Yudam-ni and cut them off from their supply lines to the south. On the east end of the reservoir, Regimental Combat Team 31, hastily formed from components of the US 7th Infantry Division, was of lesser strength than the west side. These troops were also heavily attacked by the Chinese. "Of the two-thousand, five-hundred men in Task Force Faith, only about one thousand filtered through to the friendly lines at last; of them, only four hundred were fit to be formed into a provisional formation and sent back into the firing line."[368] Marine and Naval air support would not only provide military close-air support in the retreat, but also supplies for the UN troops that were surrounded.

Once the Chinese forces were located, the 1st Marine Division formed to confront the Chinese Army and to assist MacArthur's troops, now in great danger of being overtaken. They sacrificed caution to assist the thirty-six thousand soldiers at the bottom of the Chosin Reservoir, roughly sixty miles south of the Yalu River itself. Eight thousand United States Marines and several thousand army and ROKA soldiers were seriously at risk of being captured.

As the Marines fought their way south on November 29, one thousand British Commandos then proceeded to "fight its way north from Koto-ri to Hakawoo-ri"[369] to protect the United Nations forces who were in a state of total withdrawal. Two-thirds of these men were lost in the fighting, though their assistance saved hundreds of retreating soldiers. "The Chinese attacked inside the United States Army perimeter. The heavy field of fire for the Americans was putting them in grave danger. General Almond finally realized the Chinese attackers had at least two divisions and needed help to avoid being completely overrun."[370]

Mao realized his forces were inferior to the United States Army and were wary of them. Nevertheless, he infiltrated the enemy lines, which was a courageous but necessary move. MacArthur began to understand the jeopardy his forces were under. He felt foolish that he had underestimated the presence of Chinese forces and their intent to destroy his units before he could withdraw to safer ground.

At the end of the first phase, the Chinese troops simply marched north in long columns and were not pursued. The Chinese were making their retreat obvious, though the advances south had been (and very soon would be) made in stealth. United States intelligence now correctly perceived that the Chinese were quietly infiltrating North Korea, though the exact troop strength was not fully known and was the subject of significant debate due to the range of estimates from various intelligence sources.

MacArthur did get his wish to commence a bombing campaign of "supply dumps, railheads, roads, and bridges" along the Yalu River, which finally commenced on November 8, 1950. Though the campaign was considered successful, the freezing of the Yalu in the coming months and establishing pontoon bridges to cross the river would keep Chinese supply lines intact.[371]

The Second Phase of the Chinese Offensive (late November 1950)

On August 20, 1950, Premier Zhou Enlai warned the United Nations that Korea was China's neighbor and that they were prepared to support North Korea until the US and UN troops were totally thrown out of the Korean Peninsula. Enlai said the Chinese people insisted the Korean question must be resolved. He further warned that in safeguarding Chinese national security, they would intervene against the United Nation's command in Korea.

For most of November, the Chinese had halted their advance south, leading both American military and civilian leadership to speculate as to why their movement had halted and even reversed in some areas.[372]

Despite a clearly changed situation on the battlefield and growing doubts around the true strength of the enemy Chinese forces in North Korea, MacArthur viewed his orders from the Joint Chiefs of Staff (JCS) of early October as the operating instructions he should live by: "[in the event of] open or covert employment anywhere in Korea of major Chinese Communist units," to proceed as long as there was a "reasonable chance of success."[373]

Meanwhile, political leaders and the JCS were looking for diplomatic solutions and favored a holding of existing territory until a better assessment of the situation could be made. They were, however, hesitant to overrule MacArthur, given his current position as commander in chief of the Far East.[374]

What the UN forces had not realized was that Mao's army had intentionally stalled to establish supply routes, and the retreat itself was a tactic that he had used in previous military engagements during the Second Sino-Japanese War and the Chinese Revolution. Mao's tactics were summed up in a slogan well-known in the study of irregular, guerrilla warfare:

> Enemy advances, we retreat.
> Enemy halts, we harass.
> Enemy tires, we attack.
> Enemy retreats, we pursue.[375]

During the lull, the 1st Marine Division under General Oliver Smith was tasked with resuming the march north toward the Chosin Reservoir from the coastal territories around Hamhung. Smith did not fully believe the prevailing intelligence that reported fewer than thirty-thousand Chinese had entered Korean territory. He had received reports of his own that large amounts of Chinese matériel were flowing across the Yalu River, which the pilots described as "heavy, very heavy, tremendous, and gigantic."[376]

The Chinese surprise resumption of the offensive that began on November 24, 1950, stunned Truman. He now understood that his preparations would come to nothing after anticipating the first victory over communism. Instead, American troops were being destroyed.[377]

The morning Truman had received news of the Chinese offensive, November 28, 1950, General Omar Bradley, the chief of the NSC, mapped out the disposition of forces in North Korea for Truman and his staff. He emphasized the fact that an unexpected two hundred thousand Chinese troops were in North Korea heading for South Korea. He further recommended that no new orders be provided to MacArthur until the military situation was clarified. They had to determine whether their intelligence was exaggerated. In his report, Bradley described a new defensive point of view over the difficult terrain in which American forces had to retreat. He also indicated that a new American division was to arrive in the theater within seventy-two hours, which would assist in the retreat.[378]

Bradley determined that there needed to be American air power over the entire battlefield to provide cover for their retreating forces. The Chinese had approximately three hundred bombers in Manchuria that had to be considered.

General Marshall, the army chief of staff, then provided his report to the administration. As a result of Chinese Communist aggression, he advised that they must maintain the United Nations coalition and resist expanding the war. That would change Soviet strategy to an active role in the war. Secondly, there was to be no entry into Chinese territory. Marshall suspected MacArthur would want to cross the Yalu River into China.

Truman was in full agreement with Marshall regarding the intent of limiting the expansion of the war. Truman later said, "There was no doubt in my mind . . . that we should not allow the action in Korea to extend to a general war. All-out military action against China had to be avoided, if for no other reason than because it was a gigantic booby trap."[379]

The strategic disagreement between Truman and MacArthur would have to be held in abeyance. Marshall then ordered MacArthur not to enter any engagement in which Chinese national forces (from Taiwan) would be utilized, as it would only prolong the war with the Chinese Communists. This belief that MacArthur wanted to wage a general war with China was another assumption made about MacArthur's intentions.[380]

Though the administration and military leadership in Washington, DC, disagreed with MacArthur's strategic plans of expanding the war with China, General Marshall recommended that they should not interfere with MacArthur's tactical plans. Any direct commands to MacArthur should, therefore, not occur from his superiors who were eight thousand miles away from the Korean theater. According to H. W. Brands, "MacArthur didn't get new orders. All he got were recommendations from the joint chiefs, who couldn't bring themselves to issue a direct order."[381] General Marshall compared Korea with the Battle of the Bulge in the Second World War. No hour-by-hour reports by the defense secretary or chief of staff occurred in that battle. That was to be repeated here because the joint chiefs of staff were far away and understood that they couldn't possibly have the same battlefield intelligence as a commander on the ground.

Truman's vice president, Alben Barkley, had close ties with members of Congress. He described Congress's comments that they were outraged by MacArthur's empty promises prior to the Chinese attack. This boastfulness now seemed not just empty but crazy. Why did he make the comments? Did he know what was going on? If he knew, why did he say that American soldiers would be home by Christmas?[382]

MacArthur did not know what the Chinese Communists were doing. Omar Bradley had a theory about MacArthur's predictions, specifically that the general's boast that American troops would be home by Christmas was a statement for Chinese consumption. It was still a rash statement for Omar Bradley, as well as many others in defense and Congress.

Truman went along with Bradley's advice during Truman's communications with the theater commander and gave no sign that would suggest displeasure with MacArthur's performance. Truman even defended MacArthur in the press, saying, "[The press] are always for a man when he is winning, but when he is in a little trouble . . . they all jump on him with what ought to be done, which they didn't tell him before."[383]

Politically, Truman could not damage MacArthur's prestige at this point. Marshall felt MacArthur's comments were an embarrassment, as did President Truman. The Chinese invasion across the Yalu River into North Korea and beyond, with one hundred thousand to two hundred thousand soldiers, Russian tanks, and heavy artillery, apparently was a huge surprise to MacArthur.[384]

Vice President Barkley felt that they could not survive if the Chinese Communists continued the all-out war. They could not become totally involved in Korea with all the other commitments around the world. Marshall felt it was important to understand how the United States could get out of Korea with honor.

Joe Collins, the Army chief of staff, reported that there were no ready units to send, at least not until March 1951. Individual soldiers could be inserted, but there could be no full unit replacements. The United Nations allies could assist by filling in the shortfall, but the United Nations units were over 30 percent short, according to MacArthur.[385]

Joe Collins felt the current situation was manageable, but American forces had to retreat as far south as possible and dig in to a defensive strategy. This would only be feasible if the X Corps were not cut off by a Chinese encirclement maneuver. MacArthur could hold the line in that case. Dean Acheson addressed the diplomatic issues raised by the current crisis. He spoke bluntly that the events of the last few hours had moved them very much closer to a general war. In Acheson's opinion, the US forces under MacArthur should take a more conservative approach than MacArthur's desired strategy of a naval blockade of China and bombing the Chinese mainland.[386] Acheson declared that the prudent course of action was for MacArthur to "find a line that [he] could hold, and hold it."[387]

Acheson's fears were based on China's invasion and America's potential lack of success in thwarting it. Therefore, the military objective was to hold an area and terminate the fighting until United Nations forces could get out. This action would assure the survival of the American military and bring the focus on keeping Western Europe free.[388]

Truman agreed with Acheson's analysis. Success in these undertakings was central. Truman stated that it was the Soviet Union, not China, that was America's principal enemy. America's forward defense was the defense of Europe, not South Korea. To Truman, Korea was symbolically vital, but America could not alienate its allies in Europe under any circumstances. Truman liked the consensus by both military and civilian leaders that came from the meetings to work out their strategy in Korea following the Chinese invasion. He was satisfied but uncertain about MacArthur and his ideas about American strategy. MacArthur would certainly disagree with much of the present discussion. Implementation of MacArthur's strategy would overrule this consensus and the will of the elected leaders.[389]

US Marines march along the Funchilin Pass in North Korea
The Battle of Chosin Reservoir, November 26 to December 13, 1950[390]

The Battle Resumes for the Eighth Army

The US Eighth Army (EUSAK) was attacked on November 25, 1950, in a surprise move that focused on the vulnerable South Korean soldiers of the 1st ROKA Infantry division to the east of American forces. These soldiers had, in some cases, been recruited only days earlier from the South Korean cities and countryside and had very little in the way of training for war. The first group of Chinese penetrated the lines and set up barriers behind the ROKA to prevent their retreat. Once the next line of Chinese, who were battle-hardened, commenced their charge, the ill-prepared ROKA forces "broke and ran, tossing rifles and other equipment aside in a frantic attempt at survival."[391]

The other UN divisions fared only slightly better than the ROKA divisions. The Chinese were generally attempting an encirclement to prevent their retreat to the south. The lack of effective communication combined with the Chinese element of surprise meant that the UN forces were not able to organize and coordinate to take advantage of their superior firepower. In all, the EUSAK forces, who were outnumbered and outmaneuvered, lost tens of thousands in casualties and retreated thirty kilometers south to nearly half the distance to Pyongyang.[392]

On October 15, Chinese troops invaded South Korea. To do this successfully, Mao again requested that Stalin provide air forces and supplies. Mao and his generals feared America's military capability in the war on land, air, and sea simultaneously. For this reason, Mao also wanted the Soviets to supply arms to include air power. Only then would he decide to take the offensive. Key to Mao's strategy was receiving consistent Soviet military cooperation.

The Third Phase of the Chinese Offensive

By the end of the Second Phase Chinese Offensive on December 13, 1950, the UN forces had begun their retreat south, though the Chinese forces had paused their attack to regroup. On December 16, 1950, President Truman declared a national emergency with a presidential proclamation, No. 2914, 3 C.F.R.99, which remained in force until September 14, 1978. On December 17, 1950, Kim Il-Sung was removed from command of the North KPA by China. This action ensured the Chinese command of the invasion.

Ultimately, six United Nations divisions were now attacking at Hagaru-Ri, the point of the Chinese attack. If they did not quickly retreat, the American headquarters, poorly defended, would be overtaken.

The Chinese had sought to overwhelm United Nations forces by utilizing night attacks. The result was the United Nation's fighting positions were encircled and then assaulted by numerically superior troops who had the element of surprise. These surprise attacks included psychological elements: loud trumpets and gongs for facilitating tactical communication and mentally disorienting the enemy. As a result, United Nations troops tended to panic, leave their weapons, and retreat south. The New Year's Offensive on December 31 overwhelmed the United Nations forces. This allowed the Chinese and North Korean troops to again conquer the South Korean capital of Seoul in January 1951.

With the arrival of General Matthew Ridgway after the passing of General Walker in a car accident on December 23, 1950, the esprit de corps of the retreating 8th Army immediately began to improve. Their retreat continued through the territory north of Suwon, which stabilized the battlefield as the Chinese People's Volunteer Army (PVA) began outrunning their supply lines. Ridgway reacted by instituting a reconnaissance mission known as Operation Round-up on February 5, 1951. The information provided by Operation Round-up about the enemy's location allowed a full-scale Army X Corps counterattack.

General MacArthur's Retreat

By December 24, 1950, the Navy had arrived to assist in the evacuation of the 8th Army. This intervention, known as the "Miracle of Christmas," made it possible for 193 shiploads of UN forces and matériel, with approximately 105,000 soldiers, 98,000 civilians, 17,500 vehicles, and 350,000 tons of supplies to be evacuated. One ship, the SS *Meredith Victory* had evacuated 14,000 refugees in one loading.[393] This was to be one of the largest rescue operations by a single ship, especially unique because it had been designed to hold fewer occupants and matériel. Before escaping, the United Nations command forces razed most of Hungnam City, especially its port facilities, by detonating a cache of frozen dynamite and 1,000-pound bombs on the dock.[394]

Just south of the thirty-eighth parallel, the UN forces had a chance to regroup and attempt to form a more solid defensive stance. The Chinese

PVA had achieved an initial victory at Hoengsong on February 13, though the Chinese forces were then stopped by the IV Corps positions at Chipyong-ni a few days later on the fifteenth, both east of Seoul. The US Second Infantry "Warrior" Division, Thirteenth Regiment Combat Team, and a French Battalion reversed this initial victory, which was a short but desperate battle that broke the attack's momentum. It would become known as the Gettysburg of the Korean War. Five thousand six hundred South Korean, US, and French troops were surrounded but overcame the enemy, creating an impasse in the war.

With a revitalized 8th Army, they succeeded in reoccupying the territory south of the Han River in northern South Korea and in IX Corps capturing Hoengseong due east of Seoul. The operation was known as Operation Ripper and was launched on March 7, 1951. It was "intended to drive a broad wedge into the center of the enemy line and separate the Chinese in the west from the North Koreans in the east."[395] The goal was Chunchon, which was northeast of Seoul, near the thirty-eighth parallel. As a part of this operation, the 8th Army attacked, expelling the PVA and the KPA from Seoul on March 14, 1951. This was the fourth such transfer of power in Seoul. It also allowed the stabilizing of the United Nations command south of the thirty-eighth parallel.[396]

In March 1951, Mao again sent a request to the Soviets requesting an air presence. The need for air cover was particularly dire as supply lines and troops were threatened by UN air superiority. In the Soviet response via ciphered telegram, Stalin agreed to send "two fighter divisions . . . [to] Korean territory to cover the Sino-Korean rear . . . ." Stalin also commented on the need to supply materials for more temporary landing strips, as well as antiaircraft guns, and six thousand trucks.[397]

The PVA troops in Korea continued to suffer severe logistical problems throughout the war. The Chinese leaders did not necessarily fear the enemy, but they did fear having no food, ammunition, or trucks to transport wounded soldiers to receive medical care. Zhou Enlai tried to respond to PVA's logistical concerns, but increasing Chinese production and improving supply methods were never sufficient.

MacArthur's Dismissal and the Limited War Doctrine

President Truman related this intent and explanation to the American people in a radio address after MacArthur was relieved of his duties: "I believe that we must try to limit the war to Korea for these vital reasons: to make sure that the precious lives of our fighting men are not wasted; to see that the security of our country and the free world is not needlessly jeopardized; and to prevent a third world war."[398]

At the outset, Truman's goals in Korea were limited to protecting the South Korean people from being taken over by the North Koreans. The Limited War doctrine as a part of Cold War foreign policy had its origins in Europe, though its influence can clearly be seen in Korea with this goal in mind. When the possibility of taking over the entire Korean peninsula came about through MacArthur's ambitions to drive northward, Truman and his administration had not explicitly stated the follow-on goal that had emerged when China entered the conflict. This second goal was to limit the escalation of the war into what might have become the Third World War.

Truman also demonstrated his understanding through the action of firing MacArthur that his responsibility was not that of a conqueror seeking his own glory. Rather, his responsibility was to the interests of the American people and those of the military.

Carl von Clausewitz talks about the balance that must be maintained between the three parts of the trinity, and in this case, the government and military leadership had not been in sync. Clausewitz mentions in *On War* that "friction caused within the trinity due to the stress felt during the war, chaos with the social, economic, or other elements of society may certainly develop. If this friction does not end, usually, through communication and better understanding, a conflict leading to severe disagreements between the elements of the trinity will arise." One could say that the communication link between the government and the military was certainly at risk of deterioration. With his address to the people, Truman ensured the link between the government and the people remained strong.

The Path to Peace

After MacArthur's continued opposition to Truman's policies regarding the war, Truman replaced General MacArthur on April 11, 1951, with Lieutenant General Matthew Ridgway.[399] Specifically, Truman grew increasingly displeased with MacArthur's approach to the war. MacArthur had crossed the thirty-eighth parallel in direct opposition to Truman's orders not to move north. MacArthur believed that "total victory was the only honorable outcome," while Truman wanted a more limited approach to the war. MacArthur wanted complete surrender by the Chinese, while Truman was "extremely pessimistic about MacArthur's chances of success once he was involved in a land war in Asia." Further, "Truman felt a truce and then, an orderly withdrawal from Korea would be a valid solution. Such a truce would make South Korea remain free and send North Korea and China home."[400]

In congressional hearings in May and June 1951, following the firing, the members ruled that MacArthur had defied the orders of the president and had violated the US Constitution by that defiance. Therefore, MacArthur was relieved primarily due to his determination to expand the war into China, which other officials believed would needlessly escalate the war and consume too many already overstretched resources.[401]

March 28, 1951: Men of the 187th US Regimental Combat Team prepare an assault.[402]

Truman's concerns were that such a strategy would provoke the Soviet Union into entering the war. Russia had thirty-five Russian divisions totaling some five hundred thousand troops in the Far East, as well as eighty-five Russian submarines surrounding the Korean Peninsula.

Once General Ridgway became the theater commander following the dismissal of MacArthur, he reorganized the UN forces for successful counterattacks. General James Van Fleet, the commander of the US 8th Army, was able to slowly deplete the PVA and KPA forces beginning in April 1951.

The Chinese Spring Offensive started close to the end of April and continued until the end of May 1951. The Chinese PVA, under Field Marshall Peng Dehuai, moved three field armies of seven hundred thousand men close to the thirty-eighth parallel, with the intent of removing UN military forces from the Korean peninsula for good.[403] The plan was to establish air superiority by building or repairing airfields close to the parallel, though this superiority was never truly established to protect their troops. The allied air forces, under Brigadier General

James E. Briggs, intended to "withhold B-29 strikes until the fields were about to become operational. He intended to bomb the fields out of action at that time and to keep them neutralized with attacks just heavy enough." This strategy proved successful, as these airfields were never made operational.[404] The plan for ground troops was to capture Seoul by May 1, which Peng intended as a "May Day gift" to Mao.[405]

Within the scope of the Spring Offensive, the Imjin River was the northernmost line for the UN forces. This was known as the Kansas Line and stretched across the peninsula, approximately twenty miles north of Seoul. Just south of this was the Delta Line, halfway between the Imjin River and the latitude of Seoul. The last line, known as the Nevada Line, was bookended by Seoul on the west of the Korean peninsula, and Taepo-ri on the east coast would only be crossed temporarily at the Soyang River, but this territory would not be held.[406]

Notable among the battles during the Spring Offensive are the Battle of the Imjin River, April 11–25, 1951, and the Battle of Kapyong, April 22–25, 1951. Both were successful for UN units in halting the PVA's movement south.[407] The 8th Army used ground and airborne units to trap Chinese forces between Kaesong and Seoul. As a part of Operation Tomahawk, the 187th Airborne Regimental Combat Team, the "Rakkasans," would perform the last Airborne operation of the war. The Rakkasans were named after the Japanese term for "falling down umbrella" or "parachute," a nickname they earned during Pacific theater operations during World War II.[408]

The result of the battles in April ultimately changed Chinese expectations of how the war would end for them and for their North Korean allies.[409] During the first week of the offensive alone, the PVA lost between thirty-five and sixty thousand casualties as compared to four thousand UN forces.[410] The reason for the difference was due to General Van Fleet's use of superior firepower in the form of air bombardment, artillery, and tanks.

During the western campaign, UN forces would "withdraw only a short distance per night, the distance that the short-supplied [Chinese] troops could travel overnight, in order to maintain close contact with Chinese attacking forces throughout the next day."[411] With their movement on the western side of the peninsula halted by the end of April, Peng refocused on Seoul.[412]

The first two weeks of May "was similar to the eye of a hurricane," as James Stokesbury called it.[413] The Chinese had regrouped ten miles north of their farthest reach south in order to resupply as fast as they could and to let their troops rest. They had also begun moving troops from the west to the east to approach Seoul. On May 15, 1951, the Chinese Spring Offensive attacked the ROKA and the US X Corps east of the Soyang River. The Chinese experienced initial success but were halted by May 20, 1951, as the US 8th Army successfully counterattacked, thus regaining Line Kansas just north of the thirty-eighth parallel.

The remainder of the war was characterized by a stalemate that lasted until 1953, when the armistice agreement was reached. Bombing of North Korea continued leading up to the start of negotiations on July 10, 1951, which took place at Kaesong, northeast of Seoul. Some combat operations took place during the two-year-long negotiations. Twelve specific battles were designed by the PVA to put pressure on the UN command and make them withdraw without successful agreement. These twelve "battles of the stalemate" were as follows:

- The Battle of Bloody Ridge: August 18–September 15, 1951
- The Battle of the Punchbowl: August 31–September 21, 1951
- The Battle of Heartbreak Ridge: September 13–October 15, 1951
- The Battle of Old Baldy: June 26–August 4, 1952
- The Battle of White Horse: October 6–15, 1952
- The Battle of Triangle Hill: October 4–November 25, 1952
- The Battle of Hill Eerie: March 21–June 21, 1952
- The Sieges of Outpost Harry: June 10–18, 1953
- The Battle of the Hook: May 28–29, 1953
- The Battle of Pork Chop Hill: March 23–July 16, 1953
- The Battle of Kumsong: July 13–27, 1953.[414]

Why were the Chinese unsuccessful at dislodging the United Nations command positions, even with their initial success in routing United Nations forces out of North Korea? The PVA had a very large size advantage over the UN forces, though with the Spring Offensive, "Peng rushed a half-million men to the front without air cover, training, or essential supplies." As a result, their plan to outnumber the UN forces at least four-to-one turned into a casualty rate of "10-15 to 1 (about 3 to 1, according to Chinese official statistics)."[415]

The US leadership also began to catch on that these operational pauses, such as the one during the first two weeks in May, were due to PVA logistical challenges. The Soviets were also unable to support the PVA militarily to the satisfaction of Chinese leaders.[416]

The Long Road to an Armistice: Truce Talks Begin

On June 23, 1951, Adam Malik, the Soviet UN ambassador, "unexpectedly called the US government's Soviet Union expert, George Kennan, proposing discussions leading to a cease-fire and armistice that would end the Korean conflict."[417] The Truman administration was eager for peace, so they signaled to General Ridgway that talks could commence. Ridgway suggested a Dutch hospital ship in Wonsan harbor, deep in North Korean territory, though the Chinese and North Koreans countered with Kaesong, just below the thirty-eighth parallel.[418]

The talks commenced on July 10, 1951, in Kaesong, and other than an overall agenda for the talks, which was agreed to by July 25, chief among the issues to be settled was the demarcation line.[419] Ridgway was adamant that the cease-fire not commence until this line of advance was agreed upon by all parties. Therefore, fighting by the troops continued while their leadership haggled for what seemed to be just a few more miles of land. The UN negotiating team, led by Admiral C. Turner Joy, proposed to the Communist negotiators that the current battle lines north of the thirty-eighth parallel should be the demarcation line due to the superior air, naval, and firepower of the UN troops. This wasn't well received, as the other side believed the line should reflect the original demarcation line, the thirty-eighth parallel.[420]

The talks became stalled and ultimately moved to Panmunjom a few months later, in October, because on August 23, the "Communists charged that UN planes had bombed the site of the talks and broke off negotiations."[421] At the October meeting, the Communist negotiators seemed to relent on the drawing of the demarcation line, making their proposal match closely with the UN negotiating team. The ownership of the ancient city of Kaesong ultimately went to North Korea, though this was hotly contested as well.[422] The final demarcation line and border were very close to these proposals, though fighting continued for nearly two more years.

The last main issue of the talks was the return of prisoners of war (POW) and whether they would have freedom of choice regarding repatriation. This was a suggestion the United States introduced in January 1952 to members. As a result, approximately one-third of North Korean prisoners and a larger contingency of Chinese POWs refused to return to their countries.[423]

Ultimately, South Korea, still led by Syngman Rhee, refused to sign any armistice "that did not provide for a united Korea, with [Rhee] in control."[424] He had also "threatened to withdraw the ROKA forces from the UNF Command and continue the war alone," though this would likely have resulted in a disastrous defeat for the ROKA. In a further act of defiance, Rhee released 25,000 North Korean POWs to a South Korean territory that had refused repatriation. By one account, nearly 4,000 more escaped when the ROKA guards of the POW camp opened the gates the following two nights.[425] US guards quickly replaced these ROKA guards, subsequent to Rhee's orders to release them. Ultimately, Rhee agreed not to delay or block the armistice, though he refused to sign it.[426] In the end, South Korea was promised aid by the US, and "Rhee agreed to behave."[427]

In the meantime, the Chinese leadership was not enthusiastic about Rhee's actions and was willing to continue fighting to strengthen their position at the negotiations. Some of the fighting was the fiercest of the entire war between mid-June and July 23, when the final demarcation line was agreed upon by the Communists and the UN military leaders.[428]

The Communists pursued two separate and costly offensives in June–July 1953 that failed. The Americans pursued ways in which they could stop the violence with violence. The Air Force was ordered to bomb huge irrigation dams necessary for 75 percent of the North's food production. Also, the Communist air forces had restocked their planes in North Korea, though many of these would become fodder for US pilots, as seventy-four MiG-15s were downed in this time.[429]

In the end, many American historians felt the final decision to make peace occurred because of Joseph Stalin's death on March 5, 1953, the American bombing of North Korea, and threats to put atomic weapons into the mix. This was publicized widely by the American press. Ironically, MacArthur's intent to use nuclear weapons, with or without formal approval, had been a major reason Truman fired him two years earlier.[430] "To this day there remains a debate on whether Truman's limited war strategy was correct or whether MacArthur's strategy was what should have been pursued."[431]

The POW question was settled as well, which paved the way for a signed armistice agreement. Though Rhee's actions inflamed the Communists, they ultimately agreed to allow POWs who resisted repatriation to be handed over to the newly formed Neutral Nations Repatriation Commission. Until January 1954, the Communists attempted to encourage over 22,000 resisting POWs to return to China and North Korea. Only 628 were, for whatever reason, finally convinced to change their mind. The rest settled in either Taiwan or South Korea.[432]

Finally, a day—July 27, 195—was chosen as the day of signing: "Precisely at ten, General Harrison entered the building from his side, and Lt. Gen. Nam Il of the North Korean People's Army from his end. They sat down at the center of their respective tables and signed the copies of documents in front of them . . . Neither general spoke; neither offered to shake hands. They got up, looked coldly at each other, and walked out."[433]

B-26 Invaders bomb logistics depots in Wonsan,
North Korea, 1951[434]

*All great wars are tragic—the fact that there was no victor made
[the Korean War] even more tragic.*
—Author unknown

CHAPTER SIX

THE VIETNAM WAR

Vietnam War protest at Florida State University, 1970[435]

The Vietnam War, fought between 1954 and 1975, with the US involvement primarily stretching from 1960 to early 1973, is characterized by three major wartime components: a revolutionary war, a regional war, and a global war (the Cold War). This war within a war understandably generated a constant interplay between the different belligerents as each generated its own unique friction. Political objectives translated into military strategies.

For the US, the development of a coherent wartime strategy by its civilian and military leaders proved extremely difficult, if not impossible.

With confidence in the immense power of the United States, Robert McNamara, the secretary of defense under both President Kennedy and President Johnson, believed that any enemy foolish enough to compete with the United States military on the field of battle could be easily overwhelmed. This confidence lacked a truly comprehensive assessment of US goals and objectives regarding the overall will to fight and win.

The United States' adversaries in this conflict included the people, government, and military of North Vietnam, their "revolutionary" extension in South Vietnam, and their guerrilla army, the Vietcong. Any military entering a war should know who their enemy is in every respect. The United States did not understand its enemy, although the Communists seemed to know America very well.

Only a practical, objective net assessment would have been sufficient to understand the answers to these future challenges. American senior leaders did not make serious consideration for assessing whether to invade Vietnam. This early failure eventually led to an inglorious defeat, much like it had for the French during the French-Indochina War.

After twelve years of war, the United States reduced the Vietcong's presence in South Vietnam by 80 percent, but the cost to Vietnam was the destruction of its environment through napalm and other chemicals delivered through the air. There were deaths of an estimated one million civilian and military Vietnamese[436], as well as nearly three hundred thousand US and allied military deaths.[437] All this destruction and loss of life was without any progress toward a cessation of hostilities.

Robert McNamara did have a theory for the victory that evolved into a strategy. He believed with proper political and military persuasion measured by bombing missions designed to intimidate and destroy selected North Vietnam targets that the North Vietnam leadership would eventually agree to peace terms.[438] Because Robert McNamara used complex statistical management models in his business, it was natural to use statistics as a measurement of progress in defeating this enemy.[439] He believed that the measure of success was through quantifiable indicators, such as kill ratios, bomb tonnage dropped, and the number of training sessions held. However, all turned out to be useless in measuring the enemy's willingness to resist regardless of the force used against them.

The Complex Nature of the Vietnam War

Any interpretation of decisions made regarding direct intervention in the Vietnam War must begin with a good understanding of the complex nature of the Vietnam War. At its very core, the war was a revolutionary war, with multiple political elements characterized by assassinations and the use of other terrorist acts for political gain on both the North Vietnam and South Vietnam sides. From this revolutionary war, a regional component evolved as the United States came to South Vietnam's aid.

The government of North Vietnam also found its benefactors, if not allies, in the People's Republic of China and the Union of Soviet Socialist Republics (USSR). Both provided North Vietnam with heavy armaments and munitions.

These multiple elements, or layers of war, generated constant friction between belligerents for the duration of the war. It also made the development of a coherent United States strategy extremely difficult, if not impossible.[440]

The dilemma for the United States, as it attempted to develop a viable strategy to move forward, was found in any course of action that might be effective in winning the regional war. Direct attacks on North Vietnam through invasion were not allowed, as they might affect the global coalition war with the escalation of involvement from the Soviet Union and the People's Republic of China on North Vietnam's behalf.

Focusing on the revolutionary element by attacking the Vietcong in the South might have defeated that guerrilla foe. But that effort might have only exhausted the United States forces without affecting the real center of gravity in the war, North Vietnam.[441]

It was feared that committing sufficient forces to succeed in putting down the revolution in South Vietnam and the regional war against North Vietnam might bring the Chinese and the Soviet Union into the war, as well as unintentionally take needed US forces from Europe, a similar dilemma that had occurred in the Korean War. Even twenty years after the end of World War II, the US still feared putting Europe at risk of an invasion from the Soviet Union.[442]

The United States Decision Process for Intervention

The reasons the United States intervened in Vietnam were both simple and extraordinarily complex. They involved discussions by the Kennedy and Johnson inner circle of senior civilian staff about the many pros and cons related to engaging themselves in another land war in Asia. Comparisons of value versus risk and a seemingly superficial view of the future enemy's capacity to resist were not significant elements of the United States' decision process for intervention.

A more complicated response to why the United States ultimately committed itself to what they assumed would be a limited war was to protect a fledgling country from its northern neighbor. Although numerous civilian and military leaders warned against it, their ultimate decision to intervene was related to the more significant issue of containing worldwide communism.[443]

The 1954 Geneva Accords had split the country into two nations, with North Vietnam under the control of the Communist leader Ho Chi Minh. The overarching issue of limiting communism translated to the commitment to defend this small, little-known country of South Vietnam from being overrun by the Communists in North Vietnam. This commitment was to ensure "South Vietnam would remain independent and non-Communist."[444] It took the United States twelve years of war before they understood they would not be successful.[445]

The reoccurring question became whether the value of committing American forces in South Vietnam was equal to the potential sacrifices to be made. Alternately, could the United States stand by and watch it be overrun by a Communist enemy in the middle of the Cold War?

Was the United States' intervention valuable enough to offset its cost? Other arguments seemed to heavily outweigh those of standing down from its obligations as the leader of the so-called free world. One such rationale used to bolster the value versus cost discussion was that its value came from the issue of containment of worldwide Communism. It also came from the containment of Communist expansion in Asia and the avoidance of a frequently expressed fear that the fall of South Vietnam would cause the eventual fall of Cambodia, Laos, Malaysia, Thailand, Indonesia, Burma, and even the Philippines, like a set of stacked dominoes.[446]

Analysts often drew a direct line between Vietnam and these countries, using the rationale that if we did not stop this "cancer," it would spread a unified Communist influence throughout the rest of what had formerly been called Indochina and beyond. This line of reasoning was accepted at the time by many clear-thinking Americans both in and out of government. However, in time, other significant portions of the American people would openly rebel and bring the United States government to its knees.

Carl von Clausewitz emphasizes the critical imperative to link the people with the actions of both the government and the military based on his Trinity theory. Without this linkage, the war cannot continue—and this was ultimately proven in Vietnam.[447]

The Possible Consequences of Not Intervening

Other early analysts compared the fall of South Vietnam to the hypothetical loss of West Berlin to the Soviets and its adverse effect on the future course of the Cold War in Europe. One report maintained that losing South Vietnam would soon have a crippling effect in Southeast Asia and Asia in general, much like the loss of West Berlin would have on Europe.[448]

Once the decision was made for the US to support South Vietnam with weapons, supplies, and equipment, several thousand military and civilian advisers were sent. Some compared it to the proverbial slippery slope, others a swamp never to be exited—the theoretical foundation for using military means for our political aims. Some believed that war was merely politics in different ways and that the use of these military means may be inappropriate for meeting individual political objectives.[449]

Why the United States continued to pursue victory in this small Asian war is an even more complicated story. The United States government deemed it necessary to take that crucial first step, a step Carl von Clausewitz had warned about over one hundred and fifty years before. "Use of military means may be inappropriate for achieving the desired political end-state. Some of the ways in which force is employed may generate counterproductive political effects."[450]

Direct United States Intervention Begins

Once the intervention was underway, as early as 1950, with President Harry Truman's approval of National Security Council Memorandum 64,[451] the United States found it difficult to withdraw from its commitment to South Vietnam. This action would provide the French with several thousand military and civilian advisers to train and supply South Vietnam as they fought off the Communist North Vietnam aggressors and their growing Viet Cong guerrilla movement in South Vietnam.

After South Vietnam proved they were unable to make progress in driving out the surprisingly resourceful insurgents, hundreds of thousands of United States military personnel were progressively transferred in to prevent the defeat of those it had intended to assist.

By the time Lyndon B. Johnson became president upon the assassination of John F. Kennedy, he and his senior staff found it extremely tough to retreat from this commitment, even though the South Vietnamese government and military were less than ideal allies. If the United States had conducted a truly comprehensive initial and ongoing assessment of Vietnam and its belligerents, it might have realized the United States had little or no chance of winning this war. They would have realized that they were fighting an enemy that was willing to lose everything to throw the French colonialists out during the First Indochina War (also known as the French Indochina War). They would do the same to the Americans.

The facts of this previous war should have alerted United States political and military leaders to the difficulties ahead. They knew what they had to do but disregarded their best instincts. Because of the overwhelming force that the United States could bring to the war, senior American leaders were confident the enemy could be defeated. This belief in its systems and its confidence in its leaders and soldiers proved disastrous to the American war effort.

Senior civilian leaders, led by Secretary of Defense McNamara, projected their confidence during briefings with senior American leadership. They believed that the combination of America's awesome military power and their faith in precisely how to measure success on the battlefield made them confident they were pursuing the proper course. They, unfortunately, designed strategies for victory in a vacuum, without any significant understanding of who the enemy was and what its capabilities were. These leaders were confident because of US military power, as demonstrated by America's successes in the Korean War and the Second World War in particular.[452]

During the first significant battle of the Vietnam War at Ap Bac, Colonel John Paul Vann provided a unique perspective on the enemy as well as the South Vietnamese army. American soldiers on the ground during the battle began to understand and respect the enemy's true capabilities. However, senior leaders like General Harkins, commander in chief of United States Military Command, Vietnam, the secretary of state, and others, ignored the adverse reports presented to them by Colonel Vann and other American leaders on site. General Harkins and McNamara believed they knew the proper course to victory but failed to adhere to even those beliefs at Ap Bac and throughout the war.[453]

Severe Policy Limitations

The United States fought despite severe policy limitations placed on its military; self-imposed restrictions placed on the military that were deemed necessary if they were to avoid unwelcome entry into the war by third parties, such as the People's Republic of China and the Soviet Union. These policies equated to a limited war.

Perhaps the United States leadership should have asked one additional question before committing to any form of war in Southeast Asia: "If the option of force was selected, were policy limitations placed on the use of its military? If so, were these limitations so stringent as to reduce the chances of success?"[454]

Civilian advisers, and perhaps President Johnson himself, ultimately realized that they were not going to win this war with such restraints intact. Therefore, the cost of waging war far outstripped the value of the objective, a "free" South Vietnam. These realities, like many others, were set aside as the war continued.

With the cost-versus-value question answered throughout the war, why did the United States continue to commit both its human and material resources to a war effort that was going nowhere? One explanation was that to withdraw, leaving the South Vietnamese to fend for themselves, would not be honoring America's commitment to them. It would be a dishonor to both countries and put up the question of how reliable the US was going to be with their many obligations around the world. These factors and others made an early withdrawal difficult. And Senior American leaders convinced themselves that their overwhelming firepower, even with severe constraints in effect, could defeat this enemy.[455]

The Restricted Focus on South Vietnam

Due to limited war restrictions, the United States was to bring the combat focus solely on engagements in South Vietnam. Attacks on the North had to be directly approved by President Johnson. His mandate was to attack North Vietnam solely to bring them into peace negotiations.

With these constraints, the military had no recourse other than to concentrate their efforts almost exclusively on South Vietnam. With ever-increasing violence from the air and on the ground, over time this policy ensured the destruction of South Vietnam without hope for ultimate victory against North Vietnam.

The center of gravity was in the North, not the South. Because this "war with no purpose" lasted for twelve violent years, the costs exceeded the value of the object. The inability to leave and the inability to end this war translated to the United States neither winning nor withdrawing.

The Civil-Military Disconnect

The civil-military disconnect created a mismatch between policy and strategy, where military tactics did not subordinate to political objectives. As Clausewitz said, "War cannot be divorced from political life, and whenever this occurs in our thinking about war, the many links that connect the two elements are destroyed, and we are left with something pointless and devoid of sense. No other possibility exists, then, than to subordinate the military point of view to the political."[456]

The issue with Vietnam was that the military was not a part of the president's trusted inner circle, where all the critical political and military strategy decisions took place. It was not surprising then that the military concept of fighting and winning the war never fully matched the political strategy held by President Johnson and Secretary of State McNamara. Policy drove strategy, but the military only grudgingly followed the civilian lead.

Clausewitz had envisioned quagmires like the American experience in Vietnam, writing, "In rare occasions, even if the war is subordinated to political life, that subordination can and did drastically affect the military instrument to the point that it was not free to bring an end to the war, let alone be victorious."[457]

McNamara's "Theory of Victory"

American senior civilian leadership did not allow itself to acknowledge North Vietnam's strategy. Leaders such as Johnson and McNamara believed US military strategies based on increased ferocity would likely persuade the enemy to surrender. They calculated that North Vietnam's leaders would come to the table and ultimately agree to peace terms—terms based on the withdrawal of their troops from South Vietnam.

This United States policy, as counterproductive as it became in South Vietnam, was used as an incentive for the enemy to stop pouring troops and supplies into South Vietnam. These incentives might have resulted in other enemies waving the white flag of surrender and negotiating from a position of weakness. But this enemy would not surrender under these circumstances. Leaders on the ground who understood the reality of the war, such as Colonel John Paul Vann, observed an enemy with an absolute adherence to fighting and dying regardless of the cost.

The United States' strategies were to use planned and measured attacks in the form of search-and-destroy missions in the south, with controlled bombing and artillery attacks in the north, always reaching out to President Johnson for final approval of the bombing plans. These strategies destroyed thousands of the enemy but ultimately did not alter North Vietnam's objectives.[458]

The Transfer of Vast Military Resources and Expertise Proved Insufficient

The United States was slow to develop a coherent strategy early in the war. They supported the South Vietnamese government and military with American military advisers, political leadership, and weaponry, as well as large sums of ever-increasing US dollars.

With this assistance, the United States had some influence on the day-to-day South Vietnamese military battle strategy. However, as advocates for South Vietnam, American military advisers, those in a position to see firsthand the South Vietnamese military's faults, began to develop a negative attitude about their ability and desire to fight the Vietcong effectively.

Colonel Vann observed that the senior leadership accepted South Vietnam's senior military and political leaders' claims of battlefield successes—but those successes did not actually exist. Efforts by the advisers to bring a more realistic view of the war to the American generals and their staff proved difficult, if not impossible.[459]

Seeking a Winning American Strategic Policy

The United States had awesome military power. It also had a self-perceived feeling of invincibility. Because of this, the senior civilian and military leaders did not believe a strategy was even necessary. Their military could simply overwhelm enemy forces with this power.

Critical to understanding why the United States failed to win the Vietnam War is acknowledging the early failure of the United States to comprehend the enemy's plan and capability for victory. They also seriously failed to understand the South Vietnamese government and its military's inability to resist North Vietnam's aggression.

This early failure to understand the nature of the war at the ground level continued through the tenure of the first and subsequent commanding generals of the Military Assistance Command, Vietnam (MAC-V). They preferred to believe more optimistic views of the war and transmit those views to their superiors in Washington, DC. Negative, independent estimates of how the war was progressing were considered far too grim and were rejected.[460]

Adverse news on the war was not allowed to affect the overall view of progress in winning the war by the president and his senior officials. President John F. Kennedy and his successor, Lyndon Johnson, routinely accepted the "good news" from the theater commander and the theater commander's chain of command. Information was usually filtered to them by their secretary of defense, Robert McNamara.

The reporting system had no room for reports that did not include progress toward victory. The established reporting formats were full of words such as *progress, enemy kill ratios, successful engagements with the enemy,* and *training efforts*. There was also a concerted effort to withhold negative information. It kept the American public unaware of what was happening in Vietnam, especially the data that showed failure rather than success.[461]

The Battle of Ap Bac

Though we will not focus on the individual battles of the Vietnam War as much as we have in other chapters, the lesser-known Battle of Ap Bac proved to be pivotal and is worth exploring to understand its impact on the rest of the war effort for the Communists, the United States, and its South Vietnamese ally. It not only demonstrated the unwillingness of the Army of the Republic of Vietnam (ARVN) to fight an aggressive war but also the unwillingness of US military commanders to tell the full story about the war. It also showed the chaotic, often dysfunctional relationship between the US military leadership and the ARVN.[462]

It's safe to assess that North Vietnam and the Viet Cong had widely divergent military objectives and strategies from the United States and South Vietnam. Clearly, North Vietnam and their Viet Cong counterparts in the South wanted to unify Vietnam under Communist rule. The South Vietnamese government and US goal was, on the surface, to ensure South Vietnam's freedom, though beneath the surface, the president of South Vietnam, Ngo Dinh Diem, was largely focused on self-preservation and maintaining a loyal, standing army to fend off the danger of a military coup. For this reason, the ARVN were quite reluctant to be aggressive on the battlefield.[463]

From the viewpoint of the ARVN and the US military, Ap Bac was fought against the VC on January 2, 1963, and on the next day, with the ARVN unintentionally fighting themselves. Ap Bac was a small hamlet south of Saigon where ARVN intelligence had determined through the interception of radio transmissions that a small VC contingent was stationed there. Colonel John Paul Vann, a US Army advisor to the ARVN 7th Infantry Division, was tasked with planning the assault with the ARVN military commanders.[464]

It should be said that ARVN troops were far less motivated than their VC and North Vietnamese counterparts. They were conscripted against their will, many for multiple years, with little hope of returning to their lives, their farms, and their families. This led to exceedingly low morale and a reluctance to fight at the troop level. ARVN military officers were also unwilling to see their troops lost in battle, not necessarily out of altruism. More realistically, because President Diem was wary of a military coup, he wanted to keep the highly loyal ARVN intact to stay in power. The approach of troop preservation remained a significant strategy of ARVN military leadership as a result.[465]

Ap Bac had relatively few casualties as it was fought on the scale of battalions. The South Vietnamese ARVN suffered around two hundred casualties while the VC around sixty. In addition, three Americans were killed, with eight wounded. For the Americans, ten CH-21 "Flying Bananas" were used to move troops on and off the battlefield, while five

UH-1 "Huey" gunships were used to provide covering fire and rescue attempts. In the end, five of these helicopters were shot down during the battle due to their vulnerability to machine gun fire in open terrain.[466]

The VC, for the first time in the war, had decided to dig in and repel the oncoming force, where previously they would retreat to fight another day when faced with a militarily superior ARVN opponent. The VC ranks, as opposed to the ARVN conscripts, were filled with veterans of their war against the French, and especially in the case of the 261st VC battalion, they were considered an elite unit with significant experience. Their foxholes, dug along the tree line to the west of Ap Bac, as well as their positions in the fruit groves in the vicinity of Ap Bac proved to provide ample concealment, improving their overall survivability, though they were outnumbered by an estimated five-to-one ratio.[467]

The plan called for troops to be delivered by American helicopters early on the morning of January 2. Fog and the fact that only ten CH-21s were available to deliver troops meant that the ARVN strength would build up slowly enough to provide the VC an advantage and remove any element of surprise.[468]

The first contact came between the ARVN and the VC when the fog- and terrain-concealed VC position was stumbled upon by the ARVN infantry. The ARVN leadership was quickly neutralized, and the troops were stuck on the ground, with little hope of survival or of resuming any positive military action.[469]

Evacuation attempts of these troops by the US helicopters proved disastrous as well, as several were downed and disabled during these attempts. Colonel Vann had implored the ARVN mechanized battalion with armored personnel carriers (APC) to move in to support this first troop movement, but the commander outright refused to do so. Only when this ARVN commander, Captain Ly Tong Ba, had been occupationally ("I'll tell your boss") and physically ("I'll have you shot") threatened by Vann did Ba reluctantly move his APCs into battle.[470]

Later in the battle, another ARVN commander refused to drop airborne troops behind the VC in Ap Bac to prevent the VC retreat and instead dropped them to the west, behind the APCs. This unwillingness to meet the enemy head-on would prove to be a theme for the entire war, crippling the southern war effort. When the ARVN airborne troops were finally deployed, many were dropped a half mile away from the intended drop zone, and the ones that got stuck in trees were quickly eliminated by VC troops.[471]

Although clearly a disaster for the US and its allies, Ap Bac was declared a success by General Harkins, and on the following day, more military action was planned, as he determined that they finally had the VC in a vulnerable position. ARVN field artillery, which was largely absent the previous day, started a barrage on what they believed were the enemy positions, albeit eighteen hours too late, and in error, they targeted ARVN troop positions. Little did anyone realize that the VC had fully retreated silently in the night and were in no danger of being attacked whatsoever.[472]

Journalists Neil Sheehan and Nick Turner, war correspondents who were touring what they believed to be a dormant battlefield with Brigadier General Robert York, were in more danger than the VC, having come under this artillery fire, which killed several ARVN troops.[473]

Stanley Karnow describes the Ap Bac battle from both the United States and Vietcong perspectives in his book *Vietnam: A History—The First Complete Account of Vietnam at War*. The Vietcong encampment at Ap Bac, viewed from the air by spotter aircraft and landing helicopters alike, appeared as natural vegetation. Vietcong resourcefulness included the use of irrigation ditches for safe communications and transport. Keeping a low profile when submerged in this muddy channel was a small price to pay for the Vietcong, as it was crucial for communication with their units and regular supplies, and the ditches provided a safe means of retreat if that became necessary.[474]

The Battle of Ap Bac proved to be a microcosm of the entire war effort in that it characterized the differences in the opposing sides and the frustrations that existed between the US and the South Vietnamese military and political leadership. Even with a VC adversary that was scraping by with arms imported clandestinely from the NVA, scavenged from US stockpiles left behind in battle, and on the black market, the militarily superior ARVN and US forces were challenged by the VC.[475]

When examining the question of why the United States was destined to leave Vietnam without meeting any of its strategic goals, the battle of Ap Bac serves as an excellent example to clarify how the North Vietnamese and Vietcong were ultimately victorious.[476] Of course, South Vietnam contributed heavily to its own demise, but ultimately the answer lay in how the two sides viewed the conflict.

Chopper wreck at the Battle of Ap Bac, Vietnam[477]

The Enemy is Gaining Strength

If the ARVN soldiers and their officers were not willing and able to defend their country, American efforts would never be able to compensate for that failure. By January 1963, the Vietcong main force and regional guerrillas had seized—or purchased on the Saigon black market—enough modern American weapons to stand and fight in ever-increasing numbers.[478]

What was a typical Vietcong platoon or company configuration was becoming battalion and brigade. An abundant supply of United States weaponry was available to aid in this unit expansion because of the outposts the ARVN evacuated due to the attacks by the Vietcong and the North Vietnamese Army. General Harkins had neglected to have these outposts dismantled. Once available, the weapons left behind became weapons of the enemy.

Virtually all the enemy platoons in South Vietnam—both the NVA and the Viet Cong—had a wide assortment of weapons, including both light and heavy machine guns, grenades, and a variety of ammunition. As they accepted battle, rather than retreat to fight another day (in an ambush or another minor contact), they came to expect that they would be able to compete and maneuver on their own, especially after they expanded into battalion-sized and larger units. These units required great discipline among the ranks and had specialized skills in establishing defensive and offensive battlespaces.[479]

The Viet Cong Find Their Voice

Colonel Vann described how the Vietcong learned at Ap Bac that they could survive even the lethal American technology. With success on the battlefield, they were unwilling to accept the possibility that their revolution might fail. With ample protection and concealment, as well as the art of ambush, they could succeed. The sheer depth of the foxholes allowed the Vietcong to duck down and escape harm from the fighter bombers and artillery.

During the battle, not only did they escape serious harm, but they destroyed five helicopters trying to bring in reinforcements for the South Vietnamese Army. They stood down a civil guard battalion and frustrated the American military advisers who saw an ally incapable of defeating a well-armed, well-entrenched enemy one-fifth its size and without air support. This initial success was unprecedented but repeated many times during the war. Of course, the Vietcong would also suffer enormous casualties and were willing to sacrifice more.[480]

The Army of the Republic of Vietnam (ARVN) Showed Their Weaknesses

The United States had armed their South Vietnamese partners with all the weapons necessary to succeed: Browning automatic rifles (BARs), clip-fed light machine guns, plenty of bullets and grenades, field artillery, H21s from the Korean War, and airpower from helicopters to attack fighters and bombers. But the Battle of Ap Bac made clear that the defeat of the Vietcong was going to be a lot more complicated than the South Vietnamese and most United States counterparts had ever believed.[481]

Sixteen individual eyewitness accounts of ARVN performance against these guerrillas brought out in detail many of the ARVN weaknesses that had to be improved if they were to succeed in their defense of South Vietnam, its government, and its people.

Some of the American advisers already knew what their weaknesses were. For others, it became apparent during and just following the battle.[482]

None Are So Blind as Those Who Will Not See

If only their superiors at the MAC-V headquarters would have read and taken these battle reports seriously. The critical comments were endorsed by the local American brigadier general, who forwarded the document to the commanding general and his staff. Many of the failings had to do with ARVN conduct—the failure to stand and fight the enemy. Those providing eyewitness comments regarding the ARVN performance confirmed this.[483]

Adviser observations, in short, were quite negative. One US adviser, Colonel Porter, in his report to the general staff at MAC-V, described the results of their efforts with the terms *failure, unwillingness,* and *futility.* According to Neil Sheehan, Colonel Porter "did not have a single redeeming comment to make."[484] The colonel further described their allies' conduct as "repetitive weaknesses." The cause of their failure, of course, was their reluctance to face the enemy.[485]

The ARVN Dereliction of Duty and Viet Cong Rise to the Occasion

Before the Battle of Ap Bac, the Vietcong units throughout South Vietnam (platoons or smaller) were able to conduct general asymmetric guerrilla operations. Afterward the Vietcong operated in larger, more lethal configurations. They were actively preparing to face their enemy as military equals. At Ap Bac, a South Vietnam civil guard unit had attempted to dislodge the Viet Cong from their massive entrenchment without success.

Colonel Vann assembled battle reports. One dereliction was from the commander of the South Vietnam Civil Guard, who surprisingly did not order his second battalion into the battle. It was an action that would have assured at least a concerted and coordinated attack by his forces. He also did not take any action to correct the unsuccessful targeting by his artillery, even after an American lieutenant begged him to do so. The lack of coordination with higher headquarters, as well as a lack of genuine will to win, was noted by the American advisers. The commander in chief, MAC-V, received the American adviser's report for review.[486]

The Army of Vietnam is Failing the Test

As part of the American military observers' on-site analysis, they wrote that the "South Vietnam military had sufficient armaments, but not the will to use them against the North Vietnam military." That would become the key problem throughout the war, "the South Vietnamese failure to fight for their country's freedom willingly." Although this does not describe every South Vietnamese unit, it does describe most groups.[487]

Colonel John Paul Vann, who had observed the conflict in its entirety from a low-flying L-19 spotter plane, had a clear vantage point from which he could assess the performance of ARVN forces and of the VC's strategy during the battle. Vann gave these observations to the press, which he summarized as "a miserable damn performance." He continued, saying, "These people won't listen. They make the same . . . mistakes over and over again." News headlines in papers in the United States stated how "the

Saigon forces had disgraced themselves."[488]

After journalists had passed on these observations through the press and added a few of their own, Arthur Krock, an AP syndicated columnist, would write that "no amount of US military assistance can preserve independence for a people who are unwilling to die for it."[489]

Prophetically, journalist David Halberstam summarized the extant issues in an article written a month prior to the battle. He observed that Vietnam was "a war fought in the presence of a largely uncommitted or unfriendly peasantry, by a government that has yet to demonstrate much appeal to large elements of its own people. The enemy is lean and hungry, experienced in this type of warfare, patient in his campaign, endlessly self-critical, and above all, an enemy who has shown that he is willing to pay the price."[490]

It appeared to be a case of journalists covering the war acknowledging—or at least understanding—the truth behind the war effort, where US military leadership was either willfully deceitful or, at the very least, ignorant in their assessment of the fundamental issues of the war.

Push Back on Reality

The American advisers received a hefty pushback on their negative insights of the battle report of Ap Bac. These observations, as well as the press' depiction of them, if taken as reality, would have been proof that this army—that Colonel Vann had to guide—was ludicrously inadequate for the task. Commanding General Harkins, MAC-V, received the report and after having time to digest its contents, reacted with great disapproval of it. His first reaction was to call for the firing of the report's primary author, Colonel Vann. General Harkins believed that Ap Bac had been a great victory for his South Vietnamese units.

Field officers like Colonel Vann knew better. He believed this battle's results would affect the course of the war unless the United States took direct control of the war and developed a winning strategy with far less reliance on the corrupt and inept ARVN force and its government.[491]

The commander in chief, MAC-V, General Harkin's inability to recognize the effectiveness of the enemy was not only his failing. In 1963 there were twelve American generals in Vietnam responsible for implementing strategy and developing specific goals and objectives in the theater that required an accurate assessment of the enemy. The preconceived assumptions of the generals regarding the enemy's so-called limitations were not correct in the case of the North Vietnamese military or of their guerrilla fighters in the South, the Vietcong. In effect, General Harkin's determination that the Battle of Ap Bac was a victory for the ARVN because their leaders said so bordered on a dereliction of duty.[492] Brigadier General York, who was a brief target of friendly fire by the misdirected ARVN artillery rounds on the second day, also gave a report that came to a different conclusion than that of his superior. General York's reaction that Harkin had declared the battle a success for the ARVN and the US was one of astonishment, much like the journalists that were present.[493]

The question remained, for journalists and military leaders such as Colonel Vann and General York, whether General Harkins truly believed that Ap Bac had been a success. Journalist Neil Sheehan, having been directly involved in the second day of the battle, wondered as well whether Harkins had believed ARVN General Cao that the VC were still in Ap Bac the next day, even though Vann had made it clear that they were gone. The morning after the battle, Harkins was asked by Peter Arnett of the Associated Press and David Halberstam of the *New York Times* what he thought of the battle, to which he replied, "We've got them in a trap, and we're going to spring it in half an hour."[494] They knew this was not true and was contrary to their observations. In Sheehan's estimation, Harkins tended to believe what reinforced his own beliefs.[495] The general's overinflated opinion of the American war machine and the South Vietnamese army's capabilities would only support this confirmation bias and may have falsely linked American power with that of his ARVN units, as they were trained and supplied by members of that same American war machine. General Harkins also assumed the fundamental inferiority of the Vietcong.[496]

Finally, did America's senior generals have preconceived assumptions about their enemy that were now being tested? The commonly held view by historians was that they tended to be veterans of the Korean War and the Second World War. These experiences managed to prevent them from seeing the current reality. They believed their military was nearly invincible. Furthermore, they believed that the training provided to South Vietnam was also superior. The problem was that ARVN units were not superior. Unless leadership came to a real understanding of the South Vietnam government and military, continued failure was inevitable.[497]

Tet Offensive: Accelerating Loss of Public Support

What the Battle of Ap Bac did for exposing the ARVN as inadequate for the job of defending South Vietnam, the Tet Offensive showed that the ARVN was unable and unwilling to defend major cities as well. The Tet Offensive was a large-scale military operation launched in South Vietnam by the NVA and the Viet Cong after months of planning. The Tet holiday marks the beginning of the lunar new year, symbolizing a fresh start to the year, and lasts a week. The VC had agreed to a Tet holiday truce in 1968, which some in US military and intelligence leadership believed was just a regrouping for a renewed offensive after the holiday. Instead, the NVA and the VC would attack in the middle of the holiday, breaking the truce.[498]

The planning had started in the fall of 1967, led by General Le Duan, a former peasant who had risen through the ranks of the North Vietnamese Army during action against the French. Ho Chi Minh and General Giap feared heavy losses due to this Tet plan, though both were largely excluded in planning due to political maneuvering within the Communist Party and existing medical ailments that allowed other senior members of the party to begin taking the lead. The Soviets and the Chinese also voiced concerns with the plans.[499]

The offensive targeted two dozen military bases and major cities in South Vietnam, with the attacks being carried out mostly by Viet Cong in the south and NVA troops further north. Some elements of surprise had been lost because a radio transmission that was to be played in anticipated captured radio stations around the country was intercepted by ARVN troops. And the overall effort was further hindered by the VC's own intention to keep the offensive a secret by withholding details from their own troops for as long as possible.[500]

Militarily, the intention of the NVA and VC was to destroy three to four ARVN divisions and to cause a general uprising that Le Duan earnestly believed would occur once NVA and VC troops arrived. This uprising did not occur, and some have speculated it was due to the people not being convinced, for good reason, that the military assaults would lead to victory.

Of the major targets, Saigon was by far the most important but arguably the least successful of the assaults. In downtown Saigon, many of the VC troops became lost while moving to their respective starting lines because of the size of the city but also because they were not as familiar with the streets. The assaults began at one thirty in the morning on January 31, targeting several key civilian and military locations. The largest siege took place at the US Embassy, where nineteen Viet Cong commandos stormed the compound just before three in the morning. They blew a large hole in the compound wall that provided entry while the two military policemen at the gate closed and barred it while fending off an attack. At the first sign of trouble, the South Vietnamese guards fled into the city. The attack was not successfully repelled until far into the morning, and in the end, all the VC and five Americans were killed.[501] The embassy was seen as a humiliation for the Americans, as much of the press was covering the attack from their bases of operations in Saigon. Tan Son Nhut was the strategically important air base in Saigon, and North Vietnamese leadership knew that it was important for not only controlling the skies around Saigon, but also troop movements in the South. It was attacked early in the morning on January 31. The main gate and the petroleum storage tanks were the primary targets. The attack was repelled by early afternoon, with around fifty US and ARVN killed and around seven hundred VC killed.

The Battle of Hue City was the most symbolically relevant and, some would say, the most successful assault for the NVA and Viet Cong. Hue is an ancient, imperial capital of Vietnam that was taken initially unopposed on January 31, 1968. The NVA and the local VC contingent walked into the city with very little resistance, though later, the action of the US Marines and ARVN to retake the city would lead to a long, bloody urban conflict. During the occupation, however, the NVA troops and VC massacred thousands of people they believed to be enemies. There would also be damage to the city's history, including parts of the citadel and the enclosed palace. It would take three and a half weeks for the US and ARVN to retake the city, which occurred on February 24, 1968.[502]

Just to the west of Hue was the US military base at Khe Sanh, which General Westmoreland had focused on in preparation for coming NVA assaults. There was the justified belief that the NVA would attempt to create another Diem Bien Phu, which is where the NVA had decisively defeated the French in 1954, thus ending their war with France. The assault on Khe Sanh by the NVA started earlier than the others, on January 21, and lasted for seventy-seven days. The NVA had Khe Sanh surrounded to block all resupply routes to the base, though the base had been stocked ahead of time in anticipation of military action by the NVA. During the siege, airlifts became critical for resupply, and airstrikes and artillery strikes were common on NVA troop positions. The siege finally broke when Operation Pegasus opened a path to the base by US forces. Over two hundred US Marines were killed and another 1,600 were wounded during the siege, while an estimated ten to fifteen thousand NVA troops were killed during the battle.[503]

Leading up to Tet, the US military was becoming more desperate to hand off the reigns to the ARVN. The Tet Offensive was not the most confidence-inspiring performance for the ARVN. The US had stepped up its military presence in the country through a large influx of US troops that was assisted by the advent of the military draft that lasted from 1964 to 1973.

Tran Do, a Lieutenant General in the NVA, confessed after the war that "in all honesty, we didn't achieve our main objective, which was to spur uprisings throughout the south. Still, we inflicted heavy casualties on the Americans and their puppets, and that was a big gain for us. As for making an impact in the United States, it had not been our intention, but it turned out to be a fortunate result."⁵⁰⁴

What Tran Do was alluding to was that NVA leaders would later realize that, though they failed militarily, they succeeded in destroying the American people's will to win the war and in precipitating the fall of President Johnson in an election year.⁵⁰⁵

The Trinity of War and the Failure of Leadership?

Why did the United States end up losing the war? In *On War*, Clausewitz speaks of three key elements of a modern war, especially in a democracy where the people's support provides legitimacy for the actions of the executive and the congress. That support is even more critical in the case of a long-term war.⁵⁰⁶

"The Executive swears allegiance to the people who they are there to protect. Congress is the closest to the people in that it legislates in their name. That provides the political and legal structure in which the people reside."⁵⁰⁷ Particularly in the case of Vietnam, this breaking of trust between the American people and the government led to eventual defeat.

It was the only way that America's effort to stem the tide of Communist expansion in Vietnam could occur. President Johnson's approach to the American public and his shunning of the advice of his senior military leaders ran directly counter to Clausewitz's trinity of war. This final element of friction is often described as civil-military relations. The key to the Clausewitz trinity is the need to achieve the proper equilibrium between these three pillars of the trinity. There were avenues to obtain American public support, as well as ways to gain its opposition. In the final analysis, President Johnson and his senior executive team accomplished the latter, causing both extreme civil disobedience and a situation in which time ran out on whatever strategies the United States might have implemented in Vietnam.⁵⁰⁸

The first of three specific significant leadership errors—the breakdowns that were to sabotage the war effort—was President Johnson knowingly withholding essential information to both the people and the military about the significant expansion of the war. He attempted everything possible to avoid the American population's inquiries about troop strength and potential troop increases. Successes or failures on the battlefield, the battleworthiness of the South Vietnamese military, and the critical transition from a South Vietnamese-led war to an American-led war would prove to be America's downfall in this war.[509]

As the war dragged on without resolution, and especially after the Tet Offensive in 1968, the American people began to speak out about this failing leadership. Ultimately overwhelmed, President Johnson's conduct regarding the conflict proved enormously inadequate, and media coverage of Tet and its aftermath was the final catalyst to jumpstart the anti-war movement. Both the *doves* and the *hawks*—those for and against the war—within the people and Congress began pressuring the Johnson administration for an end to the war effort, to withdraw summarily, or to obtain an honorable way to negotiate an end to the United States' involvement. These leadership mistakes set in motion the end of his presidency and the end of the United States' participation in this twelve-year war.

Michael Handel points out in *Masters of War* that Carl von Clausewitz's trinity needed to be in harmony and that it was impractical to deceive the people for success in war.

> War and politics could not be separated as was often assumed; that military victory does not automatically guarantee ultimate political victory; that all wars, in particular those that are prolonged, require the political support and consensus of the people in whose name they are waged; that the military is only one of the three elements essential for success in war; and that without a harmonious balance among these three elements essential for success in war (the others being the government and the people), and that without a harmonious balance among these three elements, wars cannot be won no matter how just the cause or how great the effort invested.[510]

Clausewitz seemed to foretell this conflict between the elements of the trinity as it related to the Vietnam War: "The friction caused within the trinity due to the stress felt during the war, chaos with the social, economic, or other elements of society may certainly develop. If this friction does not end, usually, through communication and better understanding, a conflict leading to severe disagreements between the elements of the trinity will arise."[511]

Handel acknowledges that the weight of each element of the trinity need not be completely equal, which was certainly the case in Vietnam: "The intricate [complex] relationships among the three dominant tendencies define the nature of war. The three dominant tendencies rarely carry equal weight; their relative intensity and relationships change according to the circumstances of each case."[512]

Although the three may not exist with equal weight at any given time during the war, if there exists such a large imbalance, especially in the case of a war like Vietnam, the imbalance in the relationships can become destabilizing over time. One element can become less supportive over a longer period of time because they have lost faith in the other two elements, and as a result, a successful conclusion to the war becomes less likely. More balance and agreement between the three elements can only help to pursue a stable war effort focused on the initial objectives of the war.

Public demonstrations against the war were quickly expanding in both sheer ferocity and the number of people directly involved throughout American cities. The American people became President Johnson's and then President Nixon's center of gravity, which was quickly spinning out of control.

A theory that ignored the relationships between the government, the military, and the people would conflict with the social reality and become useless. An effort to develop an approach that maintains a balance between the three pillars must occur. This achievement would ensure a clear relationship between the government, the military, and the people. Some South Vietnamese units, as well as the United States government and military, as brave as they were on the battlefield, did not balance within the South Vietnamese society or the American culture during the Vietnam War.

Marines riding atop an M-48 tank southwest of Phu Bai[513]

The Beginning of the End

Despite the fact that the war spanned the administrations of four presidents, it became Lyndon Johnson's war as he took specific actions to exclude the people, the congress, and the military from his management of it. Prior to Johnson's presidency, the US's involvement in the war was limited to an advisory capacity for the South Vietnamese government. Under JFK's administration, American casualties had been limited, as "less than 120 had been killed, and the number of men wounded seriously enough to require hospitalization had not yet reached 250."[514] Johnson chose to escalate the war, taking the initiative to increase the US's involvement in the way he desired, which was to exclude Congress, the public, and, for the most part, the Joint Chiefs of Staff in decision-making.

When real scrutiny began in Congress regarding the costs of the Vietnam War, as well as questions about the strategy that would bring an end to the war, the public became suspicious. That interest climbed when congressmen and the people understood that numerous members of the Joint Chiefs of Staff and the Vietnam theater commander were meeting in Congress to answer questions from the congressmen.

During these hearings regarding the progress or lack of progress in the war, President Johnson and his senior civilian staff required the top military leaders from the Joint Chiefs of Staff also to be present. The Johnson administration successfully convinced these senior military leaders to provide both misinformation and lies regarding specific details of the war. "In the days before the president made his duplicitous public announcement concerning Westmoreland's request [for more troops], the Chiefs, with the exception of the commandant of the Marine Corps Green, withheld from congressmen their estimates of the amount of force that would be needed in Vietnam. As he had during the Gulf of Tonkin hearings, [chairman of the Joint Chiefs of Staff, General Earle] Wheeler lent his support to the president's deception of Congress."[515]

This misinformation happened even in the face of the dramatic transition from a South Vietnamese–led war to a United States–directed war that necessitated the transfer of thousands of soldiers from the United States and Europe to Vietnam.

The senior executive branch attendees, as well as the senior military leaders, failed to meet their constitutional mandate by not providing clear and truthful answers to congressional questions. The war effort was fast becoming needlessly destructive, pointless, and without political meaning.[516]

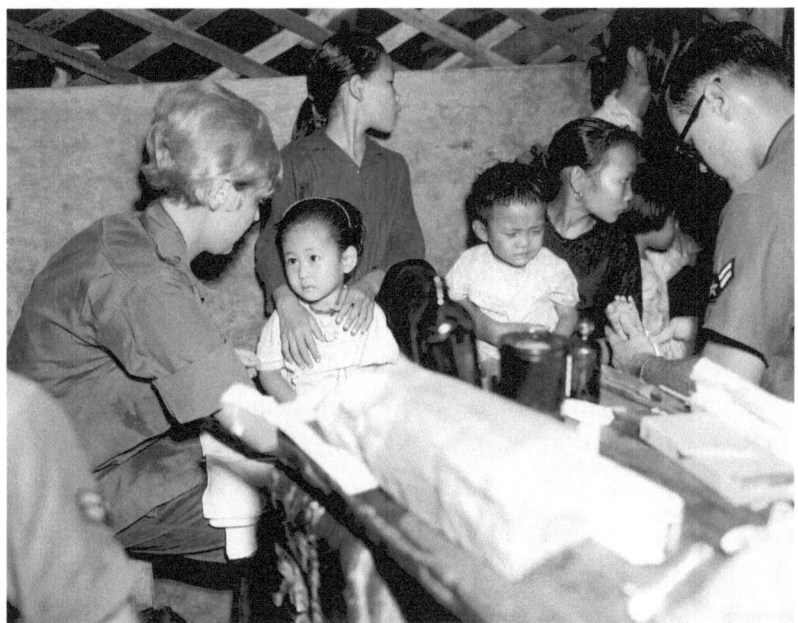

US Medical Staff Assist Vietnamese Children[517]

Presidential Leadership: The Buck Stops Here

Why did the United States lose the war? Was it due to poor presidential leadership? There were ways to obtain this support, as well as ways to gain increased opposition. In the final analysis, President Johnson and his senior executive team accomplished the latter, causing both extreme civil disobedience and a situation in which time ran out on whatever strategies the United States might have implemented. This opposition continued to gain traction into the next presidential administration.

When American soldiers, sailors, and airmen were coming home from serving in Vietnam, they faced a hostile American public. Rather than receiving treatment as heroes, as they had in past wars, the opposite occurred. The American public considered them villains responsible for the defoliation of Vietnam and the death of countless innocents.[518]

The "buck" stopped with President Johnson. He had lost his mandate to lead the fight in Southeast Asia against this small but determined enemy long before. In opposition to Clausewitz's advice, President Johnson had never defined a clear mission for the military.[519]

President Johnson relied totally on his trusted senior civilian advisory team throughout the war. When members of the Joint Chiefs of Staff provided a list of measures considered "essential" for victory, they were not successful in gaining his support. Several of the proposals were to attack previously restricted areas in North Vietnam, the real center of gravity for the enemy.

The Joint Chiefs of Staff recommended the mobilization of the reserves, the increased bombing of North Vietnam, and the mining and bombing of North Vietnam's major port, Haiphong. However, these recommendations did not meet President Johnson's requirement for a limited war strategy.[520]

Despite Johnson's retrospective assertion that his administration may have been wrong, he claimed his senior civilian and military leaders agreed with him throughout the war. His government was, as historian George Herring observed, "both wrong and divided." Since then, the Joint Chiefs of Staff and other military leaders have been heavily criticized for not insisting that their recommendations agreed with the United States Constitution and their duties within it.[521]

Johnson refused to accept the military leadership's preferred strategy—the total invasion of North Vietnam. To keep the Joint Chiefs of Staff's attention, he gave them only enough information to suggest they might get more later. The senior military leaders could not change the strategy. By July 1965, even with decisions for significant troop commitments being executed, there remained deep divisions over strategy.[522]

Then secretary of state Robert McNamara sensed, in retrospect, his partial responsibility for not getting these two crucial pillars of the trinity to work well together to resolve the war effort's fundamental challenges: "I clearly erred by not forcing, then (1965), or late in either Saigon or Washington a knock-down, drag-out debate over the loose assumptions, unmade questions, and thin analysis understanding our military strategy in Vietnam. I had spent twenty years as a manager identifying problems and forcing organizations, often against their will, to think deeply and realistically about the alternative course of action and their consequences. I doubt I will ever fully understand why I did not do so here."[523]

This admission partially attempts to come to grips with how he managed the Vietnam War. It implies that military and political strategy was formed by himself and a few inner circle senior civilians in coordination with the president. He alludes to having left out the most apparent decision-maker, the top military leadership. The military leaders were required by the US Constitution to provide direct advice about the conduct of the war. Both the Johnson administration and the military were derelict in forcing that to happen.[524] However, regardless of what McNamara believed were his failings, it may have been impossible for him to encourage President Johnson to accept any plan beyond Johnson's limited war strategy.

President Johnson was interested in only one thing: his advisers reaching a consensus, not necessarily an agreement, about the strategy going forward. He would agree to some of the requests by the military, but he never approved enough to amount to an effective military plan for moving forward. That remained in his hands alone. It was like he would throw them a bone solely to put them in agreement with the consensus. Real differences were never addressed.[525]

Finally, he left out the people and the congress—thus ensuring a long and destructive war that ended very badly. In this way, the Battle of Ap Bac was the first act in a play that would run for twelve years. The Battle of Ap Bac possessed elements that were to be repeated time and time again throughout the war. These elements began to paint a picture of why we lost the battle. The ARVN leaders failed their people, and they failed themselves by continuing to be overcome by greed, corruption, and military ineptitude. The United States should have expected more from them. Instead, it accepted the ARVN's failings and fought the war on its own.

The US leaders also failed to win the support of the South Vietnamese people, especially the rural farmers. The loss of this major center of gravity, the Vietnamese people, was not reversible. In time the United States gave up efforts to reduce governmental corruption. It also gave up relying on a native military that, although fully armed by the US, found that they could not prevent their failure to meet the challenge of an unrelenting and dedicated enemy. The United States found themselves in a position where they could not accomplish victory with or without the South Vietnamese government and military. The United States tried but ran out of time. The people insisted America depart from Vietnam.[526]

Conclusions

There were severe political constraints on the military strategy that significantly inhibited actions that might have defeated the enemy. We were never allowed to invade North Vietnam with the central military power it possessed. The United States had the incorrect strategy for defeating North Vietnam and the Vietcong, and as a result they lost the war; North Vietnam had the correct procedure for beating the United States and South Vietnam, and they won the war.

During the Vietnam War, 46,163 Americans were killed in combat, 10,298 died of noncombat causes, and around 1,800 Americans were declared missing in action. Astoundingly, over 300,000 were wounded in action. Among the South Vietnamese, 635,357 people were killed, with over two-thirds (415,000) being civilians. Also, 1,434,026 were wounded, while two-thirds of those (935,000) were civilians. There is more debate about casualty figures for the Vietcong and North Vietnamese, as the estimated number of killed in action ranges from 666,000 to 924,048. Civilian losses in North Vietnam are estimated at 65,000.[527]

In a conversation in Hanoi in April of 1975, a United States Army colonel said to a North Vietnamese colonel, "You know you never defeated us on the battlefield." The North Vietnamese colonel pondered this remark a moment. "That may be so," he replied, "but it is also irrelevant."[528] The Vietnamese colonel may have been correct that the success of the North Vietnamese made those lost battles irrelevant, though that doesn't disguise the fact that all parties to the war lost a staggering number of countrymen. It is also important that all of the people who were lost in this conflict are mourned.

US Army Soldiers led by Major Bruce Crandall on a "Search and Destroy" mission with a supporting UH-1 "Huey" Iroquois[529]

CHAPTER SEVEN

THE IRAQ WAR

During the great debate surrounding the invasion of Iraq in 2002, a set of assumptions were made that proved to be supremely flawed. They resulted in a policy-strategy mismatch. Months of planning focused on building a coalition for the commencement of the invasion and focused almost exclusively on military operations necessary for the attack and the subsequent beheading of the Iraqi government. Little if any of the planning developed a vision of post-war Iraq, such as determining what roles the United Nations, nongovernment agencies (NGOs), and elements of the United States government would have.[530]

A vast majority of planning time focused on military operations and how soon those operations would be complete. By the time President George W. Bush announced military operations were ending, events within Iraq made it evident that the real challenges of the war were just beginning. The hard reality was that once military operations were complete, the business of nation-building would begin.

Richard Cheney went from providing prophetic words, as secretary of defense in 1992, about the specific issues that would have to be addressed before any political goals could be met to supporting the invasion of Iraq in 2003 as vice president. Just eighteen months after the first Iraq War ended, Cheney had asked, hypothetically, "Once we had rounded him up and gotten rid of his government, then the question is, what do you put in its place? You know, you then have accepted the responsibility for governing Iraq." He had also asked, "Now what kind of government are you going to establish? Is it going to be a Kurdish government, or a Shi'ia government, or a Sunni government, or maybe a government based on the old Baathist Party, or some mixture thereof? You will have, I think by that time, lost the support of the Arab coalition that was so crucial to our operations over there."[531]

In Iraq in 1992, Cheney understood the great challenge associated with any invasion of Iraq. For whatever reason, he put those concerns aside and supported the full-blown military attack of 2003 despite his earlier apprehensions. This plan would have to include all members of Iraq's society and one government that could defend itself and its people. The American government and military belatedly realized no real planning had occurred regarding war termination. If they had completed their preparation, they might have made the decision not to invade Iraq in the first place or at least planned for the need for nation-building.

In the Iraq War, a series of faulty assumptions led the United States and its coalition of allies to decide to go to war. These assumptions proved to be a series of ill-advised adjustments that cost America dearly in both lives and resources.

It was presumed by government officials that the United States would have to overthrow the Iraqi president and prime minister Saddam Hussein, or they would have to bring democracy to Iraq at gunpoint. It is now understood that "building a new state needed to be done by the Iraqis themselves."[532] However, the Kurds had one answer, the Shia had another, and the Sunnis had still another. The population needed essential services for the people to be secure. Hussein was heading in the opposite direction. For most Iraqis, with or without Hussein, the future was not bright, and the invaders would have to assist them. However, the primary reason America wanted to invade had to do with Saddam Hussein's threats to use weapons of mass destruction (WMDs) on its enemies, not improving the lives of the Iraqi people.[533]

Reaching a Decision

The Bush administration began planning for war as early as 2001. The rationale for going to war started with the 2002 UN Iraqi Resolution, which authorized the use of military force and gave as its rationale that Saddam Hussein's government was developing weapons of mass destruction. The resolution increased in importance with Saddam Hussein's continued support of international terrorists.[534]

President Bush feared waiting too long to decide to invade, which he deemed disastrous, believing the WMD violations and the widespread support of terrorists would make delays to the attack devastating. George W. Bush was convinced there was an immediate need for action against Iraq's efforts to develop WMDs, stating, "We cannot wait for the final proof, the smoking gun that could come in the form of a mushroom cloud."[535]

President Bush also related the current issue of invading to the 9/11 terrorist attacks. If he waited for the danger to fully develop, it would be too late. He resolved to confront the threat from Iraq one way or another. He then coordinated with other world leaders to tell them about his decision. These allies had mixed feelings regarding going to war. All but Great Britain would not send soldiers.

On November 8, 2002, the United Nations Security Council wrote Resolution 1441. All fifteen members agreed to give Iraq a final opportunity to comply with its WMD obligations. According to the Resolution, Iraq had to disarm. The United States and the United Kingdom continued to argue that Saddam Hussein was developing weapons of mass destruction. They agreed that this was a significant threat to his neighbors and the United States. The United States believed Iraq's failure to comply with UN Resolution 1441 would require both military force and an end to Saddam Hussein's regime. The United Kingdom agreed force would be necessary, but not for a regime change.

President Bush believed that Iraq was armed and dangerous and that Hussein's regime had to end. The House and Senate then passed a joint resolution authorizing the president's power to call the United States military forces to duty during a time of national crisis. In taking this action, President Bush expressed nationwide once again in October 2003 that Iraq was armed and dangerous and that Saddam Hussein should be removed from power.[536]

American public opinion was overwhelmingly behind him, with 72 percent believing an invasion was necessary. They, too, believed Saddam Hussein had been involved in plans for the 9/11 attack. President Bush continued to demand that Iraq comply with UN sanctions but ultimately declared that America could not wait for any final proof.[537]

President Bush was convinced that Saddam Hussein would never resign, nor would he ever divulge the facts about his production of WMDs. The United Nations Monitoring and Verification Commission and the International Atomic Energy Agency assumed the responsibility to inspect any facility at any time and question anyone to ensure compliance. However, if they did not prove there was no manufacture of these weapons, the United States would have to go forward alone.[538]

The American public supported President Bush, but the same could not be said for the rest of the world. The United States and Great Britain ran counter to opinion polls around the world that showed that people of nearly all nations opposed a war without a United Nations mandate. Ultimately, that would not affect America's plan to invade.

The United States believed Iraq's noncompliance constituted a danger to world peace and significantly increased the likelihood of Iraq WMD attacks. It was becoming increasingly clear that America was headed to war, regardless of world opinion. It was even the conclusion of the United Nations Secretary-General Kofi Annan, who thought the Iraq War was illegal. In his view, America's invasion was not in conformity with the Security Council rules and regulations. His position was ignored by the Bush administration, and war commenced.

A Gallup poll conducted between January 11–14, 2002, indicated most United States citizens supported the military option. The progression in war planning reached a certain point in which President Bush met with the German chancellor to discuss the potential for an invasion. President Bush told the chancellor that "the military option was the last choice, but [he] would use it if necessary." This may have been a ploy to obscure his intentions until the military forces were ready to proceed.[539]

The Neoconservative Influence

The Neoconservatives, a political interest group that emerged in the late 1960s, were gaining traction within the American government. Neoconservatives pushed for the promotion of democracy throughout the world and encouraged military intervention in international affairs. During the Cold War, the Neoconservatives had supported war as the first alternative. Eventually, President Bush accepted their premise as it related to war. He stated, "We are in a conflict between good and evil by its name, and we will lead the world in opposing it."[540]

War would become a passion not only for Neoconservatives but for President Bush as well. Their ideas of a new world order were soon accepted not only by President Bush but by others like Vice President Cheney and high-level subordinates within the administration as well. President Bush dropped many of the previous beliefs he had promoted during the campaign and replaced them with policies largely adapted from Neoconservative writings.[541]

The Neoconservatives held morality as their guiding light. They believed the United States' power and the superior performance of its free-market system was the primary source of good in the world. When nations were overrun by communism, there was, at least until 1989, no second chance. Morality was the issue. "The weapon was American moral authority versus the Soviet system that enslaved minds and bodies for most of a century." Much to the chagrin of the Neoconservatives, regime change took place in Moscow without one battle with the North Atlantic Treaty Organization (NATO). Their view was that without a military attempt to free nations around the world, the United States' moral authority would be seriously at risk.[542]

Neoconservative Beliefs and Objectives

Stefan Halper and Jonathan Clarke, in *America Alone*, describe today's Neoconservatives as united under three tenets: (1) "The human condition is defined as a choice between good and evil. Political character is to be found in the willingness of the good to confront the evil;" (2) "The fundamental determinant of the relationship between states rests on military power and the willingness to use it;" and (3) "The Middle East and global Islam [is] the principal theater for American overseas interests."[543]

In putting these assertions into practice, Neoconservatives analyzed moral categories as black-and-white and absolute. The Neoconservatives focused on military force as the first, not the last, option of foreign policy. They repudiated the lessons of Vietnam, which they interpreted as undermining American will toward the use of force, and embraced the "lessons of Munich," where France and the United Kingdom had allowed the Nazi German occupation of the Sudetenland as an appeasement to Adolf Hitler in September of 1938 in an effort to avoid war. They understood establishing the virtues of preemptive military action as a key lesson for America.[544]

However, there was some political opposition to these objectives. Secretary of State Colin Powell believed the Neoconservatives had taken American international relations on an unfortunate path. This belief would not be understood by the country until the war failed to make Iraq's transition to a free, democratic nation.[545]

The Neoconservatives took particular interest in Saddam Hussein and his administration's program to influence Libya and other nearby Arabic nations. The Neoconservatives came to believe the effort was momentary and containable if the United States took immediate action against Saddam Hussein and his administration. They thought America, for the first time since the Second World War, was suffering a crisis of international legitimacy. America had to end the crisis. They considered using the power of the United States and its military forces as the first option of international policy.[546]

The Neoconservatives disagreed with diplomatic agencies such as the State Department and their current country-specific, diplomacy-first focus. As expressed in the National Security Strategy of 2002, which some consider the clearest espousal of applied Neoconservative doctrine that exists, it states that "it has taken almost a decade for us to comprehend the true nature of [the weapons of mass destruction] threat. Given the goals of rogue states and terrorists, the United States can no longer solely rely on a reactive posture as we have in the past. The inability to deter a potential attacker, the immediacy of today's threats, and the magnitude of potential harm that could be caused by our adversaries' choice of weapons do not permit that option. We cannot let our enemies strike first."[547] The Bush Doctrine, which included preemptive action against whomever the US deemed was a threat to US safety and sovereignty, was now in effect. Although these examples tend to be both simplistic and radical, they are relevant to the way Neoconservatives tended to view the world and America's position in it.

In that way, Neoconservative political thought was similar to the prevailing thought patterns of the United States' leadership during the Cold War. Neoconservatives observed what they concluded were fundamental flaws in the despotic elements of the world's political landscape.[548] Cold War leaders, many well before the Neoconservatives, believed in the "fallibility of the Communist system." In 1947, George Kennan had already described the Communist regime as the "seeds of its own decay." The leaders in Neoconservative thought believed in the fallibility of their enemies as well.[549]

The Neoconservative Intent

Neoconservative focus was on the utilization of power in any foreign policy. Military force was the tool used to begin the procedure of change in Iraq. They viewed America's Vietnam experience as self-defeating. They looked to the lessons of the Second World War and the Munich appeasement as their map to completely remake Iraq in their image. "Former Iraq leadership would be tried and disposed of so that power in the new government, chosen by them, would rule this new republic."[550]

Neoconservatives abhorred diplomatic agencies such as the State Department. They rejected the use of diplomacy to gain international accommodations, such as through treaties. Their ultimate theme was "global unilateralism." Because, in their view, the United States was superior to any other nation in the world, they believed they could install a system containing "American virtues." This view also allowed the freedom to disclaim international criticism.

Though some Neoconservatives may have believed that Ronald Reagan fit the profile of a Neoconservative president, this could not be further from the truth. Balance-of-power politics, where diplomacy and treaties were sought to limit the power of any one country, were a staple of American foreign policy during the Cold War. Once the Cold War ended during G. H. W. Bush's tenure, Neoconservatism would emerge from the ashes. After the Cold War, there was no real threat to American military superiority, and the United States' path to unilateral dominance in world politics, as the Neoconservatives sought, was assured.[551]

How Much Was George W. Bush Influenced by Neoconservative Thinking?

Neoconservatives offered a blueprint for a comprehensive revamping of American foreign policy around their objectives.[552] Once the Neoconservatives caught the ear of the president regarding these objectives, they began to heavily influence him and the impending march to war.

Neoconservative contributors offered a strategy for victory in Iraq if the president and his administration chose to follow it, establishing "the standard of a global superpower that intends to shape the international environment of its own advantage." In operational terms, this would require an "American foreign and defense policy that [was] unapologetic, idealistic, assertive, and funded well beyond existing appropriations. America must not only be the world's policeman or its Sheriff, but it must also be its beacon and guide."[553]

Neoconservatives were becoming a powerful political interest group within the American government. Eventually, even President Bush accepted their premise, as it related to the war in Iraq.

Neoconservative concepts became a passion for President Bush, Vice President Cheney, and high-level subordinates within the administration. President Bush dropped many of the previous beliefs he had campaigned on during his run for president. Having prominent Neoconservatives holding high government positions helped facilitate their point of view.

Possession of Weapons of Mass Destruction: An Intelligence Failure

"Accusations of faulty evidence and alleged shifting rationale became the focal point for critics of the war." They charged that the Bush administration purposely fabricated evidence that would justify the release of American military power. The Central Intelligence Agency (CIA) and other intelligence organizations were required to provide information as they knew it, not what the government wished to hear. They were required to abide by the Biblical quotation, "And ye shall know the truth; and the truth shall set you free." Because of the pressure from the Bush administration and their interest in time, the American government tended to go to weaker intelligence organizations, not the CIA, for their information.[554]

Because the intelligence community wavered in their analysis of Iraq's possession of WMDs, the intelligence agencies had to decide whether to comply with the will of the administration or not. Once they complied, the American and British governments were free to continue with their false narrative regarding Iraq's possession of these weapons—weapons that supposedly could harm any nation Saddam Hussein chose. This narrative led to the American and British governments' eventual loss of credibility.

Vice President Cheney and the CIA would rely solely on raw intelligence. Cheney and the hawks in the administration believed that information that was not fully validated or corroborated would have to be used if the government's strategy to invade was to continue. Eventually, George Tenet, chief of the CIA, testifying in the United States Senate, was forced to admit his agency's findings that Saddam had obtained nuclear materials from an African nation had been false.[555]

Within the Pentagon there also existed a secret unit, the Office of Special Plans. This unit belonged to the undersecretary for policy, Douglas Feith. The office had the freedom to reinterpret as it reviewed intelligence material. They elected not to go through a rigorous analytic process. They preferred relying on their ideological preconceptions. Feith's office, on occasion, sent its findings straight to "friendly media outlets"[556] to falsely demonstrate that the information was credible.[557]

The administration avoided the Pentagon's professional standard by obtaining information that validated their views. According to one anonymous intelligence officer, "You cannot just cherry-pick evidence that suits your case and ignore the rest. It is a cardinal rule of intelligence."[558] Creating such an analysis would fail to meet the standards of accurate knowledge. Lacking independently found data, senior government leaders could choose what they wanted to believe—and President Bush wanted to believe Iraq was a clear and present danger.[559]

The Bush administration utilized intelligence agencies that did not require the presentation of the whole truth about Iraq's possession of WMDs. Consequently, President Bush was free to rely on his assumptions of the intelligence data provided. That would prove to be disastrous to the government's credibility. A similar fate befell the prime minister of Great Britain for proof of a link between Iraq and certain terrorist groups, namely Al-Qaeda.[560]

Prime Minister Tony Blair tried to improve his position with a disbelieving populous. He attempted to heighten the immediacy and magnitude of the threat, claiming that Saddam Hussein possessed WMDs and could deploy them within a few minutes. To be accepted, this claim required accurate intelligence information to be rewritten to produce a politically palatable conclusion. In September 2002, a dossier in the United Kingdom entitled "Iraq's WMD" was found. The document was proven wrong, much to the embarrassment of the prime minister and intelligence services. The record, along with WMDs and the suicide of David Kelly, the lead scientist on WMDs in Great Britain, led to further legal scrutiny.

These events brought on a court of inquiry. Prime Minister Blair was brought to trial to explain the suicide and the problem with the Iraq WMD inquiry. The prime minister and intelligence services received enormous damage to their reputations over these issues in Great Britain and internationally.

The problem between London and Washington was what the political authorities wanted their intelligence services to say about the Iraq threat. There was an absence of available intelligence containing "hard, rigorously sourced intelligence." This intelligence did not exist.[561]

It took a long time for intelligence organizations to overcome their failures to provide concise information that was true to their profession. Ironically, it took the United States and Great Britain a long time to explain the needless death and devastation of the Iraq War as well.

The Policy of Containment

Iraq had suffered numerous sanctions generated by the United Nations Security Council. First, there was the enforcement of Iraqi no-fly zones declared by the United States and Great Britain in 1992. The no-fly zone had been established to protect Kurds in Iraq and Kurdistan from aerial attacks by the Iraqi government.[562] Then, in October 1998, ongoing inspections to remove Iraq WMDs began. This was only one month after the bombing during Operation Desert Fox. During the 2003 State of the Union address, President George W. Bush said, "We know that Iraq, in the late 1990s, had several mobile biological weapons labs."[563]

Nevertheless, the United States continued to rely on the authority of the United Nations Security Council with Resolutions 678 and 687, passed in 1990 and 1991, respectively, which required Iraq to cease all development of nuclear weapons, chemical bombs, and any other WMDs.[564]

Leading up to the decision to invade, the United States and the United Kingdom argued Saddam Hussein was developing weapons of mass destruction, posing a significant threat to his neighbors and the United States. The weapons report given in response to UN resolution 1441 passed on November 8, 2002, was, according to Donald Rumsfeld, a "contemptuously incomplete declaration of their weapons program."[565] He added that "nothing seemed to result from their noncompliance with the earlier resolutions, [so] Iraq concluded, not unreasonably, that it could safely respond to this latest, UN Resolution 1441, with still another shrug."[566] According to Rumsfeld, there had been "no fewer than seventeen UN resolutions demanding that Saddam comply with various requirements since 1991," and that these were all met with noncompliance.[567]

The United States government, led by President Bush and others, became convinced that action should be taken, though some allies, such as Great Britain, believed a final warning should be made through a separate UN resolution.[568] It was becoming increasingly clear that America was headed to war with Iraq, regardless of world opinion. Even the conclusion of the United Nations Secretary-General Kofi Annan that a war with Iraq was illegal and not in conformity with the Security Council was ignored. Accusations of faulty evidence and alleged shifting rationale were also becoming more prevalent.

It is safe to assume the idea of invading Iraq came up some time after the attacks on 9/11, with General Tommy Franks being asked for and giving recommendations as to how military action would look to remove Saddam Hussein as early as December 2001. Though when the decision was made by President Bush is not entirely clear, after he made his case for an invasion in front of the UN General Assembly in September 2002, Congress passed the Iraq Resolution in October of 2002 authorizing the use of force.[569] The United States would later officially declare its combat role in Iraq with a warning to give Saddam Hussein forty-eight hours to leave Iraq on March 17, 2003, which he refused, and then with the invasion that began on March 20, 2003.[570]

Early Plans for War

The preparations for war began well in advance of the final, official decision to invade, which came in January 2003. With the American people seemingly supporting the war, Franks planned for an attack in early 2002, over a full year before the actual invasion that would put the Baathists, the military and political organization serving Saddam Hussein, off balance.[571]

In planning the timing of the war, General Franks understood the secretary was reflecting the White House pressure to be ready as soon as possible, though he had warned Secretary Rumsfeld that "because of the summer heat, he did not want to start fighting on the ground in Iraq any time after April 1."572 If Franks's warnings were to be heeded, the invasion would have occurred in the autumn of 2002 at the earliest.573

President Bush had developed a full range of options on how to deal with Iraq. The policy of regime change was something the Bush administration might have to consider doing alone, however. Countries around the world did not support direct military action against Iraq.574

President Bush ordered a military timeline strategy regardless of the final decision. General Franks named the process "Generated Start." As pressure mounted for the potential date of the attack, Secretary of Defense Rumsfeld had to coordinate the timing for an attack on the Iraq homeland.575 Like Secretary of State Colin Powell, Vice President Cheney normally stayed away from military planning. However, he began studying the Iraq Army training schedules throughout the year. "The Iraq military was at full strength from October through November. Iraq units would be winding down their training schedule from December through February, when their combat strength would be at its lowest. The weather would also be a problem before December. Midsummer, the temperature would be up to one hundred thirty degrees Fahrenheit."576 During a discussion between Vice President Cheney, President Bush, Secretary Rumsfeld, and General Franks, the president asked if they could go earlier than October or November. General Franks's answer was: "We could, but it would be ugly."577

Vice President Cheney followed these discussions with a coordination trip to London to consult with Prime Minister Tony Blair, then went to Jordan in March 2002. During these trips, as well as a trip to Turkey, it became clear to Cheney that Iraq's neighbors were very aware of the possibility of war between Iraq and America. He understood that his next move would have to be with the Turkish government. Ultimately, he met with the chief of the Turkish general staff. After Cheney's return from his trip, he stated, "I think we failed to understand the magnitude of the shift that was taking place in Turkey."578

In that meeting, Cheney found out that the Turkish people were overwhelmingly opposed to another war in Iraq. They feared the possible breakup of Iraq and the establishment of an independent Kurdish state would encourage secessionist actions among the Turkish Kurd population. During the meeting with the chief of the Turkish general staff, Cheney also discussed the Bush administration's attitude about war; his comments were that "We are an administration that, when we say we are going to do something, we mean it; that we are resolved to fight the war on terror; that this is not a short strategy for us; that we understand history has called us into action; and we are not going to miss this opportunity to make the world more peaceful and freer."[579]

That was the message he provided the Turks. In it, he tended to lump the issue of terrorism with the Iraq invasion. That turned out to be the approach to gaining Turkish approval for the attack. General Franks and staff continued to plan for the invasion. He learned from the Joint Chiefs of Staff that the war was going to happen. General Franks, in an earlier meeting on Afghanistan, was informed that the chief's military responsibilities would also include the war with Iraq.

The planning continued. General Franks met with the president at Camp David on Saturday, April 20, and again on May 11. At the May meeting, President Bush stressed that it was essential to "portray the invasion as the liberation of Iraq."[580] The president also emphasized to Franks that messages should highlight the importance of moving to free Iraqis from Saddam Hussein. The president said to Franks that, at the time, the US was "not interested in becoming occupiers."[581]

On June 1, 2002, Bush was in West Point to deliver the commencement address for newly graduated cadets. In this speech, and in an earlier State of the Union speech, he made it clear he was selecting war. He believed the US must take the battle to the war on terror. It would not be won on the defensive. If they waited for specific threats to appear, that would be too late. These speeches were meant to begin changing the mindset of the cadets and the nation.

As part of President Bush's policy, he supported preemptive action to defend freedom and lives, and he and his administration were quickly focusing on war. Some internationally and some in America believed available intelligence and specific facts were leading to the policy of war. There was no turning back.[582]

In a meeting that would be recorded in what is now known as the Downing Street Memo, British foreign secretary Jack Straw was quoted on July 23, 2002, as saying he believed the US National Security Council had no patience with the UN approach to Iraq pursuing WMDs, whether atomic bombs or fatal poisons.[583] Jack Straw stated that it seemed "clear that President Bush had made up his mind to take military action." He also felt the case for war was "thin" and that "Saddam would continue to play hardball with the UN."[584]

On January 13, 2003, President Bush had a meeting with Colin Powell in the Oval Office. "I really think I'm going to have to take this guy out," he said to the one member of his cabinet who had shown the most resistance to the idea.[585] Powell had publicly joined in on the criticism of Iraq. He also believed Saddam Hussein would become receptive to the United Nations' oversight of their WMD development due to this pressure. That would mean Saddam Hussein would have to agree to weapons inspections from United Nations inspectors, or the invasion would commence.

Once the decision was made, however, President Bush allowed General Tommy Franks thirty days advance notice before the commencement of the invasion. In response, General Franks requested an additional sixty days to deploy the necessary forces. Three to six divisions, with 275,000 troops total, would be required. There would also be simultaneous air and ground attacks.

Prelude to War

Since the 1991 Gulf War, the United States and the United Kingdom had been engaged in attacks on Iraqi air defenses while enforcing Iraqi no-fly zones. The no-fly zones were opposed by several prominent world leaders, including UN Secretary-General Boutros-Boutros Ghali and French Foreign Minister Hubert Vedrine. China and Russia also took the position that these actions violated Iraqi sovereignty.[586]

Part of the preparation for going to war was the selection of targets meant to "disrupt the military command structure in Iraq."[587] By mid-2002, this shift in enforcement of the no-fly zone became a part of what was internally called Operation Southern Focus.

Externally, rhetoric was used to attempt to disguise this shift in tactics by pointing out how the volume of airstrikes had decreased as compared to the days of the Clinton administration. This information had been used to dispute the theory that the Bush administration had already decided to go to war against Iraq prior to his election. The bombing during 2001 and 2002 laid the groundwork for the eventual invasion in 2003. However, information obtained by the United Kingdom Liberal Party showed the coalition had dropped twice as many bombs on Iraq in the second half of 2002 as they did during the whole of 2001. The tonnage of United Kingdom bombs dropped increased from zero in March 2002 and 0.3 in April 2002 to between seven and fourteen tons per month from May to August, reaching a war peak of 54.6 tons in September, before the United States Congress's October 11 authorization of the invasion.

The September invasion included a hundred-plus aircraft attack on the main air defense site in western Iraq. According to an editorial in *New Statesman*, a British political and cultural news magazine, this was "located at the furthest extreme of the southern no-fly zone, far away from the areas that needed to be patrolled to prevent attacks on the Shias. It was destroyed not because it was a threat to the patrols but to allow allied special forces operating from Jordan to enter Iraq undetected."[588]

Tommy Franks, commander of the Coalition Forces from the beginning of the Iraq invasion, belatedly admitted that the early bombing of various locations in the country, ordered by senior officers in the Pentagon, was designed to degrade Iraqi air defenses in the same way as the air attacks that began in the 1991 Gulf War. These "spikes of activity" were, in the words of the British Defense Secretary Geoff Hoon, "designed to put pressure on the Iraqi regime," or, as the British periodical *The Times* put it, it was meant to "provoke Saddam Hussein into giving the allies an excuse for war."[589]

Another attempt at provoking the war was mentioned in a leaked memo from a meeting between George W. Bush and Tony Blair on January 13, 2003, as Bush allegedly told Blair that "the United States was thinking of flying U2 reconnaissance aircraft with fighter cover over Iraq, painted in United Nations colors."[590] If Saddam fired on them, he would be in violation of the UN resolution. On March 17, 2003, President George W. Bush gave Saddam Hussein forty-eight hours to leave the country along with his sons Uday and Qusay or face war.[591] Not only did Saddam refuse, he appeared on Iraqi television in full military uniform, and his eldest son, Uday, urged "President Bush to give up power in America with his family."[592]

In February 2003, Secretary of State Colin Powell addressed the United Nations General Assembly. His objective was to gain authority and UN support for an invasion. Secretary Powell was armed with intelligence provided by Rafid Ahmed Alwen Al-Janabi, an Iraqi immigrant living in Germany. His code name was "Curve Ball." Much to Secretary Powell's surprise, the intelligence information turned out to be false.[593]

President George W. Bush and Prime Minister Tony Blair's objective was to rid Iraq of WMDs, prevent Saddam Hussein's support of terrorist organizations, and advocate for the freedom of the Iraqi people. They deemed this the final opportunity to remove alleged nuclear, chemical, and biological weapons from Iraq.

A CBS poll in January 2003 indicated that 64 percent of Americans approved of military action in Iraq. However, 63 percent wanted President Bush to seek a diplomatic solution first.[594] America's allies, such as France, Canada, Germany, and New Zealand, believed there was no evidence of WMDs in Iraq. They felt due to the absence of verifiable intelligence of an active WMD program sufficient to endanger its neighbors or their close allies, the coalition's intention to continue the Iraq intervention was not justified and should stop. Within the context of the United Nations Monitoring and Verification Commission inspections, their February 12, 2003 report found only five thousand chemical warhead shells. They had been built but were abandoned during the 1991 Gulf War. The Verification

Commission also believed the significant existence of chemical weapons did not support the American Government's current rationale.[595]

A month before the invasion, there was a peace rally in Rome, Italy. Three million protesters were present. This was the largest single anti-war rally in history.[596] On January 3, 2003, there were three thousand war protests in various countries across the globe, all to no avail. Despite these worldwide protests and the growing United Nations' lack of support for an invasion, the United States and its senior leaders, led by President Bush, had no intentions to change the military course they were on. The war would soon begin.

April 9, 2003: Statue of Saddam Hussein is toppled in Firdos Square[597]

Phase I: The Invasion of Iraq

The invasion began on March 19, 2003, with a "shock and awe" campaign to rapidly dominate the Iraqi military by overwhelming them with superior US military capabilities and firepower. This initial invasion lasted until May 1, 2003, when US leadership prematurely declared victory.[598] The United States led the coalition in troops, which totaled some 199,400 military personnel in Iraq and surrounding countries and bodies of water. There were also approximately 23,000 non-US coalition forces made of twenty-seven countries, most notably Australia, Great Britain, and Poland.[599]

The Army began the primary invasion by crossing the Kuwait-Iraq border on the seventeenth, with small skirmishes along the berm, or artificial ridge, which separated the two countries as they crossed into Iraq. This berm had been erected after the first Gulf War to help prevent Iraq from invading Kuwait again.

The coalition air forces flew "between 1,500 and 2,000 sorties a day,"[600] and naval forces launched 500 cruise missiles in the first few days, destroying various targets. Strikes on senior leadership, command and control, air defense capabilities, and other targets were meant to ensure a smooth march to Baghdad.[601]

The Command and Control of the Iraqi army was severely damaged early in the war, with stealth aircraft providing much of the destructive power to take out communications infrastructure and targeted strikes on high-value targets, meaning "senior Baath leaders and officers of the Special Security Organization and the Special Republican Guard,"[602] using GPS guided bombs that enabled hitting a target with a six-foot margin of error.

The invasion also began with a decapitation strike that aimed to topple the regime on March 19, though this was not successful. It would take several months to capture Saddam Hussein and his sons, Uday and Qusay, who were the heirs to Saddam's dynasty. General Tommy Franks would later recall that President Bush would not authorize the regime-ending strike to take place before the forty-eight-hour deadline, though the opportunity presented itself.[603]

The US also attempted to secure oil fields, though this was done a day sooner than planned, as some half a dozen oil fields had been set ablaze by Iraqi forces in an act of attempted sabotage. Marines successfully gained control of these oil fields and Persian Gulf oil platforms to prevent a larger environmental disaster such as the one that occurred when Iraqi forces set fire to multiple oil fields in Kuwait during the first Gulf War.[604]

In the north, Special Forces were used to stabilize the Kurdish Autonomous Zone, and in the west of Iraq, they were used to prevent any potential SCUD launches against surrounding countries like Israel,

Jordan, Turkey, or the Kurds in the north. The general tactic of the Iraqi military, with the exception of the Fedayeen, Republican Guard forces, was to "just melt away" and show little, if any, resistance.[605]

The coalition occupied Baghdad by April 9, then Kirkuk in the far north, securing Kurdish areas by April 15. The 173rd Airborne Brigade had been deployed near Kirkuk on March 26, and they were joined by Special Forces, which gave the area task force the capability to conduct surgical operations while also holding ground. This presence was intended to reassure the Turkish and Kurdish in the region, which it accomplished.[606]

The Battle of An-Nasiriyah

An-Nasiriyah was a key stop along the way because it had access to several important bridges in the center of the town, as well as a regional airport, Tallil Airfield, that could be used to resupply and reinforce. The Army 3rd Infantry Division had been tasked with taking the Tallil airfield and did so with little trouble on March 21. This was the first significant battle for the 3rd Infantry Division and consisted mainly of using artillery to defeat Iraqi armor that protected the base. They were also able to capture an Iraqi Air Force Brigadier General, who had with him intelligence of the Iraqi battle plans as well as information about senior leadership, all of which proved useful in the coming weeks.[607]

The most difficult fighting of the invasion came just after the Marines took the oil fields of southern Iraq and began the push north to Baghdad. Though the battle took several days, the worst of the days was March 23, when an army supply convoy took a wrong turn into the city rather than remaining on the outskirts. Eleven soldiers were killed, and seven were taken as prisoners of war, though one, Pfc. Lori Piestewa, perished and became the first Native American woman to die in battle.[608]

The 1st Marine Division also entered the city on March 23, though, with the intent to secure several bridges in the center of the city that crossed the Euphrates River. Eighteen Marines died securing it in fierce fighting, though some of these were later attributed to friendly-fire incidents.

The Approach to Baghdad

One of the intelligence failures of the invasion was the poor assessment of the terrain leading up to Baghdad. Intelligence had not considered that the area southwest of Baghdad, which was known as the Karbala Gap, was mostly urban sprawl, which, as was seen in Somalia, is kryptonite for air assets like attack helicopters that fly close to the ground. The only failed battle within the first month was the attack on the Karbala Gap on March 23, 2003, known as the "Darkest Day." The Karbala Gap was occupied by the well-trained Iraqi Republican Guard, Medina Division, which was able to neutralize the thirty-two AH-64 Apache attack helicopters with a well-planned ambush. One Apache was shot down, and another crashed shortly after takeoff. All but one of the returning helicopters were heavily damaged by small-arms fire, and the 11thArmy Attack Helicopter Regiment was out of commission for a month. For the Apache helicopter that was shot down, the two pilots who were taken captive were later rescued by Marines.[609]

The Battles of An-Najaf, As-Samawah, and Karbala

As-Samawah, just south of An-Najaf, had largely been bypassed on the way to An-Najaf, though it became another key city along the way that was captured by the US Army. This was also the first significant encounter with the Fedayeen, a militia of martyrs willing to fight to the death, who were more formidable than invasion planners had anticipated. The Fedayeen showed during the capture of As-Samawah that they were willing to use civilians as human shields and force other militias, such as the local Al-Quds militia, to fight by threatening them and their families. Fighters would also show their tendency to fight in civilian clothing, which made following Rules of Engagement more difficult.[610]

Reaching and securing As-Samawah marked the halfway point, geographically, between Al-Basra in the far south and Baghdad, though time-wise, they were at the beginning of the invasion. Predictably, the march to Baghdad would begin to slow down due to urban sprawl and allow time for supply lines to catch up, while also securing lines of communication from ambush.[611]

Like An-Nasiriyah and As-Samawah to the south, An-Najaf was also a key point on the march to Baghdad. An-Najaf had several key bridges that crossed the Euphrates that the US Army was attempting to secure between March 25 and April 4, 2003. There were two main pushes, first to surround the town and then to enter the town to clear the Iraqi army, the Republican Guard, the Fedayeen, and several militias.[612]

It would take ground troops from April 2–7 to secure the area of the Karbala Gap, which came a full two weeks after the helicopter attack that had failed. The Karbala Gap was a twenty-five-mile gap between the Euphrates River and Lake Razazah that served as a natural chokepoint, an area that must be passed through to make progress. In reality, because the Euphrates River valley was filled with marshland, the ideal land area to go through the gap was even narrower, around a mile wide (1.8 kilometers).[613]

Though well disguised in the available terrain, a feint by the 3rd Infantry Division to move across the Euphrates instead of through the gap encouraged the Iraqi tanks and artillery to reposition, which uncovered them, making them vulnerable to air strikes. The Medina division and the Fedayeen were thus attacked, and what remained of the Medina force moved back to defend the western part of Baghdad. Once through the Karbala Gap, the path was open for an almost entire encirclement of Baghdad. "By 1 April, the Medina Division—originally composed of two armored brigades, one mechanized infantry brigade, and supporting assets—was largely destroyed."[614]

The Battle of Baghdad

Taking Baghdad was divided into several tasks, which started with the logistical objective of taking Saddam International Airport, later renamed Baghdad International Airport. Once the airport was taken, there were two Thunder Runs, which were raids of armed convoys of twenty to thirty M-1 Abrams tanks and M-2 Bradley fighting vehicles that were used to gain intelligence about defensive postures in the city. These were designed to test the defenses but also had a psychological effect against the regime because contrary to the propaganda, the US forces seemed to come and go into the capital as they pleased.[615]

The first raid took place on April 5, starting south of Baghdad and curving westward toward the airport, skimming the protected downtown regime area. Some RPG and small-arms damage needed to be repaired the following day in preparation for the second Thunder Run on April 7. This run went deeper and instead of turning left toward the airport, went into the heart of the regime's protected area, which included the palace and various government buildings. On the second run, Colonel David Perkins, the architect of the raids, set up a command post, which was attacked but was then broken down and repositioned in a more protected area. In the attack, three American soldiers were killed by a rocket with a 280-kg payload warhead. Two foreign reporters were also killed, fourteen soldiers wounded, and twenty-two vehicles destroyed.[616]

With such a well-positioned start to the battle, the 3rd Infantry Division surrounded the city on the left hemisphere, and the 1st Marine Division surrounded the right hemisphere of Baghdad. The city would fall in six days as the US forces slowly made their way into the city. Many of the Republican Guard and Fedayeen either deserted or disbanded and resorted to Guerrilla tactics, which would become more common in the years to follow. In all, several dozen US military personnel were killed, while over 2,500 Iraqis were killed.[617]

Post-Invasion Iraq

The view of the United States leadership was that no war ever goes the way it's planned. However, that did not absolve the president's advisers of their duty to prepare carefully and consider the possible dangers. By March 2003, there was already growing opposition to the war in America. President Bush had to face the American people, especially those arguing against military action.

President Bush needed to address not only the war but the peace following the initial combat action. President Bush, Secretary Rumsfeld, and others working closely with the Pentagon foresaw the potential problems in a post-Saddam Hussein Iraq. Winning the war was one thing, but winning the peace after an enemy regime had been removed was quite another matter. Defense Secretary Rumsfeld was concerned with the current strategy for promoting a new government in Iraq. A democratic government needed to represent the entire multi-cultured nation. The Sunni, Shia, and Kurdish cultures had to be brought into the government. If they were not, wars between them would certainly occur. Civil war had to be avoided at all costs.

Defense Secretary Rumsfeld began rethinking the strategy for the future. He sent draft notes to the president in the autumn of 2002, as well as the National Security Council, containing the basic elements of a new post-war strategy. His intent was for a comprehensive discussion of the draft of his proposed strategy to take place. It could then be the map of any post-war strategy for peace. Rumsfeld entitled the draft "Parade of Horribles."[618]

His list resulting from the invasion was intended to generate serious early thinking regarding potential risks and what might be done to reduce them. It engendered a discussion between President Bush, Vice President Cheney, Secretary of State Rice, and Secretary Tenet.

Secretary of Defense Rumsfeld provided a list of specific dangers as the US proceeded with nation-building:

1. There could be another rogue state that could take advantage of United States preoccupation with the Iraq War, nations such as North Korea, Iran, or the People's Republic of China;
2. There could be higher than expected coalition deaths. Iraq's use of WMDs might be used;
3. Fortress Baghdad could prove to be long and unpleasant. The NSC brought up serious risks that, in fact, materialized;
4. the United States could fail to find WMDs on the ground in Iraq, and that would affect international opinion;
5. Rather than a post-Saddam Hussein effort requiring two to four years, this effort could take eight to ten years. It could deplete the United States' financial resources;

6. Iraq could experience ethnic strife among the Sunni, Shia, and Kurds;
7. World action against preemption could inhibit the United States' ability to engage with other countries to deal with problems of common concern;
8. In the future if WMDs were not found, it could affect the president and his administration's credibility.[619]

General Franks's battle plan was not only based on the finding of WMDs. It included preparations for a possible invasion, shaping the battle space with the start of air operations, decisive offensive and major combat operations, and post-hostility stabilization and reconstruction.

May 1, 2003: President Bush signals the end of major combat in Iraq aboard the USS *Abraham Lincoln*[620]

Democracy

The war appeared just about over on April 9. The next question was how the Bush administration would transition the country into a federalist and democratic state. They would first have to work together to change the old patterns of living under a despot. The television announcement in the US stated, "The Iraqis have been liberated from a monster," as a sign of how the Iraqis would deal with these changes. Suddenly, an American soldier with an American flag appeared on camera as a statue of Saddam Hussein standing in Firdos Square in the heart of Baghdad was toppled. That flag was quickly replaced with the Iraq flag, symbolizing the Americans' intentions to develop a free society, but with Iraq as a new state with its own flag—not the American flag.

Although the invading forces were initially successful, the war was also significantly changing to a long, drawn-out guerrilla war with ever-increasing casualties to Iraq and coalition forces. The symbolism of the American flag and the toppled statue did not bode well with the Iraqi people.[621]

Mission Accomplished?

The Al-Jazeera Media Network's publications spread propaganda that worried the people of Iraq. More evidence was available that the Iraqis were worried about the United States' ultimate takeover of the Muslim world. They worried that America would take Iraq's oil. The American plan was to establish Iraqis as the core of a new interim government. It was hoped that this interim government would help avoid the Iraqi perception that the United States would develop Iraq as a colony of America. General Franks announced the first step to creating the Iraq Interim Authority, which included key Iraqi participation.

Unfortunately, the American press reported that the Department of State planned to delay the establishment of the Iraq Interim Authority, which complicated the situation. Secretary of State Condoleezza Rice was pushing for a senior diplomat to head the reconstruction agency. She appointed a senior Department of State official to represent them in Baghdad.[622]

It was noted by the American press that discussions of a major conflict about the composition of the Iraq Interim Authority were occurring. Would it take the form of Iraqi representatives, or would it take some other form? The stability of Iraq was now in question.

Reconstruction of Iraq's power grid, manufacturing base, water and sewer systems, oil drilling, and refining capacity was underway. Of course, it would take hundreds of millions of dollars to accomplish these important elements of Iraq's society. The degrading of these elements of the country had been in effect well before the invasion, with the war only damaging these systems further. If there was an improvement to be made, it would take the invaders, as well as the members of the Sunni, Shia, and Kurds, to make the new Iraq a success.

It would also require the formation of an Iraq provisional government so that they could begin learning how to govern this complex nation. Of course, the transformation from a long-term dictatorship to a democratic state would simply take time. In truth, it might take decades before Iraq was able to develop any semblance of progress toward a democratic society. Americans might not have the patience or resources to wait for such progress.

The president and his administration already had a growing number of detractors of the war effort for a multitude of reasons, such as increased casualties and the division of the Iraqi people. Detractors believed it was questionable that the alliance could stay the course. A further complication was brought up—that it was culture, not politics, that would determine the success of a society. That was certainly true in this case.

Too Many Hands on the Steering Wheel

The United States military was also experiencing a crisis of leadership. Lieutenant General Ricardo Sanchez, a new military commander who was installed as commander of all ground forces in Iraq in June 2003, would only last ninety days. He was well thought of within senior civilian and military circles; however, he had problems dealing with the complexities of commanding 170,000 Allied troops as his division in Germany had been roughly one-tenth that size. He also ran up against Ambassador Paul Bremer, who had different views on how to integrate Iraqis into any future government. Ambassador Bremer, speaking to Secretary of Defense Rumsfeld, stated that they would take their time putting a face on the Coalition Provisional Authority (CPA).[623]

The CPA was the temporary governmental body appointed by President Bush to oversee the "policies, plans, and budget for the reconstruction of Iraq and its return to sovereignty." Bremer was assigned to this task and "reported to the president through the secretary of defense."[624] The sheer magnitude of what Bremer and the rest of the group were tasked with would prove to be overwhelming. "Because Bremer's fledgling CPA was ill-organized and lacked sufficient State Department volunteers to act as provincial advisers, during the summer of 2003, the American and British battalion commanders acted as the de facto mayors of all Iraqi cities, re-establishing services and jump-starting governance."[625]

Secretary Rumsfeld believed they were "running out of time to put an Iraqi face on the CPA."[626] Ambassador Bremer believed there could only be one government at a time, the CPA or an Iraqi one, but not both, as a power-sharing arrangement between the coalition and Iraqis would not work.[627] Because Ambassador Bremer had the authority, he chose to create a long delay before he made such a decision. This complicated the quick process toward an independent Iraq. Rather than two to four years, it would take four to eight years or more before Allied forces could leave Iraq.

Disagreements between the State Department and the Defense Department continued, at least at the Iraq level. Local military commanders knew money was required to offset the long years of neglect at the ground level. Any delay in that regard would bring the Iraq insurgency and the Allied military in direct opposition.

Ambassador Bremer also refused to use money from seized assets coming from Saddam Hussein's government as a resource. The military would have to make do with the funds they had, which were insufficient for the reconstruction of a devastated country. This impasse would continue, as would the empowerment of the insurgency.[628]

Fallujah and the Al-Anbar Campaign

The Iraq War in Anbar Province, also known as the Al-Anbar campaign, consisted of fighting between the United States military and Iraq government forces. Sunni insurgents in the western Iraq province of Al-

Anbar also participated on the side of the Iraq government forces.

Although the Iraq War officially lasted from 2003 to 2011, most of the fighting and counterinsurgency campaigns in Anbar took place between April 2004 and September 2007. The fighting initially consisted of heavy urban warfare between insurgents and US Marines.

These Iraqi insurgents later focused on ambushing the American and Iraqi security forces with improvised explosive devices (IEDs). Almost 9,000 Iraqis and 1,335 Americans were killed in this three-year campaign. Insurgent attacks would become the principal way Iraqis would attack the invaders. Casualties grew with the assistance of the Iranians and their more advanced IEDs.[629]

Although there were numerous battles throughout Iraq after the allies defeated the Baathists and Saddam Hussein, none illustrate the development of the insurgency better than the Battle of Fallujah. There were 1,500 insurgents in Fallujah alone. One hundred fifty-three Americans and thousands of Iraqi lives were lost in the city during the twenty months of battles spanning 2003 and 2004.

After the death of Saddam Hussein in April 2003, twenty million Iraqi Shiites and Kurds refused to believe they had lost power. This former regime was an essential element in the growing insurgency. They also turned and joined forces with radical Islamic fundamentalists in both Fallujah and throughout Iraq. In the summer and fall of 2003, this united front focused on winning the hearts and minds of the Iraqi people.

The citizens of Fallujah tended to be poor, unemployed men with no money, no jobs, and no opportunity to improve their lives. They were susceptible to recruitment by the growing numbers of insurgents due to their poverty. The US military could not provide any countermeasures due to the absence of resources.[630]

Fallujah: "The Most Dangerous City in Iraq"

In March 2004, four American contractors from the Blackwater security company were taking a shortcut during a Marine supply run through the city of Fallujah. This was a city where the US did not have a direct presence, so traveling through it in broad daylight was a risky endeavor at best.[631]

The contractors were former military with impressive wartime credentials, including one ex-Navy Seal, Scott Helvensten; a former Ranger, Wesley Batalona; a former paratrooper, Jerry Zovko; and an Army Bronze Star recipient, Michael Teague. The contractors were ambushed by insurgents. Their cars, which did not have armor, were shot with small-arms fire, and their bodies were burned with gasoline by the mob that had accumulated. Following that, their bodies were dragged through the streets and hung up on a bridge for all the world to see.[632]

President Bush was infuriated and demanded that Fallujah be taken immediately. The American military would now have to organize their units for a long battle to destroy the insurgents and gain support from the population. Lieutenant General Ricardo Sanchez took command of American Joint Task Force 7 (JTF). Lieutenant Colonel Suleiman Al Marawi, a commander of the Iraqi National Guard west of Fallujah and a native of Fallujah who would battle against the insurgency, took command of "a poorly trained Iraqi Battalion in Fallujah."[633] He believed the key to victory would be keeping US troops out of Fallujah to avoid inflaming the situation. He also believed Abdullah Al-Janabi, a businessman and a fundamentalist Sunni cleric, was leading the citizens of Fallujah into open rebellion.[634]

Winning Hearts and Minds

The British leaders believed the attack on Fallujah was creating more insurgents among the residents of the city. "The lid of the pressure cooker has come off," British Foreign Secretary Jack Straw told BBC Radio a few days later. Straw continued, "It is plainly the fact today that there are larger numbers of people, and they are people on the ground, Iraqis, not foreign fighters, who are engaged in this insurgency."[635]

It became apparent, not only to the Iraqis but to US allies as well, that the Coalition was failing to win the hearts and minds of the Iraqi people. The Marines of the 1st Marine Expeditionary Force, who took over for the Army's 82nd Airborne division a week before the attack, were planning on humanitarian-weighted missions. While still stateside they had packed gifts for the people of Fallujah, including soccer balls, teddy bears, and other toys. Because of the growing number of attacks against US military personnel, they had to repack their gear for a more militarily minded mission.[636]

Operation Vigilant Resolve: The First Battle of Fallujah

Once the decision was made to clear Fallujah of insurgents, the Marines encircled the city on April 4 and began fierce house-to-house fighting for the next five days. During this time two hundred insurgents were killed, with several key strategic areas for the insurgents cleared and areas for the insurgent retreat cut off. The tactic of attack and retreat was a well-worn strategy of the Viet Cong in Vietnam, and the Marines had learned from this and had trained heavily in urban combat leading up to their deployment. Twenty-seven Marines were killed, though Fallujah had been nominally cleared of insurgents—for the time being.[637]

At the end of the battle, Fallujah was handed over to the Iraqi Security Forces, though the situation would steadily deteriorate again. These security forces were not trained to keep order as police forces would have been trained, and the training they did receive was woefully inadequate.[638]

Operation Phantom Fury: The Second Battle of Fallujah

The second battle took place six months after the first had ended, in November 2004, and in total lasted for six weeks. Most of the fighting, however, happened in the first six days, in the initial clearing of the city. The rest of the time was spent uncovering and clearing smaller pockets of resistance throughout the city. By December 23 the city had been cleared of insurgents. In total, 95 US military personnel were killed, and an estimated 2,500 insurgents were killed.[639]

This engagement differed from the first battle in that some materials had been captured by the insurgents during the first battle, including M14s and M16s, as well as some uniforms and body armor. The insurgents were also made from fighters all over the Middle East, including volunteers from Chechnya, Saudi Arabia, and Syria. Some of the houses were also prepared as booby traps by the insurgents, as they had started to learn about house-clearing tactics of the Army and Marines.[640]

By the end of the battle, Fallujah became a quiet industrial city, though insurgent activity in the country increased. In January 2005, a new National Assembly was elected to form a new government and to produce a constitution that would serve all Iraqis. The Sunni areas boycotted the election, as the clerics had urged them to do so. Nevertheless, over 60 percent of the population that was eligible to vote turned out for the election.[641]

An Inefficient Way of Operating

Before the war, General Tommy Franks had convinced Secretary of Defense Donald Rumsfeld that once the war in Iraq was over, post-war Iraq needed to stay under a central command. His issue was the need for a unity of authority—one chain of command led by the military. General Franks noted, "In combat, there had to be one line of authority." He had learned this critical lesson in the Vietnam War: any development of post-war Iraq had to remain under the military's command, not the State Department or any other entity.[642]

American commanders had a full slate of duties in the city of Fallujah. They were economic administrators, political advisers, and the court of final appeal for the Iraqi citizenry. Unity of command was paramount to the American strategy, an essential principle.

Although the war seemed over at this point in 2003, Iraq was plagued by uncontrolled mobs destroying government buildings and stealing ancient artifacts. Unlike in Vietnam, President Bush decided to change controls to his envoy, Ambassador L. Paul Bremer III, and the Department of State. Ambassador Bremer assumed control on May 10, 2003. His mission was to administer the Coalition Provisional Authority (CPA). He was vested with the broad policymaking and budget authority necessary to build a "new" Iraq.[643]

As the military had feared, the chain of command was now broken into two pieces between the military and the State Department. Before his retirement, General Franks agreed with the change of a civilian leader running the reconstruction. He believed that by removing the position of "deputy [Central Command] commander for reconstruction,"[644] a military position, and replacing it with Bremer in his position as head of the CPA, more attention and money would flow to the important task of helping Iraq to rebuild. The military-backed off, and the State Department took charge, in opposition to General Franks's earlier opinion regarding a single line of authority.[645]

General John Abizaid disagreed with the change as the new commander of Central Command (CENTCOM). He assessed the problem as a classical guerrilla campaign requiring a joint command, not a divided one. Far from being over, the Iraqi war was continuing as an insurgency. Ambassador Bremer now had the responsibility and the money to create Iraqi security forces. He was empowered to make any security model he saw fit. However, he had no authority to approve, veto, or comment on US military operations. It was now a divided chain of command once again.[646]

To further complicate the leadership conundrum the US found itself in, Ambassador Robert Blackwill was appointed in October 2003 as the deputy assistant to the president, in charge of the newly formed Iraq Stabilization Group. This chain of command, unlike the others, flowed to the president through Dr. Condoleezza Rice, the National Security Advisor. This group was specifically designed to "coordinate Iraqi policy from inside the White House." The goal was to exit Iraq as soon as possible, leaving behind a viable country and political system, "transitioning to an Iraqi government, with eventual elections."[647]

In contrast, the other two leaders, Bremer and Abizaid, considered to also be "powerful and strong-willed personalities,"[648] in their own right, would be focused on the economic, political, and military stability of the country. The overlap and dependency between these three leaders' responsibilities, and that they each brought their own particular priorities, solutions, background, and capabilities, made their coordination a challenge. They were three separate individuals with three different reporting structures, and this made the task almost as impossible as it was inefficient.[649]

Looking at the American Revolution, the US had developed a

government that not only had American values as its foundation, based on classical liberal ideology, republicanism, and democracy, but the US had a strong set of leaders, headed by George Washington, that could overcome military challenges the young country faced, but also worked effectively with both the congress and locally, in the interests of the state governments. Iraq did not have this, as they were being led through a process of democratization they were not familiar with and for which they were not fully prepared. This also ignored the real issue of who should oversee the destiny of the country, which few would disagree, should ultimately be the Iraqi people.

The differences in priorities that emerged from having three different decision-makers would be the principal challenge that faced the new nation. General Abizaid focused primarily on defeating the insurgency and called it a "classical guerrilla-type campaign." Blackwill's priority was simply to remove the US from Iraq as soon as possible, though defeating the enemy and getting out was not a linear path because of the growing insurgency and the unmet needs of the people. We can discern Bremer's focus from his proposed budget to Congress for Iraq in 2003, which asked for "$18 billion for Iraq, of which 80 percent was allocated for development (electricity, sewage, schools, and the like) and 20 percent for security (police, the army, and border guards)."[650] Bremer's plan assumed that Abizaid's problem was already solved, thus the percentage allocation.

Though very capable, as he was well-versed in the mechanics of Washington and also as a diplomat, Paul Bremer was faced with the most daunting task of rebuilding the country, and "the span of control and the enormity of his duties were staggering."[651] Bremer had the authority to create Iraqi security forces, but the trainers were military. As a result, the Iraqi Security Forces were very poorly trained. "Once the CPA agreed to Wolfowitz's request, Abizaid directed the US divisions in Iraq to use the money to recruit, train, and pay for the new Iraqi National Guard. They were initially called the Iraqi Civil Defense Corps. Unfortunately, Fallujah was near the bottom of the list of cities to receive such a battalion. National Guard soldiers did not arrive there until February 2004."[652]

Only a few recognized that the Iraqi people needed security above all else and that provincial police forces were the best way to address this need. One senior CPA advisor would correctly assert that "If you build a strong police force, you have a republic. If you build a strong military, you have a banana republic."[653]

As they were far away geographically and far removed from what was happening on the ground, Rumsfeld and Rice were not equipped to act as appropriate advisors to the local decision-makers. They were simply too high on the food chain to understand the realities on the ground.

Post-War Iraq: Who Won the War?

Did the United States win the war? Former Secretary of Defense Leon Panetta felt the United States and the Iraqis "sort of won."[654]

The United States and Great Britain had developed a long-term relationship with Iraq after more than eight years of war, and it was a very questionable exit of military forces, perhaps before their work was complete. As a result of this abrupt exit, it is not clear whether the US, Iraq, or its neighbors "won" the war.

The United States alone lost 4,074 soldiers and civilians, with thousands crippled or wounded. The financial cost was heavy. It spent a couple of trillion dollars on Iraq with very questionable results. President Obama ordered the evacuation of troops in the middle of considerable chaos. In the resulting vacuum created by the exit, thousands of additional terrorists entered Iraq to take advantage of the resultant disorder. Therefore, the issue of the United States and Great Britain winning the war is highly questionable.

Secretary of Defense Leon Panetta further clarified his assessment. "A political entity follows its own path." An ambiguous statement, to say the least.[655] Panetta's analysis of the results of the war, however, clearly summarizes the effort. "They [the Iraqis] virtually allied themselves with Iran, not the United States . . . unsupportive of American geopolitical dreams. We will trade with Iraq, selling military gear to Iraqis. President Bush went to war and all we got was a low-rent dictatorship turned into a low-rent, semi-police state."[656]

Peter Van Buren, a civilian tasked with the reconstruction of Iraq, expressed doubts that his organization's efforts would have a significant impact and whether the US military would be allowed to stay long-term.

He highlighted, as well, how the US didn't meet both military objectives, as well as civilian reconstruction objectives. "Who won the war, Iraq? They were defeated by the US military and its allies. Civil society was pulled apart. Iraq had its civil society dismembered. Eight years of sectarian civil war, two hundred thousand Iraqis killed, and the entry of Al Qaeda adds up to Iraq not winning the war. The United States left without brokering a deal between the Kurds and the Arab Iraqis, leaving massive civil discord."[657]

The United States seriously failed to establish stable borders for the Kurds, resulting in Iran attacking Kurdistan from the east consistently for the past twenty years as it fights a Kurdish rebellion that has spilled into its borders. America's NATO ally, Turkey, has dropped bombs on Kurdistan for decades. Those attacks sewed social disruption in that area that remains to this day. The United States, an ally of the Kurds, has sat silently as the Turks have attacked.

Fighting a civil war between the Sunnis and Shias, the dwindling American force of less than ten thousand could not have a positive effect on its outcome and could not be expected to intervene. Daily news from Iraq described an ongoing, steady occurrence of suicide bombings and targeted killings. It had become a normal part of life for Iraqis. Bottom line: Iraq was hardly a winner.

The US intelligence community, concerning their involvement in the war, could be judged as having lost their part of the war. Nearly a year after the invasion, former chief weapons inspector David Kay, in his testimony to the Senate Armed Services Committee, called for an independent inquiry into the veracity of the prewar intelligence, though he also stated that he "did not believe the Bush administration had pressured intelligence analysts to exaggerate the threat."[658]

Though there is debate as to the extent to which the intelligence apparatus of the federal government could have potentially been compromised by political forces, the sheer contrast between what intelligence predicted the US would find in Iraq and what actually was found could only cast doubt on its credibility.

Who won the war, Iran? Iran was patient while the United States hacked away at its two major enemies, Saddam Hussein in Iraq and the Taliban in Afghanistan. These wars were instrumental in clearing both its eastern and western borders at no cost to Tehran. In 2003, Iran had reached out to the United States government for a diplomatic relationship but was refused. Iran, after being rebuffed by President Bush, decided to watch the quagmire envelop America.

In his book *We Meant Well: I Helped Lose the Battle for the Hearts and Minds of the Iraqi People*, the former leader of two provincial reconstruction teams for the State Department in Iraq, Peter Van Buren, discusses the budding relationship between Iran and Iraq, describing how Iran brokered a deal with Prime Minister Nouri al-Malaki, who was exiled by Saddam Hussein, but upon returning to Iraq, served from May 2006 to September 2014. This worked to undoubtedly strengthen "economic and social ties" between the two countries. Iran also provided 9,500 barrels of fuel oil per day for Iraq's electrical needs. They brokered a $365 million "agreement to install a pipeline to import natural gas" in July 2013, and they were able to "sign an agreement to overcome all the suspended problems between both countries."[659]

Iraqi citizens were in favor of improving relations with Iran.

> In effect, Iran was playing a positive role in Iraq, and there was no objection within the Iraqi populous to the strengthening of relations between the two countries. Trade between them is good. Oil is necessary for both economies and tourism, its second major industry helping them both. Religious tourism is especially beneficial. Shia pilgrims traveling to Iran were formally not allowed under Saddam Hussein. The shrines were previously off-limits in Iraq, but it is now a huge source of economic exchange. It also creates significant people-to-people ties that Iran will be

able to exploit well into the future. Iranian travel agencies control religious tourism. Iranian travel companies associated with the local hotels are also owned by Iranians. Iranian domination also extends to security arrangements for protecting the tourists.[660]

Van Buren's State Department provincial reconstruction team became aware of the economic exchanges between Iraq and Iran during his time in Iraq. He saw large tour buses with Iranian license plates hauling tourists around the city. Peter Van Buren commented that there was "nothing weirder than to be spending one's days freeing Iraq only to run into Iranian tour agencies being the most obvious beneficiaries of that freedom." To him, these tourists were a view of the future, a picture of who the winners and losers were to be in the war.[661]

Postscript

Cheney understood the great challenge associated with any invasion of Iraq in 1992. For whatever reason, he put those concerns aside and supported the full-blown military invasion despite his earlier apprehensions. In doing so, he implicated himself in a serious strategy-policy mismatch. It was a strategy equaling the overthrow of Saddam Hussein's regime using conventional military means and policy equaling withdrawal of all forces once a democratic government was established that represented all members of the Iraq society—one that could defend itself and its people from continuous attack and perhaps civil war.

The military overthrow was feasible, but the democratization and avoidance of civil war were not—at least not without a huge cost in lives and resources. The mismatch, then, caused a drastic rethinking of the war strategy once the military invasion came to an end and the need for nation-building became apparent. This realization came to the United States belatedly, as it realized no real planning had occurred regarding war termination. If the US had completed its real homework, it perhaps would have made the decision not to invade Iraq in the first place, especially to prevent the development of WMDs, which was exaggerated for political reasons.

CHAPTER EIGHT

THE PAST AND FUTURE OF LIMITED WAR

No one starts a war—rather, no one in his senses ought to do so—without first being clear in his mind what he intends to achieve by that war and how he intends to conduct it. In war, more than anywhere else, things do not turn out as we expect.
—Carl von Clausewitz, *On War*

When a nation weighs whether or not to go to war, it must consider a number of questions that must be answered by all members of the Clausewitz Trinity—the government, the military, and the people. Those involved must understand the war's initial objectives, as well as the known consequences of both entering and not entering the conflict. Knowledge of the political goals of all belligerents is critical if they are to understand and accept the decisions on war or peace. Once the war begins, these questions must continue to be addressed because war is a dynamic process that changes frequently. If these changes are not known by the elements of the trinity, tremendous discord between its members occurs, often with catastrophic consequences.

Can political objectives be achieved by means other than military action, with a successful result?
In assessing the political aims of the nation contemplating war, all elements

must be understood. Are there courses of action—other than military force—that would meet political goals just as well, such as economic sanctions or diplomacy? Sometimes, the best decision might be to use actions short of open war and still reach a reasonable objective.

Prior to the Anglo-Irish War, Great Britain could have set up a treaty giving Ireland political freedom and then continued both political and economic ties with them. Instead, Britain insisted that Ireland remain a subordinate colony with few economic and political freedoms. The result was Great Britain losing Ireland altogether as a colony.

Even earlier than the Irish rebellion of 1919–1921, England could have allowed Home Rule, an agreement to allow Ireland internal self-government, by setting up an Irish parliament. Great Britain would have remained in control of Ireland's international trade and political and military alliances abroad. Although the British Parliament passed a Home Rule bill prior to the First World War, to begin at the completion of the war, once the war ended, there was little support for such an agreement by the British, the Irish Republican movement, and Northern Ireland.

Irish nationalists had demanded Home Rule from the British at least since the 1880s. Although Home Rule was finally approved in 1912, its day had passed, and revolution became the Irish Nationalist's solution. England lost its opportunity to settle the disputes raging for centuries. As a result of their failure to meet the aims peacefully, all belligerents chose military force.[662]

What limitations, if any, were placed on the use of force, if that direction was chosen?

If the option of using force was chosen, would it be a total or limited war? Were there limitations to the application of force that might prevent the military choice from being successful?

If the limitations to military and political goals are too stringent to reduce the chances of success, entry into these limited wars should not have occurred; political goals alone are not always possible, but ultimate defeat could prove militarily or politically disastrous. In Vietnam, the

United States placed significant limitations on itself in the use of force against North Vietnam.

North Vietnamese forces and their Vietcong guerrillas in the South had to surrender if the United States were to meet its goal of keeping South Vietnam independent of the North. With full control of the North Vietnamese government, military, and people, America would have been able to dictate a peace agreement; until that occurred, the war would continue.

That approach never materialized due to the American fear that the Soviets and Chinese would enter the war in defense of North Vietnam, despite the entry of 200,000 Chinese forces already in the North.

All aspects of war must be considered, such as the strengths and weaknesses of potential belligerents. If there are significant limitations for a combatant, not going to war may be the logical decision. The alternative actions can be decided upon.

A United States Army analyst of the Vietnam War, Colonel Harry G. Summers Jr., described the American dilemma as a "US strategic policy which called for the containment rather than the destruction of communist power." The failure of this policy resulted in American troops being bogged down in an unwinnable "quagmire."[663]

Can all parties understand and articulate the political goals of military action?

Both the political and military goals set up by a nation must be understood by all elements of the trinity. Misunderstandings of these goals before or during the war could cause chaos within the nation, even a nation previously united.

In the American War of Independence, General George Washington developed communication links with the political leaders in the Continental Congress and the individual colonies early in the war. Washington made sure his political leaders knew his strategy for victory and what supplies and military hardware would bring them success.

Washington also accepted guidance from Congress and the colonies about these military actions. As the war progressed, Washington adapted his communication with the Continental Congress as necessary to keep them apprised of progress, as well as to receive their concerns, but he also knew never to overstep the bounds of civilian authority. He made sure civilian leadership fully understood their military's capabilities. This process was to ensure that both the military and political goals were known by his subordinates as well.[664]

Is regime change necessary, or can political objectives be satisfied otherwise?

This question relates to the importance of political stability within the nation under attack. Once the political leadership and its supporting military are removed, what will replace it, the invaders, other elements within the nation that could work with the invaders, or other forces within the nation that support the change?

The United States and its ally, Great Britain, successfully toppled Saddam Hussein's regime in a matter of a month. However, the various populations within the cities and countryside unexpectedly rose up and physically tried to remove the invaders from their country, thus drastically altering the invaders' original aims. These goals included setting up a democratic government standing for all elements of the nation, the Kurdish, Shia, and Sunnis. However, these ethnic groups unexpectedly continued the war.

Although the United States intended to help all ethnic and religious elements of the nation, enough of Iraq's population resented foreign countries entering their nation that they tried to remove the invaders from Iraq and their cities.

The Bush administration failed to consider secondary issues, such as large or small armed groups revolting against them. Instead of considering only the strength of the government, the US should have considered the populous in general and the sub-elements of the society, such as the Kurdish, Shia, and Sunnis, during the initial war planning.[665]

Are the benefits and rewards worth the costs and risks that we expect to see?

All wars include costs to the invader and the nation attacked—costs in lives, damage to its economy, the overall stability of the society, and the people's acceptance of the invading force and its intentions. At a minimum, these issues must be anticipated with solutions prepared.

In the Vietnam War, the United States allied with South Vietnam with the intention that this alliance would be sufficient to prevent the North Vietnamese from overrunning the South Vietnamese. The deterioration of the South Vietnamese government and military, its inability to sustain its role in the war, and its failure to keep the support of the South Vietnamese people forced the United States to take on all aspects of the fighting at a great cost in lives and resources. As the war continued, those costs and risks became an unanticipated disaster, ending in the withdrawal of all United States forces. The takeover of South Vietnam by North Vietnam quickly followed.[666]

Are we accurately assessing our military capabilities, as well as those of our allies, in creating our strategy?

An objective net assessment of the political and military capabilities to fight and defeat the enemy must be made, as well as the political and military capabilities of the enemy. International support or opposition to any war must be considered prior to the war's commencement.

Effective objectives depend on reliable intelligence and a thorough understanding of the enemy and our own capabilities to be victorious. Does intelligence supply critical information on the prospective enemy? Does the enemy really have the capability of harming the United States, its neighbors, or international partners? War planners can only put together a sound strategy for employing various military assets to meet objectives if they have the right intelligence.[667]

Saddam Hussein's Iraq was misjudged by President Bush. Intelligence officers and political leaders were considered to have significant weapons of mass destruction that could seriously harm the United States and other nations. Other political and intelligence leaders believed atomic, various chemicals, and other WMDs Iraq might have had were not serious hazards. Intelligence sources claiming that Iraq possessed these weapons were used as a basis for the US to pursue the war, but no weapons were ever found, and the US ended up in a multiyear entanglement that cost thousands of lives and billions of dollars.

What is the quality of the intelligence, including its interpretation, that has led us to this point?

Does available intelligence supply critical information on the prospective enemy? Do they plan and are they capable of harming the United States, its neighbors, or international partners? In addition to reliable intelligence about the potential enemy, a thorough understanding of that country's government, military, and people's willingness to fight is necessary.

The United States went to war with Saddam Hussein and his Iraq based on faulty intelligence about Iraq's possession of weapons of mass destruction. By the end of the Iraq War, no trace of nuclear, significant chemical, or other deadly weapons that would endanger his Mid-East neighbors, America, or their allies were found to be available to him. Even though all but a very few United Nations members disbelieved this intelligence, America declared war purely on faulty intelligence information.

In addition to reliable intelligence of the potential enemy, a thorough assessment of that country's military, economy, and the population's willingness to fight is necessary. Achieving goals depends upon having reliable intelligence and a thorough understanding of the enemy and its capabilities.

The United States did not set up goals that would remove Hussein and his supporters and placate the three major ethnic tribes. The latter responded in Iraqi cities with guerrilla warfare against the United States and its allies for years.

Staying away from questionable intelligence might have left room for another, better solution than an invasion. President Bush's resolve to go to war fogged the realities apparent in the intelligence available; Iraq's

WMD capabilities did not call for the actions taken by the government and military of the United States.[668]

What prevents the leadership from fully integrating available instruments of war?

Will the invader be able to sufficiently supply its military with forces, supplies, and weaponry? Are those forces capable of fighting within an alien terrain? Are its forces trained in the tactics necessary to defeat the expected enemy?

As the American War of Independence grew in intensity, Great Britain responded with ten thousand regulars and the British Navy. The British failed to understand their strategy was inappropriate for fighting a war on the North American Continent, which held vast lands with forests, rivers, and a large hostile colonial population. Britain's trained soldiers and sailors were adept at fighting a conventional war, not a traditional war and a guerrilla war simultaneously.

The British also terribly miscalculated the American resolve and its military's ability to fight. That British belief was based on years of believing American soldiers were vastly inferior to their British regulars.

The British war assessment was seriously flawed because it analyzed the current capabilities of the American military rather than estimating how those abilities might change as the war progressed. They failed to take into consideration the logistics of waging war on a foreign continent, as well as the possibility of a long, drawn-out, and complicated war becoming a reality. Considering such possibilities might have aided them as they decided on war or peace.[669]

Do all leaders understand the capabilities of their military forces?

The goal is to carefully assess the strengths and weaknesses of the opponent and oneself. The collaborative involvement of the political, military, and civilian population throughout the war is essential.

War dominated by United States civilian leadership, lacking a true comprehension of its military's capabilities, showed an ongoing ignorance within the Vietnam environment. This lack of understanding of how to force North Vietnam to surrender contributed to America's ultimate failure. The lack of honest communication between the military and civilian leadership about the military's effective and ineffective capabilities was aggravated by the lack of a partnership between the government and the military, making the achievement of goals difficult, if not impossible.

President Johnson's principal architect of the strategy for victory in Vietnam, Secretary of Defense Robert McNamara, recalled in his memoirs the principal mistake, which was to not explore alternate avenues to achieve Clausewitz's "political object," the goal of going to war. In his previous life, he was a businessman who had forced "organizations, often against their will, to think deeply and realistically about alternative courses of action and their consequences." Had the Johnson administration examined the questions that remained unanswered, the assumptions they had taken as truth, and accurately assessed the enemy's will to fight to the end, they might have achieved a better result for the Vietnamese people.[670]

During the Vietnam War, civilian political leaders like Secretary of State Robert McNamara did not understand the basic concepts of Clausewitz's theory that political leadership and military leaders must understand each other's critical role before, during, and following a war.[671]

How malleable are the prewar plans in the face of military decisions made by the enemy?

To address this question, we return to Clausewitz's words: "In war, more than anywhere else, things do not turn out as we expect." Prewar plans must be developed; however, as Clausewitz indicates here, those plans are very likely to be disrupted by unexpected enemy actions—throughout the war. Therefore, war planning must continue as the war progresses to adapt to those changes.

The surprise invasions of the North Korean Army and the Chinese Army were initially devastating to both the South Korean and United Nations forces. General MacArthur and then General Ridgway had no choice but to withdraw south, re-form their forces, and take advantage of their superior air force, as well as take advantage of the long and insufficient supply lines of the enemy.

In the meantime, President Truman altered their goals from all-out war to limited war. He also fired General Douglas MacArthur, who would not agree to the president's political intent for the war. Once the new strategy came into effect, the result was repelling the North Korean and Chinese armies to North Korea, which resulted in a guarded peace still in place to this day.[672]

What pressures are exerted upon the various phases of war by international political entities?

Potential international opinion in all its forms must be considered as war planning begins and develops throughout the war. To ignore that opinion would be folly.

During the Anglo-Irish War of 1918–1921, the Irish strategy continued to be small-unit attacks on unsuspecting British units, individuals, and small groups. The Irish people were able to sustain such operations throughout the war thanks to outside support from the United States and others and from the support of the Irish population, which housed the rebels in private homes throughout Ireland. In fact, the growing support the people provided was unlike any earlier Irish rebellion.

The British slowly changed their strategy to deal with the Irish surprise attacks. They also increased the violence its units were willing to provide. The British Black and Tans committed violent counterattacks on innocent civilians, their homes, and their government and community facilities. Their various units never decreased their violent attacks, a fact that not only changed the Irish people into supporters of the rebellion but forced the British Army to finally cease operations and leave Ireland due to the English people's reaction to their violence. In the end, the prevailing system of international politics represented by the United States and European nations, especially the people and government of England, made the continued conflict impossible to sustain by England.[673]

What effects will the outcome of the conflict have on the international political environment?

It is very likely that a war's outcome will change the international environment in some way, proportionate to the interests of any given nation. All belligerents involved must understand and react to those changes.

The United States and England spent more than twenty years fighting radical Islamists in Afghanistan and Iraq, only to withdraw ingloriously. Going to war may not have been the only choice the United States and Great Britain could have taken before invading both Afghanistan and Iraq; they could have considered the limitations of fighting this war. In the case of Afghanistan, these limitations included fighting the Taliban and their allies beyond the borders of Afghanistan into at least Western Pakistan. Regardless of the reasons for not taking the war to the Taliban's "safe haven," that freedom allowed them to remain safe as they planned and executed attacks on the allies, as well as Afghan forces within the borders of Afghanistan. In Iraq, the US failed to consider the growing insurgency in time to quell the rebellion before it had taken hold of quite a few major cities, especially in the volatile Sunni Triangle.

Though we have not explored Afghanistan as we have Iraq, the effects have been eerily similar. The final impact of the war in Afghanistan is also yet to be decided, at least to the extent that it has in Iraq. This is mostly due to the reoccupation of Afghanistan by the Taliban. Certainly, the large numbers of allied soldiers and scores of loyal Afghans should have left before the Taliban reemployed its savage treatment of the Afghan people. As a result of this chaotic withdrawal by the allies and their failure to defeat or reach a settlement with the Taliban, there seems to have been a negative reaction to departing Afghanistan without ensuring the safety of those Americans, British, and Afghans who loyally fought with them but did not leave before or during the evacuation of allied military forces. Along with possible human suffering, the reputation of the allies is at stake. Throughout the world their enemies may not fear them—and their allies may not trust them—in future confrontations.[674]

How does human bias affect the decisions made by the government, the military, and the people whether or not to go to war?

Where do our beliefs and opinions come from? We tend to feel that our convictions are rational, logical, and impartial based on years of experience and objective analysis of the available information. In truth, we are susceptible to biases; some are called *confirmation biases*, where our beliefs are frequently based on information that confirms our own opinions, and we tend to ignore informants that challenge them.

President Bush stated in preparation for the Iraq War that "Iraq [Saddam Hussein] was armed and dangerous and should be removed from power." He expressed this again in October 2003, before the US entry into the war. Was President Bush's statement based on factual data from current and accurate intelligence from the CIA or a related source? There were indications that Iraq had chemical weapons during the First Gulf War, but it turned out that they were no longer available just prior to the Iraq War.

Another source indicates that President Bush was influenced by his Neo-conservative political advisers rather than any information through intelligence channels. One thing is sure: no weapons of mass destruction of any significance were discovered during or following the second Iraq invasion.

In a poll launched by CBS before the Iraq War, an estimated 64 percent of Americans approved of military action in Iraq. Were their decisions based on trust in the government or were the decisions based on an understanding of the facts available to the public? To what extent was their opinion based solely on their convictions or with rational, logical, and impartial information?

Suppose there had been little or no intelligence indicating Saddam Hussein's possession of WMDs and his ability to harm his neighbors, the United States, and his allies. Why would the United States invade Iraq? If there were other reasons, they were not emphasized over the WMDs.

During the Korean War, President Truman mentioned that the central issue for going to war was that there would be a "domino effect" if South

Korea surrendered and that it could spill over to all of Asia and beyond. This same dynamic was to affect the United States as it would soon help justify their strategy to enter the Vietnam War by repeating the fear that the United States must prevent the Communists from controlling Taiwan, Japan, Korea, Indochina, Malaysia, Indonesia, and perhaps even the Philippines. But were these fears based on hard, cold facts, or was it a bias based on previous Communist aggression?

Why did the Communists attack South Korea, and why did the United States intervene? The simple answer to both questions is that the Soviet Union shifted its attention to Asia because it feared Western strength in Europe. They also focused their attention on Asia because they believed that Asia was a low priority for the United States. With these "beliefs," the Russians' assumption that the United States would not defend a nation in Asia and the American rationale that the Russians might enter a possible atomic war with America over Korea (and Vietnam) were, at best, assumptions—and possibly a bias lacking concrete facts—that impacted the course of both wars.

What actual rational, logical, and impartial facts would bear out both sides' assumptions? If that analysis had occurred, it would have been necessary to filter out any biases to ensure the decisions were, in fact, necessary.

Clausewitz states a very basic precept in his iconic analysis of war, an analysis provided throughout this book as well: a nation should never enter a conflict without sound reasons for doing so. Its initial objectives should involve the entire nation in the necessity for war and what their involvement will be. And, even with the best planning, it still may turn out differently than expected; all involved must realize that fact. Clausewitz's thoughts imply that bias should be avoided if the decisions are to be made objectively.

My fervent hope for the world is that we can go beyond choosing between war or peace and just choose peace and fellowship. I believe that for this to come true, we must all reach into our spiritual beliefs; they will give us hope that universal peace can be realized.

ACKNOWLEDGMENTS

Two exceptional people assisted me with key elements of *Limited War*: Olivia Slayden and Dave Rogers, my daughter and son. Olivia helped me with many key areas of the manuscript, especially the Introduction, the Prologue, and most notably, Chapter 8—the chapter I am proudest of. Olivia also helped me find the perfect publisher for this new author—Koehler Books. Dave helped me focus on the essence of marketing *Limited War* to a variety of audiences and established a marketing plan, a web presence, and additionally helped with editing. They are both true professionals in so many ways. Thank you both! Finally, I thank my wife, Sandra, for her support and love.

ENDNOTES

1. Carl von Clausewitz, *On War*
2. Ibid
3. Piers Mackesy, *British Strategy in the American War for Independence.*
4. Carl von Clausewitz, *On War*
5. B. A. Lee, *Strategy and Policy Lecture: Retrospect and Prospect*
6. George C. Herring, *Cold Blood: LBJ's Conduct of Limited War in Vietnam*
7. Maxine Hong Kingston, *Veterans of War, Veterans of Peace*
8. Charles Pope, *Cheney Changed his View of Iraq*
9. Harry G. Summers, Jr., *On Strategy: The Vietnam War in Context*
10. Timothy D. Hoyt, *Strategy and Policy Lecture: Strategies and Policies of Terrorism*
11. James A. Williamson, *A Short History of British Expansion.*
12. Professor Karl Friedrich Walling, Strategy and Policy Lecture: *The Americans at War*
13. James A. Williamson, *A Short History of British Expansion.*
14. Edward Channing, *A History of the United States*
15. James A. Williamson, *A Short History of British Expansion.*
16. Ibid.
17. A. P. Newton, Ernest Alfred Benians, John Holland Rose, *Cambridge History of the British Empire.*
18. Carl von Clausewitz, *On War.*
19. Professor Karl Friedrich Walling, *The Americans at War.*
20. Professor Karl Friedrich Walling, *The Americans at War.*
21. David McCullough, *John Adams.*
22. David McCullough, *John Adams.*
23. Nathaniel Currier (c. 1846). "Tea Sabotage in Boston Port". Accessed via https://commons.wikimedia.org/wiki/File:Boston_Tea_Party_Currier_colored.jpg
24. John Adams, *Diary of John Adams*
25. David McCullough, *John Adams.*
26. Professor Karl Friedrich Walling, *Republican Empire: Alexander Hamilton on War and Free Government.*
27. N. A. M. Roger, *The American Rebellion.*

28 Karl Friedrich Walling, *Republican Empire—Alexander Hamilton on War and Free Government.*
29 A. J. Newton, Ernest Alfred Benians, and John Holland, *Cambridge History of the British Expansion.*
30 A. J. Newton, Ernest Alfred Benians, and John Holland, *Cambridge History of the British Expansion.*
31 Ibid.
32 A. J. Newton, Ernest Alfred Benians, and John Holland, *Cambridge History of the British Expansion.*
33 Professor Karl Friedrich Walling, *The Americans at War.*
34 James A. Williamson, *A Short History of British Expansion.*
35 Edmund S. Morgan and Helen M. Morgan, *The Stamp Act Crisis.*
36 William J. Bennett, *America: The Last Best Hope.*
37 Samuel Eliot Morison, *A Concise History of the American Republic.*
38 Bruce Catton and William B. Catton, *The Bold and Magnificent Dream: America's Founding Years.*
39 William J. Bennett, *America: The Last Best Hope*
40 David McCullough, *John Adams*
41 James A. Williamson: *A Short History of British Expansion*
42 A. M. Schlesinger, *The Colonial Merchants and the American Revolution, 1763–1776*
43 Thomas Paine, *On Liberty*
44 James A. Williamson, *A Short History of British Expansion*
45 Ibid.
46 Morison, Steele, and Leuchtenberg, *A Concise History of the American Republic*
47 John Ferling, *A Leap in the Dark: The Struggle to Create the American Republic*
48 Thomas Paine, *On Liberty*
49 Eric Robson, *The American Revolution in Its Political and Military Aspects, 1763–1783*
50 James A. Williamson, *A Short History of British Expansion*
51 James A. Williamson, *A Short History of British Expansion*
52 Eric Robson, *The American Revolution in Its Political and Military Aspects, 1763–1783*
53 The Navigation Act of 1663, also known as the Staple Act
54 Eric Robson, *The American Revolution in Its Political and Military Aspects, 1763–1783*
55 James A. Williamson, *A Short History of British Expansion*
56 John Trumbull (c. 1786). Accessed via https://commons.wikimedia.org/wiki/File:The_Death_of_General_Warren_at_the_Battle_of_Bunker%27s_Hill.jpg
57 George Washington's Letter to Lord Bryan Fairfax, July 20, 1774
58 A. W. Brands, *The First American, The Life and Times of Benjamin Franklin*
59 Professor Karl Friedrich Walling, *Strategy and Policy Lecture: The American War*

60   Ibid.
61   *The US Declaration of Independence*
62   Joseph J. Ellis, *American Creation: Triumphs and Tragedies at the Founding of the Republic*
63   Geoff J. Armstrong, *Moments that made America*
64   Richard Brookhiser, "The General Takes Charge: Success is in the Details," *American History Magazine: Washington in His Own Words, January 1, 2010*
65   Ibid.
66   Richard Brookhiser, "The General Takes Charge: Success is in the Details," *American History Magazine: Washington in His Own Words, January 1, 2010*
67   Karl Friedrich Walling, *Strategy and Policy Lecture: The Americans at War*
68   Richard Brookhiser, "The General Takes Charge: The Will to Carry on Must Be Found," *American History Magazine: Washington in His Own Words, January 1, 2010*
69   David Hackett Fischer, *Washington's Crossing*
70   Richard Brookhiser, "The General Takes Charge: Victory by Sheer Determination," *American History Magazine: Washington in His Own Words, January 1, 2010*; and Washington's letter to John Hancock on December 27, 1776
71   Richard Brookhiser, "Challenges of War: Armies Cannot Go Home," *American History Magazine: Washington in His Own Words, January 1, 2010*
72   Richard Brookhiser, "Challenges of War: Armies Cannot Go Home," *American History Magazine: Washington in His Own Words, January 1, 2010*
73   Carl von Clausewitz, *On War*
74   Percy Moran (c.1911) Accessed via https://commons.wikimedia.org/wiki/File:Washington_at_Valley_Forge)_-_E._Percy_Moran_LCCN92506172.jpg
75   John J. Miller and Mark Molesky, *Our Oldest Enemy: A History of America's Disastrous Relationship with France*
76   Ibid.
77   Miller and Molesky, *Our Oldest Enemy: A History of America's Disastrous Relationship with France*
78   Miller and Molesky, *Our Oldest Enemy: A History of America's Disastrous Relationship with France*
79   David Hackett Fischer, *Washington's Crossing*
80   David Hackett Fischer, *Washington's Crossing*
81   William J. Bennett, *America: The Last Best Hope, The Greatest Revolution, 1765–1783*
82   Ibid.
83   William J. Bennett, *America: The Last Best Hope, The Greatest Revolution, 1765–1783*
84   Ibid.
85   John Keegan, *Fields of Battle: The Wars for North America*

86   Benson Bobrick, *Angel in the Whirlwind: The Triumph of the American Revolution*
87   John Trumbull (c.1820). Accessed via https://en.wikipedia.org/wiki/Surrender_of_Lord_Cornwallis#/media/File:Surrender_of_Lord_Cornwallis.jpg
88   John Trumbull (c. 1820). Accessed via https://www.history.navy.mil/our-collections/art/exhibits/conflicts-and-operations/the-war-of-1812/uss-constitution-vs-hms-guerriere/uss-constitution-vs-hms-guerriere-.html
89   Alan Taylor, *The Civil War of 1812*
90   Ibid.
91   Alan Taylor, *The Civil War of 1812*
92   Ibid.
93   Ibid.
94   Ibid.
95   Alan Taylor, *The Civil War of 1812*
96   Ibid.
97   Ibid.
98   Ibid.
99   Alan Taylor, *The Civil War of 1812*
100 Ibid.
101 Ibid.
102 Ibid.
103 Geoff J. Armstrong, *Moments That Made America*
104 Alan Taylor, *The Civil War of 1812*
105 Ibid.
106 Ibid.
107 Ibid.
108 Ibid.
109 Ibid.
110 Ibid.
111 Ibid.
112 Ibid.
113 Ibid.
114 Alan Taylor, *The Civil War of 1812*
115 Alan Taylor, *The Civil War of 1812*
116 Ibid.
117 Ibid.
118 Arthur R. M. Lower, *Colony to Nation*
119 A. L. Burt, *United States, Great Britain, and British North America*
120 Ibid.

121 Geoff J. Armstrong, *Moments That Made America*
122 William H. Merritt, *Journal, 8 July 1813*
123 Ibid.
124 Alan Taylor, *The Civil War of 1812*
125 William H. Merritt, *Journal, 8 July 1813*
126 Alan Taylor, *The Civil War of 1812*
127 Geoff J. Armstrong, *Moments That Made America*
128 Geoff J. Armstrong, *Moments That Made America*
129 Geoff J. Armstrong, *Moments That Made America*
130 Jeffersonians, Robert M. Utley, Wilcomb Washburn, *The Indian Wars*
131 Alan Taylor, *The Civil War of 1812*
132 Geoff J. Armstrong, *Moments That Made America; and Alan Taylor, The Civil War of 1812*
133 Ibid.
134 Geoff J. Armstrong, *Moments That Made America*
135 Geoff J. Armstrong, *Moments That Made America*
136 Geoff J. Armstrong, *Moments That Made America*
137 Geoff J. Armstrong, *Moments That Made America*
138 Alan Taylor, *The Civil War of 1812*
139 Alan Taylor, *The Civil War of 1812*
140 Alan Taylor, *The Civil War of 1812*
141 Ibid.
142 Robert M. Utley, and Wilcomb Washburn, *Jeffersonians: Indian Wars; and Samuel Eliot Morison, Henry Steele Commager, and William E. Leuchtenburg, A Concise History of the American Republic*
143 Edward Percy Moran (c. 1911). Accessed via https://commons.wikimedia.org/wiki/File:BattleofLakeErie.jpg
144 Geoff J. Armstrong, *Moments That Made America*
145 Geoff J. Armstrong, *Moments That Made America*
146 Geoff J. Armstrong, *Moments That Made America*
147 Geoff J. Armstrong, *Moments That Made America*
148 Ibid.
149 Pierre Berton, "The Invasion of Canada: 1812–1813"
150 Geoff J. Armstrong, *Moments That Made America*
151 Bradley Birzer, "Miamis," Encyclopedia of Chicago
152 Pierre Berton, *Flames Across the Border: 1813–1814*
153 William John Bennett, *America: The Last Best Hope Volume I (From the age of discovery to a world at war, 1492–1914)*

154 Geoff J. Armstrong, *Moments That Made America*
155 Elliot Cohen, *Conquered into Liberty*
156 Ibid.
157 Geoff J. Armstrong, *Moments That Made America*
158 Geoff J. Armstrong, *Moments That Made America.*
159 Geoff J. Armstrong, *Moments That Made America*
160 Geoff J. Armstrong, *Moments That Made America*
161 Geoff J. Armstrong, *Moments That Made America*
162 Ibid.
163 William John Bennett, *America: The Last Best Hope Volume I (From the age of discovery to a world at war, 1492–1914)*
164 Geoff J. Armstrong, *Moments That Made America*
165 William John Bennett, *America: The Last Best Hope Volume I (From the age of discovery to a world at war, 1492–1914)*
166 Geoff J. Armstrong, *Moments That Made America*
167 William John Bennett, *America: The Last Best Hope Volume I (From the age of discovery to a world at war, 1492–1914)*
168 John R. Elting, *Amateurs, to Arms!: A Military History of the War of 1812*
169 John R. Elting, *Amateurs, to Arms!: A Military History of the War of 1812*
170 An illustration from the book *The History of England, from the Earliest Periods, Vol. 1* by Paul M. Repin de Thoyras. Accessed via https://commons.wikimedia.org/wiki/File:British_Burning_Washington.jpg
171 Lieutenant Colonel G. Armistead, *Official Account of the Bombing of Ft. McHenry to President James Monroe*
172 Ibid.
173 William John Bennett, *America: The Last Best Hope Volume I (From the age of discovery to a world at war, 1492–1914)*
174 Robert Leckie, *The Wars of America*
175 Edward Percy Moran (c. 1910). Accessed via https://commons.wikimedia.org/wiki/File:Battle_of_New_Orleans.jpg
176 William John Bennett, *America: The Last Best Hope Volume I (From the age of discovery to a world at war, 1492–1914)*
177 Ibid.
178 William John Bennett, *America: The Last Best Hope Volume I (From the age of discovery to a world at war, 1492–1914)*
179 William John Bennett, *America: The Last Best Hope Volume I (From the age of discovery to a world at war, 1492–1914)*
180 William John Bennett, *America: The Last Best Hope Volume I (From the age of

discovery to a world at war, 1492–1914).
181　Ibid.
182　Ibid.
183　Ibid.
184　Amédée Forestier (c. 1914). Accessed via https://commons.wikimedia.org/wiki/File:Am%C3%A9d%C3%A9e_Forestier_-_Signing_of_Treaty_of_Ghent_(1814).jpg
185　Alan Taylor, *The Civil War of 1812*
186　Alan Taylor, *The Civil War of 1812*
187　Benjamin Waterhouse, *Prisoner of the British: The Journal of a Prisoner of War in the War of 1812*
188　Alan Taylor, *The Civil War of 1812*
189　Ibid.
190　Ibid.
191　Carl von Clausewitz, *On War*
192　M. L. R. Smith, *Fighting for Ireland? The Military Strategy of the Irish Republican Movement*
193　Ibid.
194　M. L. R. Smith, *Fighting for Ireland? The Military Strategy of the Irish Republican Movement*
195　*Constitution Of The United Irishmen, 1797*
196　Thomas Robinson (c. 1798) Accessed via https://commons.wikimedia.org/wiki/File:Battle_of_Ballynahinch_by_Thomas_Robinson.jpg
197　M. L. R. Smith, *Fighting for Ireland? The Military Strategy of the Irish Republican Movement*
198　Ibid.
199　Robert Kee, *The Green Flag: A History of Irish Nationalism*
200　Robert Kee, *The Green Flag: A History of Irish Nationalism*
201　Philip McKeiver, *A New History of Cromwell's Irish Campaign*
202　Robert Kee, *The Green Flag: A History of Irish Nationalism*
203　Ibid.
204　Ibid.
205　Robert Kee, *The Green Flag: A History of Irish Nationalism*
206　Robert Kee, *The Green Flag: A History of Irish Nationalism*
207　Ibid.
208　Ibid.
209　Ibid.
210　Cardinal Paul Cullen, *Public Opinion: A Comprehensive Summary of the Press*

Throughout the World

211 Robert Kee, *The Green Flag: A History of Irish Nationalism*
212 Robert Kee, *The Green Flag: A History of Irish Nationalism*
213 *Cobbett's Parliamentary Debates: Volume 191*
214 *Cobbett's Parliamentary Debates: Volume 191*
215 Robert Kee, *The Green Flag: A History of Irish Nationalism*
216 Ibid.
217 Robert Kee, *The Green Flag: A History of Irish Nationalism*
218 Robert Kee, *The Green Flag: A History of Irish Nationalism*
219 Ibid.
220 Ibid.
221 Laurence Marley, *Michael Davitt: Freelance Radical and Frondeur*
222 Ibid.
223 Laurence Marley, *Michael Davitt: Freelance Radical and Frondeur*
224 Robert Kee, *The Green Flag: A History of the Irish Nationalism*
225 Ibid.
226 Robert Kee, *The Green Flag: A History of the Irish Nationalism*
227 Robert Kee, *The Green Flag: A History of the Irish Nationalism*
228 Robert Kee, *The Green Flag: A History of the Irish Nationalism*
229 Ibid.
230 Robert Kee, *The Green Flag: A History of the Irish Nationalism*
231 Robert Kee, *The Green Flag: A History of Irish Nationalism*
232 Richard Bennett, *The Black and Tans*
233 Robert Kee, *The Green Flag: A History of Irish Nationalism*
234 Robert Kee, *The Green Flag: A History of Irish Nationalism*
235 Richard Bennett, *The Black and Tans*
236 Robert Kee, *The Green Flag: A History of Irish Nationalism*
237 Dan Breen, *My Fight For Irish Freedom*
238 Dan Breen, *My Fight For Irish Freedom*
239 Speech by Richard Francis Hayes, Dail Eireann, Volume 1 – April 10, 1919
240 Richard Bennett, *The Black and Tans*
241 W. D. Hogan (c. 1920). Accessed via https://commons.wikimedia.org/wiki/File:The_Burning_of_Cork_(9713428703).jpg
242 Richard Bennett, *The Black and Tans*
243 Richard Bennett, *The Black and Tans*
244 Thomas Perry Thornton, *Terror as a Weapon of Political Agitation*
245 Taylor, A. J. P., *English History 1914–1945*
246 Richard Bennett, *The Black and Tans*

247 Ibid.
248 Richard Bennett, *The Black and Tans*
249 Ibid.
250 Ibid.
251 Richard Bennett, *The Black and Tans*
252 Richard Bennett, *The Black and Tans*
253 Ibid.
254 Ibid.
255 Ibid.
256 General McKready, the Rt. Hon. Sir Nevil, *Annals of an active life*
257 Ibid.
258 Richard Bennett, *The Black and Tans*
259 Ibid.
260 Ibid.
261 Richard Bennett, *The Black and Tans*
262 Ibid.
263 Richard Bennett, *The Black and Tans*
264 Carl von Clausewitz, *On War*
265 Robert Kee, *The Green Flag: A History of Irish Nationalism*
266 Richard Bennett, *The Black and Tans*
267 Richard Bennett, *The Black and Tans*
268 Ibid.
269 Ibid.
270 Ibid.
271 Richard Bennett, *The Black and Tans*
272 Ibid.
273 Ibid.
274 Ibid.
275 Ibid.
276 Ibid.
277 Ibid.
278 Richard Bennett, *The Black and Tans*
279 Ibid.
280 Ibid.
281 Robert Kee, *The Green Flag: A History of Irish Nationalism*
282 Richard Bennett, *The Black and Tans*
283 Ibid.
284 Robert Kee, *The Green Flag: A History of Irish Nationalism*

285   Ibid.
286   Ibid.
287   Richard Bennett, *The Black and Tans*
288   M. L. R. Smith, *Fighting for Ireland? The Military Strategy of the Irish Republican Movement*
289   Richard Bennett, *The Black and Tans*
290   M. L. R. Smith, *Fighting for Ireland? The Military Strategy of the Irish Republican Movement*
291   Hogan's Flying Column (c.1920–1921). Accessed via https://commons.wikimedia.org/wiki/File:Hogan%27s_Flying_Column.gif
292   M. L. R. Smith, *Fighting for Ireland? The Military Strategy of the Irish Republican Movement*
293   Ibid.
294   Robert Kee, *The Green Flag: A History of Irish Nationalism*
295   Robert Kee, *The Green Flag: A History of Irish Nationalism*
296   Robert Endicott Osgood, *Limited War: The Challenge to American Strategy*
297   H. W. Brands, *MacArthur and Truman at the Brink of Nuclear War*
298   David McCullough, *Truman*
299   David McCullough, *Truman*
300   David McCullough, *Truman*
301   David McCullough, *Truman*
302   Harry Truman, *President Truman's Message to Congress, March 12, 1947*
303   Harry Truman, *President Truman's Message to Congress, March 12, 1947*
304   Robert Endicott Osgood, *Limited War: The Challenge to American Strategy*
305   Harry Truman, *President Truman's Message to Congress, March 12, 1947*
306   David McCullough, *Truman*
307   Harry Truman, *President Truman's Message to Congress, March 12, 1947*
308   Robert Endicott Osgood, *Limited War: The Challenge to American Strategy*
309   David McCullough, *Truman*
310   Hong Beom Rhee, *Asian Millenarianism: An Interdisciplinary Study of the Taiping and Tonghak Rebellions in a Global Context*
311   Robert Endicott Osgood, *Limited War: The Challenge to American Strategy*
312   Robert Endicott Osgood, *Limited War: The Challenge to American Strategy*
313   Robert Endicott Osgood, *Limited War: The Challenge to American Strategy*
314   Robert Endicott Osgood, *Limited War: The Challenge to American Strategy*
315   Allen Guttman, ed., *Korea: Cold War and Limited War*
316   H. W. Brands, *The General vs. The President*
317   Joseph C. Goulden, *Limited War: The Communists Strike South Korea; The Untold*

318 H. W. Brands, *The General vs. The President*
319 Joseph C. Goulden, *Limited War: The Communists Strike South Korea; The Untold Story of the War*
320 Joseph C. Goulden, *Limited War: The Communists Strike South Korea; The Untold Story of the War*
321 Joseph C. Goulden, *Limited War: The Communists Strike South Korea; The Untold Story of the War*
322 H. W. Brands, *The General vs. The President*
323 H. W. Brands, *The General vs. The President*
324 H. W. Brands, *The General vs. The President*
325 H. W. Brands, *The General vs. The President*
326 Robert Endicott Osgood, *Limited War: The Challenge to American Strategy*
327 Carl von Clausewitz, *On War*
328 Robert Endicott Osgood, *Limited War: The Challenge to American Strategy*
329 Harry S. Truman, *Memoirs: Years of Trial and Hope*
330 Robert Endicott Osgood, *Limited War: The Challenge to American Strategy*
331 Joseph C. Goulden, *Limited War: The Communists Strike South Korea; The Untold Story of the War*
332 Joseph C. Goulden, *Limited War: The Communists Strike South Korea; The Untold Story of the War*
333 Joseph C. Goulden, *Limited War: The Communists Strike South Korea; The Untold Story of the War*
334 Joseph C. Goulden, *Limited War: The Communists Strike South Korea; The Untold Story of the War*
335 Joseph C. Goulden, *Limited War: The Communists Strike South Korea; The Untold Story of the War*
336 Bruce Cumings, *The Korean War: A History*
337 Bruce Cumings, *The Korean War: A History*
338 Bruce Cumings, *The Korean War: A History*
339 Bruce Cumings, *The Korean War: A History*
340 Bruce Cumings, *The Korean War: A History*
341 Bruce Cumings, *The Korean War: A History*
342 Bruce Cumings, *The Korean War: A History*
343 Air and Space Museum No. 306-FS-237-2. Accessed via https://en.m.wikipedia.org/wiki/File:F4U-4B_VF-113_CV-47_1950.jpg.
344 H. W. Brands, *The General vs. the President: MacArthur and Truman at the Brink of Nuclear War*

345 Michael H. Hunt, *Beijing and the Korean Crisis*
346 Ian F. W. Beckett, *Modern Insurgencies and Counterinsurgencies*
347 Chai Zao, *Resistance: Sending troops to Korea, and American Assistance to Korea*
348 Michael H. Hunt, *Beijing and the Korean Crisis*
349 General Mao Zedong, *Mao Cable to Stalin*, 2 October 1950
350 Ibid.
351 Ibid.
352 Ibid.
353 Michael H. Hunt, *Beijing and the Korean Crisis*
354 General Mao Zedong, *Mao Cable to Stalin*, 2 October 1950
355 Michael J. Hunt, *Beijing and the Korean Crisis*
356 Ibid.
357 Ibid.
358 Telegram between Mao Zedong and Liu Shaoqi, December 18, 1949
359 Joseph C. Goulden, *Korea: The Untold Story of The War*
360 Michael H. Hunt, *Beijing and the Korean Crisis*
361 Joseph C. Goulden, *Korea: The Untold Story of the War*
362 Joseph C. Goulden, *Korea: The Untold Story of the War*
363 Joseph C. Goulden, *Korea: The Untold Story of the War*
364 Joseph C. Goulden, *Korea: The Untold Story of the War*
365 Joseph C. Goulden, *Korea: The Untold Story of the War*
366 Joseph C. Goulden, *Korea: the Untold Story of the War*
367 Joseph C. Goulden, *Korea: the Untold Story of the War*
368 James Stokesbury, *A Short History of the Korean War*
369 James Stokesbury, *A Short History of the Korean War*
370 Joseph C. Goulden, *Korea, the Untold Story of the War*
371 Joseph C. Goulden, *Korea: The Untold Story of the War*
372 Joseph C. Goulden, *Korea: The Untold Story of the War*
373 Joseph C. Goulden, *Korea: The Untold Story of the War*
374 Joseph C. Goulden, *Korea: The Untold Story of the War*
375 Joseph C. Goulden, *Korea: The Untold Story of the War*
376 Joseph C. Goulden, *Korea: The Untold Story of the War*
377 H. W. Brands, *The General vs. the President*
378 David McCullough, *Truman*
379 David McCullough, *Truman*
380 H. W. Brands, *MacArthur and Truman at the Brink of Nuclear War*
381 Ibid.
382 David McCullough, *Truman*

383   Ibid.
384   H. W. Brands, *The General vs. the President: MacArthur and Truman at the Brink of Nuclear War*
385   Ibid.
386   David McCullough, *Truman*
387   Ibid.
388   Dean Acheson, *Acheson Seminars*
389   Ibid.
390   Department of Defense Photo (USMC) A5408. Accessed via https://commons.wikimedia.org/wiki/File:A5408_Treadway_bridge_through_Funchilin_Pass_on_December_9,_1950.jpg
391   Joseph C. Goulden, *Korea: The Untold Story of the War*
392   Joseph C. Goulden, *Korea: The Untold Story of the War*
393   *Largest Evacuation from Land by a Single Ship, Guinness World Records, December 25, 1950*
394   Joseph C. Goulden, *Korea: The Untold Story of the War*; and Billy C. Mossman, *Ebb and Flow: November 1950–July 1951*
395   Joseph C. Goulden, *Korea: The Untold Story of the War*
396   Joseph C. Goulden, *Korea: The Untold Story of the War*
397   Joseph Stalin, *Ciphered Telegram from Filippov [Stalin] to Mao Zedong via Zakharov*
398   Harry Truman, *Report to the American People on Korea, Radio Address April 11, 1951*
399   David McCullough, *Harry S. Truman: The Truman Doctrine*
400   Joseph C. Goulden, *Korea, the Untold Story of the War*
401   David McCullough, *Harry S. Truman: The Truman Doctrine*
402   US Army photo. Accessed via https://history.army.mil/html/bookshelves/resmat/korea/intro/photos-and-art/photos/Rak.jpg. Enhanced by Erik Villard.
403   Xiaobing Li, *China's Battle for Korea: The 1951 Spring Offensive*
404   Billy C. Mossman, *Ebb and Flow: November 1950–July 1951*
405   Billy C. Mossman, *Ebb and Flow: November 1950–July 1951*
406   Billy C. Mossman, *Ebb and Flow: November 1950–July 1951*
407   Xiaobing Li, *China's Battle for Korea: The 1951 Spring Offensive*
408   William Weber, *Unit History of the 187th*
409   Xiaobing Li, *China's Battle for Korea: The 1951 Spring Offensive*
410   Xiaobing Li, *China's Battle for Korea: The 1951 Spring Offensive*
411   Xiaobing Li, *China's Battle for Korea: The 1951 Spring Offensive*
412   Xiaobing Li, *China's Battle for Korea: The 1951 Spring Offensive*
413   James Stokesbury, *A Short History of the Korean War*
414   James Stokesbury, *A Short History of the Korean War*

415 Xiaobing Li, *China's Battle for Korea: The 1951 Spring Offensive*
416 John Gittings, *The World of China, 1922–1972*
417 Xiaobing Li, *China's Battle for Korea: The 1951 Spring Offensive*
418 Xiaobing Li, *China's Battle for Korea: The 1951 Spring Offensive*
419 James Stokesbury, *A Short History of the Korean War*
420 James Stokesbury, *A Short History of the Korean War*
421 James Stokesbury, *A Short History of the Korean War*
422 James Stokesbury, *A Short History of the Korean War*
423 James Stokesbury, *A Short History of the Korean War*
424 Xiaobing Li, *China's Battle for Korea: The 1951 Spring Offensive*
425 James Stokesbury, *A Short History of the Korean War*
426 Xiaobing Li, *China's Battle for Korea: The 1951 Spring Offensive*
427 James Stokesbury, *A Short History of the Korean War*
428 Xiaobing Li, *China's Battle for Korea: The 1951 Spring Offensive*
429 James Stokesbury, *A Short History of the Korean War*
430 Rosemary Foot, and Burton I. Kaufman, *Korea: The Limited War*
431 Joseph C. Goulden, *Korea, the Untold Story of the War*
432 James Stokesbury, *A Short History of the Korean War*
433 James Stokesbury, *A Short History of the Korean War*
434 US Navy photo. Accessed via https://commons.wikimedia.org/wiki/File:Bombing_Wonsan_Harbor_1950.jpg
435 State Archives of Florida, Florida Memory, https://floridamemory.com/items/show/25387. Accessed via https://commons.wikimedia.org/wiki/File:FSU_protest_Tallahassee_rc01458.jpg
436 Charles Hirschman, Samuel Preston, and Vu Man Loi, *Vietnamese Casualties During the American War: A New Estimate*
437 Guenter Lewy, *America in Vietnam*
438 H. R. McMaster, *Dereliction of Duty*
439 Ibid.
440 Harry G. Summers, Jr., *On Strategy: The Vietnam War in Context*
441 Harry G. Summers, Jr., *On Strategy: The Vietnam War in Context*; and Stanley Karnow, *Vietnam: A History—The First Complete Account of Vietnam at War*
442 Harry G. Summers, Jr., *On Strategy: The Vietnam War in Context*; and Stanley Karnow, *Vietnam: A History—The First Complete Account of Vietnam at War*
443 Harry G. Summers, Jr., *On Strategy: The Vietnam War in Context*; and Stanley Karnow, *Vietnam: A History—The First Complete Account of Vietnam at War*
444 James Blight, *Vietnam If Kennedy Had Lived*
445 Professor B. A. Lee, *Retrospect and Prospect*; Harry G. Summers, Jr., *On Strategy:*

	The Vietnam War in Context; and Stanley Karnow, *Vietnam: A History—The First Complete Account of Vietnam at War*
446	Carl von Clausewitz, *On War*; and Harry G. Summers, Jr., *On Strategy: The Vietnam War in Context*
447	Carl von Clausewitz, *On War*
448	Carl von Clausewitz, *On War*; and Harry G. Summers, Jr., *On Strategy: The Vietnam War in Context*
449	Carl von Clausewitz, *On War*
450	Carl von Clausewitz, *On War*; and Harry G. Summers, Jr., *On Strategy: The Vietnam War in Context*
451	National Security Council Memorandum 64, February 27, 1950 https://history.state.gov/historicaldocuments/frus1950v06/d480
452	Stanley Karnow, *Vietnam: A History—The First Complete Account of Vietnam at War*
453	Neil Sheehan, *A Bright Shining Lie*
454	Carl von Clausewitz, *On War*
455	Lee Sorley, *A Better War: The Unexamined Victories and Final Tragedy of America's Last Years in Vietnam*
456	Carl von Clausewitz, *On War*
457	Carl von Clausewitz, *On War*
458	Neil Sheehan, *A Bright Shining Lie*; and Harry G. Summers, Jr., *On Strategy: The Vietnam War in Context*
459	Neil Sheehan, *A Bright Shining Lie*
460	Neil Sheehan, *A Bright Shining Lie*; and Stanley Karnow, *Vietnam: A History—The First Complete Account of Vietnam at War*
461	Neil Sheehan, *A Bright Shining Lie*
462	Max Hastings, *Vietnam: An Epic Tragedy, 1945–1975*
463	Max Hastings, *Vietnam: An Epic Tragedy, 1945–1975*
464	Max Hastings, *Vietnam: An Epic Tragedy, 1945–1975*
465	Max Hastings, *Vietnam: An Epic Tragedy, 1945–1975*
466	Ibid.
467	Ibid.
468	Ibid.
469	Max Hastings, *Vietnam: An Epic Tragedy, 1945–1975*
470	Max Hastings, *Vietnam: An Epic Tragedy, 1945–1975*
471	Max Hastings, *Vietnam: An Epic Tragedy, 1945–1975*
472	Max Hastings, *Vietnam: An Epic Tragedy, 1945–1975*
473	Max Hastings, *Vietnam: An Epic Tragedy, 1945–1975*
474	Max Hastings, *Vietnam: An Epic Tragedy, 1945–1975*

475 Max Hastings, *Vietnam: An Epic Tragedy, 1945–1975*
476 Neil Sheehan, *A Bright Shining Lie*
477 US Army photo (c.1963) Accessed via https://commons.wikimedia.org/wiki/File:Chopper_wreck_at_Ap_Bac.jpg
478 Stanley Karnow, *Vietnam: A History—The First Complete Account of Vietnam at War*
479 Ibid.
480 Stanley Karnow, *Vietnam: A History—The First Complete Account of Vietnam at War*
481 Neil Sheehan, *A Bright Shining Lie*; and Stanley Karnow, *Vietnam: A History—The First Complete Account of Vietnam at War*
482 Ibid.
483 Ibid.
484 Neil Sheehan, *A Bright Shining Lie*
485 Neil Sheehan, *A Bright Shining Lie*
486 Neil Sheehan, *A Bright Shining Lie*
487 Ibid.
488 Neil Sheehan, *A Bright Shining Lie*
489 Max Hastings, *Vietnam: An Epic Tragedy, 1945–1975*
490 Max Hastings, *Vietnam: An Epic Tragedy, 1945–1975*
491 Neil Sheehan, *A Bright Shining Lie*
492 Neil Sheehan, *A Bright Shining Lie*
493 Neil Sheehan, *A Bright Shining Lie*
494 Neil Sheehan, *A Bright Shining Lie*
495 Neil Sheehan, *A Bright Shining Lie*
496 Stanley Karnow, *Vietnam: A History—The First Complete Account of Vietnam at War*
497 Harry G. Summers, Jr., *On Strategy: The Vietnam War in Context*
498 Max Hastings, *Vietnam: An Epic Tragedy, 1945–1975*
499 Max Hastings, *Vietnam: An Epic Tragedy, 1945–1975*
500 Stanley Karnow, *Vietnam: A History—The First Complete Account of Vietnam at War*
501 Max Hastings, *Vietnam: An Epic Tragedy, 1945–1975*
502 Max Hastings, *Vietnam: An Epic Tragedy, 1945–1975*
503 Max Hastings, *Vietnam: An Epic Tragedy, 1945–1975*
504 Stanley Karnow, *Vietnam: A History—The First Complete Account of Vietnam at War*
505
506 Carl von Clausewitz, *On War*
507 Harry G. Summers, Jr., *On Strategy: The Vietnam War in Context*
508 Harry G. Summers, Jr., *On Strategy: The Vietnam War in Context*
509 Ibid.
510 Michael I. Handel, *Masters of War: Classical Strategic Thought*

511 Ibid.
512 Michael I. Handel, *Masters of War: Classical Strategic Thought*
513 US National Archives at College Park (April 3, 1968). Accessed via https://commons.wikimedia.org/wiki/File:Vietnam....Marines_riding_atop_an_M-48_tank_cover_their_ears_as_te_90mm_gun_fires_during_a_road_sweep_southwest_of..._-_NARA_-_532483.tif.
514 Neil Sheehan, *A Bright Shining Lie*
515 H. R. McMaster, *Dereliction of Duty*
516 Michael I. Handel, *Masters of War*
517 US Air Force photo (c. 1967). Accessed via https://commons.wikimedia.org/wiki/File:Second_Lieutenant_Kathleen_M._Sullivan_treats_a_Vietnamese_child_during_Operation_MED_CAP,_a_U.S._Air_Force_civic..._-_NARA_-_542331.jpg
518 George C. Herring, *Cold Blood*
519 Ibid.
520 Eliot A. Cohen, *Supreme Command: Soldiers, Statesmen, and Leadership in War Time*
521 H. R. McMaster, *Dereliction of Duty* and George C. Herring, *Cold Blood*
522 Daniel Ellsberg, *The Pentagon Papers* and Eliot A. Cohen, *Supreme Command: Soldiers, Statesmen, and Leadership in War Time*
523 Robert S. McNamara, *In Retrospect: The Tragedy and Lessons of Vietnam*
524 H. R. McMaster, *Dereliction of Duty*
525 Eliot A. Cohen, *Supreme Command: Soldiers, Statesmen, and Leadership in War Time*
526 Lewis Sorley, *A Better War: The Unexamined Victories and Final Tragedy of America's Last Years in Vietnam*
527 James W. Mooney and Thomas R. West, *Vietnam: A History and Anthology*
528 Harry G. Summers, Jr., *On Strategy: The Vietnam War in Context*
529 US Army photo (November, 1965). Accessed via https://commons.wikimedia.org/wiki/File:Bruce_Crandall%27s_UH-1D.jpg
530 Carl von Clausewitz, *On War*
531 Charles Pope, *Cheney Changed His View of Iraq*
532 Condoleezza Rice, *Democracy: When Tyrants Fall, Building Democratic Institutions*
533 Condoleezza Rice, *Democracy: When Tyrants Fall, Building Democratic Institutions*
534 Donald Rumsfeld, *Known and Unknown: A Memoir*
535 Jean Edward Smith, *Bush: Waging Aggressive War*
536 Ibid.
537 Jean Edward Smith, *Bush: Waging Aggressive War*
538 William Bennett, *Why We Fight: The War on Terrorism*
539 The Gallup Poll, *The Iraq War*
540 Stephan Halper and Johnathan Clarke, *America Alone*

ENDNOTES

541 Ibid.
542 William Bennett, *Why We Fight: The War on Terrorism*
543 Stefan Halper and Jonathan Clarke, *America Alone*
544 Robert Kagan, *Of Paradise and Power: America and Europe in the New World Order* and Richard Pearle and Irving Kristol, *Neoconservatism Reconfigured*
545 Lawrence F. Kaplan and William Kristol, *The War Over Iraq*
546 Robert Kagan, *Of Paradise and Power: America and Europe in the New World Order* and Lawrence F. Kaplan and William Kristol, *The War Over Iraq*
547 National Security Council, *National Security Strategy, 2002*
548 Lawrence Kaplan and William Kristol, *The War Over Iraq* and Richard Pearle; and Irving Kristol, *Neoconservatism Reconfigured*
549 George Kennan, *Sources of Soviet Conduct*
550 Robert Kagan, *Of Paradise and Power: America and Europe in the New World Order*
551 Robert Kagan, *Of Paradise and Power: America and Europe in the New World Order;* and Stefan Halper and Jonathan Clarke, *America Alone*
552 Lawrence Kaplan and William Kristol, *Present Danger: Crisis and Opportunities in American Foreign Defense Policy*
553 Lawrence Kaplan and William Kristol, *Present Danger: Crisis and Opportunities in American Foreign Defense Policy*
554 Stephen S. Hayes, *Case Closed*
555 Walter Pincus and Dana Priest, "Some Iraq Analysts Felt Pressure from Cheney Visits." *Washington Post, June 5, 2003;* and Stefan Halper and Jonathan Clarke, *America Alone*
556 Stefan Halper and Jonathan Clarke, *America Alone*
557 Stephen S. Hayes, *Case Closed*
558 Stefan Halper and Jonathan Clarke, *America Alone*
559 Walter Pincus and Dana Priest, "Some Iraq Analysts Felt Pressure from Cheney Visits." *Washington Post, June 5, 2003*
560 Douglas Jehl, *The Struggle for Iraq*
561 Stefan Halper and Jonathan Clarke, *America Alone*
562 Karen De Young, *Soldier: The Life of Colin Powell*
563 Stefan Halper and Jonathan Clarke, *America Alone*
564 Jean Edward Smith, *Bush: Waging Aggressive War*
565 Donald Rumsfeld, *Known and Unknown*
566 Donald Rumsfeld, *Known and Unknown*
567 Donald Rumsfeld, *Known and Unknown*
568 Donald Rumsfeld, *Known and Unknown*
569 Donald Rumsfeld, *Known and Unknown*

570 Tommy Franks and Malcolm McConnel, *American Soldier*
571 Tommy Franks and Malcolm McConnel, *American Soldier*
572 Jean Edward Smith, *Bush: Waging Aggressive War*
573 Tommy Franks and Malcolm McConnel, *American Soldier*
574 Karen De Young, *Soldier: The Life of Colin Powell*
575 Ibid.
576 Tommy Franks and Malcolm McConnel, *American Soldier*
577 Donald Rumsfeld, *Known and Unknown, A Memoir*
578 Dick Cheney, *In My Time*
579 Dick Cheney, *In My Time*
580 Jean Edward Smith, *Bush: Waging Aggressive War*
581 Walter A. McDougal, *American Soldiers*
582 Stefan Halper and Jonathan Clarke, *America Alone*
583 Karen De Young, *Soldier: The Life of Colin Powell*
584 Matthew Rycroft, *Downing Street Memo*
585 Jean Edward Smith, *Bush: Waging Aggressive War*
586 Tommy Franks and Malcolm McConnel, *American Soldier*
587 Ibid.
588 Tommy Franks and Malcolm McConnel, *American Soldier*
589 Michael Smith, *RAF Bombing Raids Tried to Goad Saddam into War, The Sunday Times, May 29, 2005*
590 Phillipe Sands, *Lawless World: America and the Making and Breaking of Global Rules*
591 George W. Bush and Brent Scowcroft, *A World Transformed*
592 Donald Rumsfeld, *Known and Unknown*
593 Ibid.
594 CBS, *Poll: Talk First, Fight Later.* Accessed From: https://web.archive.org/web/20070330062908/http://www.cbsnews.com/stories/2003/01/23/opinion/polls/main537739.shtml
595 Stefan Halper and Jonathan Clarke, *America Alone*
596 Guinness Book of World Records, *Largest Anti-war Rally, February 15, 2003*
597 Department of Defense, *U.S. military personnel pull down a statue of Saddam Hussein in Baghdad.* April 9, 2003. Photograph. Army History Magazine, No. 126, Winter 2023-2024, p.7. https://history.army.mil/armyhistory/AH-Magazine/2023AH_winter/AH126.pdf
598 Gregory Fontenot, *On Point: The United States Army in Operation Iraqi Freedom*
599 Linwood Carter, *Iraq: Summary of U.S. Forces, CRS Report for Congress*
600 Gregory Fontenot, *On Point: The United States Army in Operation Iraqi Freedom*
601 Gregory Fontenot, *On Point: The United States Army in Operation Iraqi Freedom*

602 Tommy Franks and Malcolm McConnel, *American Soldier*
603 Tommy Franks, *American Soldier*
604 Gregory Fontenot, *On Point: The United States Army in Operation Iraqi Freedom*
605 Gregory Fontenot, *On Point: The United States Army in Operation Iraqi Freedom*
606 Gregory Fontenot, *On Point: The United States Army in Operation Iraqi Freedom*
607 Gregory Fontenot, *On Point: The United States Army in Operation Iraqi Freedom*
608 Gregory Fontenot, *On Point: The United States Army in Operation Iraqi Freedom*
609 Gregory Fontenot, *On Point: The United States Army in Operation Iraqi Freedom*
610 Gregory Fontenot, *On Point: The United States Army in Operation Iraqi Freedom*
611 Gregory Fontenot, *On Point: The United States Army in Operation Iraqi Freedom*
612 Gregory Fontenot, *On Point: The United States Army in Operation Iraqi Freedom*
613 Gregory Fontenot, *On Point: The United States Army in Operation Iraqi Freedom*
614 Gregory Fontenot, *On Point: The United States Army in Operation Iraqi Freedom*
615 Gregory Fontenot, *On Point: The United States Army in Operation Iraqi Freedom*
616 Gregory Fontenot, *On Point: The United States Army in Operation Iraqi Freedom*
617 Gregory Fontenot, *On Point: The United States Army in Operation Iraqi Freedom*
618 Donald Rumsfeld, *Iraq: An Illustrative List of Potential Problems to be Considered and Addressed*
619 Donald Rumsfeld, *Known and Unknown* and Donald Rumsfeld, *Why We Need an IA Sooner Rather Than Later*
620 US Navy photo by PH3 Tyler Clements. Accessed via https://commons.wikimedia.org/wiki/File:US_Navy_030501-N-0000C-001_President_George_W._Bush_addresses_the_Nation_and_Sailors_from_the_flight_deck_aboard_USS_Abraham_Lincoln_(CVN_72).jpg.
621 Ibid.
622 Condoleezza Rice, *Democracy, When Tyrants Fall, Building Democratic Institutions*
623 Donald Rumsfeld, *Known and Unknown*
624 Donald Rumsfeld, *Known and Unknown*
625 Bing West, *No True Glory*
626 Donald Rumsfeld, *Known and Unknown*
627 Donald Rumsfeld, *Why We Need an IA Sooner Rather Than Later*
628 Donald Rumsfeld, *Why We need an IA Sooner Rather Than Later*
629 Ken Adelman, *Cakewalk in Iraq* and Gregory Fontenot, *On Point: The United States Army in Operation Iraqi Freedom*
630 Bing West, *No True Glory*
631 Bing West, *No True Glory*
632 Bing West, *No True Glory*
633 Bing West, *No True Glory*

634　Bing West, *No True Glory*
635　Donald Rumsfeld, *Why We Need an IA Sooner Rather Than Later* and Donald Rumsfeld, *Known and Unknown: A Memoir*
636　Bing West, *No True Glory*
637　Bing West, *No True Glory*
638　Bing West, *No True Glory*
639　Bing West, *No True Glory*
640　Bing West, *No True Glory*
641　Bing West, *No True Glory*
642　Bing West, *No True Glory*
643　Bing West, *No True Glory*
644　Bing West, *No True Glory*
645　Bing West, *No True Glory*
646　Donald Rumsfeld, *Why We need an IA Sooner Rather Than Later* and Donald Rumsfeld, *Known and Unknown: A Memoir*
647　Bing West, *No True Glory*
648　Bing West, *No True Glory*
649　Bing West, *No True Glory*
650　Bing West, *No True Glory*
651　Bing West, *No True Glory*
652　Donald Rumsfeld, *Why We Need an IA Sooner Rather Than Later* and Donald Rumsfeld, *Known and Unknown: A Memoir*
653　Bing West, *No True Glory*
654　Leon Panetta, *Worthy Fights*
655　Leon Panetta, *Worthy Fights*
656　Peter Van Buren, *We Meant Well: I Helped Lose the Battle for the Hearts and Minds of the Iraqi People*
657　Ibid.
658　Richard W. Stevenson and Thom Shanker, *Ex-Arms Monitor Urges an Inquiry on the Iraqi WMD Threat*
659　Peter Van Buren, *We Meant Well: I Helped Lose the Battle for the Hearts and Minds of the Iraqi People*
660　Peter Van Buren, *We Meant Well: I Helped Lose the Battle for the Hearts and Minds of the Iraqi People*
661　Peter Van Buren, *We Meant Well: I Helped Lose the Battle for the Hearts and Minds of the Iraqi People*
662　Robert Kee, *The Green Flag: A History of Irish Nationalism*; Richard Bennett, *The Black and Tans*; and, Carl von Clausewitz, *On War*

663 Carl von Clausewitz, *On War*; Harry G. Summers, Jr., *Defense Without Purpose*; and Stanley Karnow, *Vietnam: A History–The First Complete Account of Vietnam at War*

664 Carl von Clausewitz, *On War* and, Richard Brookhiser, *Washington: In His Own Words*

665 Carl von Clausewitz, *On War*; and, Eliot A. Cohen, *Supreme Command: Soldiers, Statesmen, and Leadership in War Time*

666 Stanley Karnow, *Vietnam: A History–The First Complete Account of Vietnam at War*

667 Carl von Clausewitz, *On War*; and Stephen Halper and Jonathan Clarke, *America Alone*

668 Stephen Halper and Jonathon Clarke, *America Alone*

669 James A. Williamson, *A Short History of British Expansion*

670

671 Stanley Karnow, *Vietnam: A History–The First Complete Account of Vietnam at War*

672 H. W. Brands, *MacArthur and Truman at the brink of Nuclear war*; and, Carl von Clausewitz, *On War*

673 Robert Kee, *The Green Flag: A History of Irish Nationalism*, Richard Bennett, *The Black and Tans*; and Carl von Clausewitz, *On War*

674 Carl von Clausewitz, *On War*; and Stanley Karnow, *Vietnam: A History–The First Complete Account of Vietnam at War*

www.ingramcontent.com/pod-product-compliance
Lightning Source LLC
LaVergne TN
LVHW041906070526
838199LV00051BA/2522